From Captives to Consuls

STUDIES IN EARLY AMERICAN ECONOMY AND SOCIETY
FROM THE LIBRARY COMPANY OF PHILADELPHIA
Cathy Matson, *Series Editor*

From Captives to Consuls

Three Sailors in Barbary and Their Self-Making across the Early American Republic, 1770–1840

BRETT GOODIN

Johns Hopkins University Press

Baltimore

© 2020 Johns Hopkins University Press
All rights reserved. Published 2020
Printed in the United States of America on acid-free paper

2 4 6 8 9 7 5 3 1

Johns Hopkins University Press
2715 North Charles Street
Baltimore, Maryland 21218-4363
www.press.jhu.edu

Library of Congress Cataloging-in-Publication Data
Names: Goodin, Brett, 1987– author.
Title: From captives to consuls : three sailors in Barbary and their self-making across
the early American republic, 1770–1840 / Brett Goodin.
Description: Baltimore : Johns Hopkins University Press, 2020. | Series: Studies in
early American economy and society from the Library Company of Philadelphia |
Includes bibliographical references and index.
Identifiers: LCCN 2019056151 | ISBN 9781421438979 (hardcover) |
ISBN 9781421438986 (ebook)
Subjects: LCSH: United States—History—Tripolitan War, 1801–1805. | O'Brien,
Richard, approximately 1758–1824. | Cathcart, James L. (James Leander),
1767–1843. | Riley, James, 1777–1840. | Prisoners of war (Islamic law)—United
States—Biography. | Prisoners of war (Islamic law)—Algeria—Biography. | United
States—Foreign relations—Africa, North. | Africa, North—Foreign relations—
United States. | Diplomats—United States—Biography. | National characteristics,
American—History.
Classification: LCC E335 .G66 2020 | DDC 973.4092/2 [B]—dc23
LC record available at https://lccn.loc.gov/2019056151

A catalog record for this book is available from the British Library.

*Special discounts are available for bulk purchases of this book. For more information,
please contact Special Sales at specialsales@press.jhu.edu.*

Johns Hopkins University Press uses environmentally friendly book materials,
including recycled text paper that is composed of at least 30 percent
post-consumer waste, whenever possible.

For all the people and organizations keeping young historians fed, sheltered, and in good company

CONTENTS

In this latest title in the Studies in Early American Economy and Society series, a collaborative effort between Johns Hopkins University Press and the Library Company of Philadelphia's Program in Early American Economy and Society (PEAES), Brett Goodin presents the lives of three sailors of the early American republic who found themselves stranded in foreign lands. *From Captives to Consuls* uses the printed captivity narratives of these citizens to explore how young men engaged in the very common activities of commercial sailing in foreign waters became captives in the Barbary States and how they suffered through the travails imposed by their captors.

But this is not a straightforward narrative, for the three white captives shared their experiences abroad just as the new United States was navigating its larger collective prospects for forging a country based on the ill-defined ideas of liberty, nationhood, and self-making. And during that heady era when such ideas were fragile, and the early republic's commercial identity was shifting ground in a world fraught with revolution and upheaval, the three central figures of Goodin's study availed themselves of opportunities to create new identities for themselves as well. Using the skills and networks they developed while captives, and then composing popular printed narratives that reflected particular elements of their captivities, the three young sailors were able to make themselves over and enjoy a certain degree of upward mobility for years after their safe return.

Although scholars have not been wrong to show how American sailors were often victims of forces beyond their control, Goodin insists that sailors were far from powerless. Captain James Riley's narrative did not dwell on the racial and religious stereotypes of Islamic peoples, but instead presented eyewitness "facts" about North African politics, geography, history, and a slave system in which white men served African masters. His wide-selling account served the scientific and antislavery communities in North America for generations. Richard O'Brien and James Cathcart rose out of their own captivities and roles as underpaid and virtually unknown sailors to become US consuls to North Africa, US state politicians, settlers and surveyors, land speculators, and federal bureaucrats.

Always adaptable, these self-made men were lucky enough to become widely read authors whose words helped to shift the early republic's production and consumption of knowledge from its elite character to something closer to the experiences of thousands of people in the new United States. As non-elite writers, Cathcart, O'Brien, and Riley helped make the notions of liberty, nationhood, and self-making more accessible. They showed how Americans might turn adversity into good fortune, albeit not great wealth, and how to manipulate opportunities to one's advantage when previous generations had taught young men to respect their given stations in life. And they did so to popular acclaim, years before Alexis de Tocqueville toured portions of the republic.

In the following chapters, Goodin traces the journeys of Cathcart, O'Brien, and Riley from Revolutionary seas, to captivity in the Barbary States, and home again to adventures in North America. He does this with a deep reading of the captives' own narratives, which is then placed in the much broader unfolding of the new nation and its place within global events.

Cathy Matson

Richards Professor of American History Emerita,
    University of Delaware
Director, Program in Early American Economy and Society,
    Library Company of Philadelphia

ACKNOWLEDGMENTS

The fear of forgetting an early mentor or of omitting a late contributor probably accounts for authors drafting acknowledgments at the last minute. Yet leaving these pages to the last minute virtually guarantees that someone will be inadvertently omitted. So, to whomever I have forgotten: I'm sorry, and I owe you dinner.

Speaking of dinner, this book would never have been fit for human consumption without the time to revise the manuscript afforded by a Margaret Henry Dabney Penick postdoctoral fellowship at the Smithsonian Institution and a Program in Early American Economy and Society (PEAES) postdoctoral fellowship at the Library Company of Philadelphia. I am especially grateful for PEAES director Cathy Matson's work and interest in this project and to Laura Davulis and Esther Rodriguez at Johns Hopkins University Press for shepherding it through the publication process. I am also grateful to JHUP's anonymous reader for pointing out some embarrassing flaws in an earlier draft of this manuscript.

This project began as a dissertation at the Australian National University, which naturally means a great intellectual debt is owed to my far-flung dissertation committee: Melanie Nolan, Doug Craig, Emma Hart, and Larry Peskin. I remain baffled and grateful that Larry and Emma accepted my cold call from the Antipodes, and I'm sorry for your suffering ever since! If you ever need a spare kidney, do not hesitate to call.

The research necessary to complete this book would have been impossible without generous fellowships from the American Philosophical Society, the Robert H. Smith International Center for Jefferson Studies at Monticello, the Huntington Library, the David Library of the American Revolution, and the Library Company of Philadelphia and Historical Society of Pennsylvania, as well as a John R. Bockstoce Fellowship, which allowed me to spend a blissful summer at the John Carter Brown Library at Brown University. Archival research can be an isolating and lonely affair, but over the years I have been blessed by the communities of scholars, library staff, and beautiful surrounds of these institutions that have made researching and writing such a pleasure.

From the earliest days of this project, Carolyn Strange has taught me to be a better writer and patiently dragged me to more persuasive approaches, arguments, and scope. It must have been an utterly miserable job, so I am all the more thankful for her continuing wisdom as I begin writing my next book. As a sign of appreciation, Carolyn, please also get in touch if you ever need a spare kidney (so long as you beat Larry and Emma to the punch—I'm not made of kidneys). Donald Ratcliffe and Fern Eddy Schultz have kindly supplied research materials from Indiana and the United Kingdom. Individual chapters have greatly benefited from the advice of Annette Gordon-Reed, Jim Sofka, Nic Wood, Christine Sears, Paul Arthur, Marcus Rediker, Linda Colley, Cassandra Pybus, and Hannah Farber.

Portions of chapter three formed the basis of my contribution to an article coauthored with Cynthia Banham and published in the *Australian Journal of Politics and History* (vol. 62, no. 2), and other parts of this chapter also appear in a forthcoming article in the *Pennsylvania Magazine of History and Biography*. Portions of chapter four appeared in an article in the *Huntington Library Quarterly* (vol. 80, no. 4). These chapters have therefore benefited from the suggestions of the journals' anonymous reviewers.

Finally, I am eternally grateful to my parents, Margo Saunders and Bob Goodin, for reading and sharing their thoughts on the several iterations of this book. And to my friends with normal jobs for never mocking me for spending my days in dusty archives musing over the dead.

From Captives to Consuls

Victims of American Independence?

This book is about three men—Richard O'Brien (1758–1824), James Cathcart (1767–1843), and James Riley (1777–1840)—whose meandering lives are an ideal lens through which to view the forces that shaped the early days of the American republic. Global conflict, diplomatic crises, international commerce, the opening of new frontiers, the emerging roles of the American military, and the carefully cultivated masculinity of the "self-made man" are all reflected in the both ordinary and extraordinary lives of these men. Their experiences— volatility and insecurity in employment, finances, personal relationships, and safety—have obvious parallels in the challenges faced by many citizens, then and now. O'Brien, Cathcart, and Riley were forced to cultivate a talent for adaptability and reinvention that was the hallmark of the self-made man. As sailors, frontiersmen, diplomats, authors, and politicians and as slaves held for ransom in North Africa, the three subjects of this book provide important insights into the making of the American nation and how ordinary citizens shaped what it meant to be an American.

Long before Henry Clay coined the phrase *self-made man* in his maiden Senate speech in 1832, generations of American men had been inventing and reinventing themselves alongside the colonies' own reinvention into a united nation. For individuals and the nation, their identities as self-made and up-wardly mobile were not wholly organic. In both cases, identity was consciously manipulated for political and self-interested ends. For individuals, this meant never letting a good crisis go to waste—always being ready to frame personal ordeals as extensions of national suffering and virtue, and thus to position one-self for subsequent employment opportunities and other preferential treatment. For the nation, this meant crafting a unified identity to transcend sectional interests and expand the new nation's military reach so as to secure opportunities in new regions and economic spheres.

O'Brien, Cathcart, and Riley were paragons of reinvention, self-making, and modest mobility. They evolved from what O'Brien and Cathcart termed "victims of American independence" into opportunists of an expanding American empire. During the late colonial era and early republic, aspiring self-made men moved sideways more than upward. Precious few experienced the meteoric rise of a Benjamin Franklin or Alexander Hamilton, who are lodged in the public imagination as paragons of the period's self-made men. Instead, typically, such men were akin to Cathcart, Riley, and O'Brien: well enough connected to benefit from family favor in securing early employment, they rose to capture the nation's attention only briefly, if at all. Their lives were far from a steady march to prosperity. Ultimately, these three men found success only through their ability to adapt to circumstances beyond their control and to change and exploit identities and patrons while navigating a dizzying array of professions. Some, like Cathcart, were never satisfied with their modest gains. Others, like O'Brien, were perfectly content. Yet, others, like Riley, pushed far beyond their station and were publicly reined in for claiming superhuman feats, such as Riley's claim to have trudged through the Ohio frontier with almost one hundred pounds of live rattlesnakes clutching to his boots.[1]

This book is anchored by these three sailors, but it is by no means a maritime history. And though the common denominator among the three sailors is that they were held captive by North African corsairs, this is not a study of piracy. Despite being referred to both then and now as *pirates*, the sailors of the North African Barbary States of Algiers, Morocco, Tripoli, and Tunis who attacked Christian shipping and coastal villages between the early sixteenth and nineteenth centuries were in fact *corsairs*. Pirates were indiscriminate in their sea banditry and attacked shipping irrespective of nationality, religion, or the state of international affairs. Corsairs differed from pirates in each of those respects. They were closer to Cathcart's and O'Brien's brief Revolutionary flirtations with privateering. Both corsairs and privateers were sanctioned by the state to attack ships from nations with whom they were at war, and shares of any prizes were divided among the state, the ship's owner, and its crew, according to rank. Unlike privateers, however, Barbary corsairs ostensibly targeted their victims on the basis of religion.[2]

The diplomatic crisis and period of hostile relations between the United

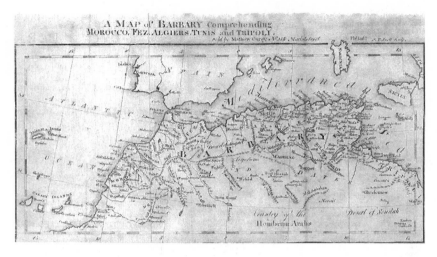

A map of Barbary comprehending Morocco, Fez, Algiers, Tunis, and Tripoli. In Mathew Carey, *A Short Account of Algiers and of its Several Wars* (Philadelphia: J. Parker, 1794), frontispiece.

Map of the Mediterranean region. In Dudley W. Knox, ed., *Naval Documents Related to the United States Wars with the Barbary Powers* (Washington, DC: US Government Printing Office, 1939), I: 140.

States and the Barbary States stretched from 1784 to 1815. But the origins of the crisis date to the same year as Christopher Columbus's first voyage to the Americas. In 1492 Queen Isabella and King Ferdinand completed the Reconquista of Spain, expelling the last Muslim ruler from Granada. Columbus's voyage was launched in celebration, while many of the expelled Moors settled in Algiers, Tunis, Morocco, and Tripoli, where they became tributaries of the Ottoman Empire. The Ottomans provided scant military or financial support to these four Barbary States, leaving Algiers, the largest and most powerful, to become a reluctant tributary of Spain. A year later, Spain imposed a series of import taxes. Algiers preferred to prosper quietly through lucrative Mediterranean trade, but the taxes were crippling. They reluctantly formed fleets of corsairs and turned to looting and extortion in order to meet the Spanish tax demands. Over the next few decades the various North African city-states passed between Spanish and Ottoman control, ultimately settling into a state of semi-autonomy.[3] Over the centuries the campaigns of Barbary corsairs that initially began as a response to Spanish taxation transformed into a default state of war against any Christian nation.

Though Christians were the targets, the driver of this war was largely economic rather than religious.[4] Writing in the unabashed literary style typical of a sailor held captive in Algiers, O'Brien articulated the corsairs' order of priorities to then minister to Paris Thomas Jefferson: "money is the God of Algiers & Mahomet their prophet."[5] John Adams and Jefferson had discovered as much for themselves three months earlier when, in March 1786, they visited the London home of Sidi Haji Abdul Rahman Adja, the ambassador of Tripoli. Adams and Jefferson were shocked when Adja advised them that Tripoli and the former American colonies were now at war. They asked how Americans had provoked war, and "the Ambassador answered . . . that it was founded on the laws of their Prophet; that it was written in their Koran, that all nations who should not have acknowledged their authority, were sinners; that it was their right and duty to make war upon them wherever they could be found, and to make slaves of all they could take as prisoners." After a presumably very awkward pause, Adja assured Adams and Jefferson that for a bargain of "30,000 guineas for his employers" (about $5 million in 2018 US dollars) and £3,000 for the ambassador (about $500,000) Tripoli would neglect this religious "right and duty" and sign a treaty of "perpetual peace." Ultimately, it took another ten years and well over 40,000 Spanish dollars (over $31 million) in cash and goods for the US government to strike a treaty with Tripoli.[6]

The corsairs mainly plucked their captives from coastal Spanish villages and merchant ships in the Mediterranean and Atlantic belonging to nations that had not submitted to the costly annual "tribute." During their peak in the early seventeenth century, corsairs even plied the Thames and raided the coasts of Ireland and Newfoundland, Canada. More than mere commerce raiders, these corsairs were frontline agents in the unique Ottoman slave trade. Some captured Europeans were held as lifelong slaves, but most were released upon payment of a ransom. Based on incomplete slave counts and informed speculation, there were approximately one million Europeans held captive in Barbary between the early sixteenth and late eighteenth centuries.[7] The years 1784 to 1815, however, were the last gasp of Mediterranean corsairs. O'Brien, Cathcart, and Riley (who came to be held captive after his ship wrecked, rather than captured by corsairs at sea) were among just 500 to 700 American sailors held for ransom.

The past twenty years has seen rapid growth in the quality and volume of scholarship on America's conflict with Barbary.[8] These scholars have all focused on a narrow period and on micro themes, either the military, comparative slavery, or the development of the American public sphere. In contrast, this book is a life history about the personal significance of macro developments upon individuals' lives. As such, it straddles the histories of politics, society, labor, race, gender, and frontiers at sea and on land. It is precisely because the history of sailors is at once the history of farmers, international commerce, literature, diplomacy, and local politics that just three well-sourced and well-traveled citizens can so effectively serve as a microcosm of ordinary citizens' influence and self-making across all of these spheres.[9]

The three biographical subjects of this book are perennial frontiersmen, laboring on the maritime frontier during the early republic and then the western frontier during the Jacksonian era. These periods coincide with the years when each of those frontiers was held to be *the* frontier in the popular American imagination.[10] The maritime frontier, which is often overlooked in conventional early American histories, is particularly significant. Though sailors were arguably more important than the young nation's few diplomats in positioning the United States within the world, they did not necessarily bind themselves to the nation's economic or political interests. Rather, sailors were more akin to merchants of the era, who Adam Smith noticed were "not necessarily the citizen of any particular country. It is in a great measure indifferent to him from what place he carries on his trade, and a very trifling disgust will make him remove his capital, and together with it all the industry which it supports, from one country to another."[11]

The one atypical experience that all three subjects of this book have in common is their captivity in the Barbary States. Their lives eerily echo historian Linda Colley's description of British captive Elizabeth Marsh, whose life "coincided with a distinctive and markedly violent phase of world history, in which connections between continents and oceans broadened and altered in multiple ways." "So," Colley writes, "this book charts a world in a life and a life in the world."[12] *From Captives to Consuls* similarly, but more modestly, aims to chart an emergent United States in three lives and three lives in an emergent United States. Like Marsh, who claimed herself a victim of "impersonal forces," O'Brien and Cathcart styled themselves "victims of American Independence." They were literally victims of Independence in the sense that they would not have been captured by Algerian corsairs if the American colonies had remained part of the British Empire, protected by the costly British tribute paid to the Barbary States.

Yet, like Marsh, they were not entirely victims because they were often the beneficiaries of the same commercial and political circumstances that put them in
danger.[13] O'Brien, Cathcart, and Riley are far from perfect representatives of the
triumphs, tribulations, expansions, or reinventions of the United States. They
cannot speak for women, slaves, Native Americans, or lifelong landlubbers. But
it is thanks to their varied careers that, in their own ways, they can so effectively
serve as exemplars of the era.

That these sailors were among the few North Americans to experience the
exceptional phenomenon of Barbary captivity does not disqualify them as can-
didates for a microhistory of (admittedly, white) American men of the era more
generally. These were simply individuals in whose lives significant forces of global
conflict, commerce, and cultural exchange happened to violently converge. That
the trio became leaders among American captives in Barbary, then diplomats,
authors, and politicians is simply the culmination of this convergence. That
they fell into captivity was random, neither self-selected nor the result of their
unique personalities or inherent abilities. This bad luck could have struck any
American sailor in the Mediterranean or outer reaches of the Atlantic. As ordinary, non-elite citizens at the time of their capture, their response to captivity
was that of any random American. Given the intense political, social, and economic circumstances of the period, many (if not most) Americans within the
former colonies also sat at the intersection of the same forces—whether they
were slaves, Native Americans, frontier settlers, writers, or participants in Shays'
Rebellion or the War of 1812. Though these forces shaped the lives of all citizens, it is unusual for them to converge so markedly in the lives of three individuals and for those three to leave behind such a trove of source material.

First drawing on the story of Barnabas Downs, an archetypal Cape Cod farmer
who wrote a book about his time as a Revolutionary privateer, this book expands into O'Brien's, Cathcart's, and Riley's early experiences as seafarers.
Drawing on Cathcart's and O'Brien's Revolutionary War pension records and
Riley's brief reminiscences, I supplement their accounts with those of biographical proxies (such as Barnabas Downs) who shared similar experiences and help
position the trio within the aggregate of their profession and of Revolutionary-
era sailors. Chapter one primarily explores the roles and motives of Cathcart,
O'Brien, and other sailors in the Revolution, arguing that their early lessons
in self-interested self-making at sea taught them to adapt to circumstances and
routinely tack their identities and allegiances toward profit and security. And
that those maritime experiences of the Revolution, celebrated for their daring
and sacrifice, were actually typical of those endured by sailors in the decades
before and after.

Like most Americans in the Revolutionary era, Cathcart and O'Brien did not throw tea into Boston Harbor. They were not members of the Continental Congress, nor were they at Yorktown when General Cornwallis surrendered to American forces. Instead, their experience of the Revolution as privateers, in state navies, and the Continental Navy was particular but also socially significant. In his early teenage years, Cathcart's career in the Continental Navy led to his first experience of captivity and mercenary reinvention. Born in Ireland, he fought for the colonies until captured by the British, when he again changed allegiances, reasserting his Irish birth and joining the Royal Navy in exchange for a pardon. Cathcart learned early that successful sailors and self-made men bend to the breeze and fly the flag of greatest convenience. Many, like Riley, only learned these lessons after repeated catastrophes. He was too young to serve in the Revolution, but the sorts of financial and physical crises he experienced in his troubled career as a merchant sailor during the Napoleonic Wars had plagued sailors since long before the Revolutionary era, despite turbulent changes in geopolitics and the practice of merchant shipping. Like Cathcart's and O'Brien's luckless Revolutionary years, Riley's early maritime career highlights adaptability as the key criterion for the success of sailors and self-made men—a skill that the trio subsequently honed during captivity in North Africa, and which continued to pay dividends throughout their lives.

Chapter two explores thematically, rather than chronologically, O'Brien's and Cathcart's experiences of captivity, arguing that their commentaries and observations from captivity are a nuanced manifestation of both American masculinity and Orientalism. With purposive prose, Cathcart's and O'Brien's dispassionate diary entries engage in traditional Othering by contrasting American values and peoples with their romanticized ethnographic observations of the culture, government, commerce, interracial dynamics, geology, and climate of Algiers. But when these observations became laced with passion and judgement, they helped establish nascent American Orientalism by distinguishing Barbary from the rest of the Muslim world, portraying its decadent and depraved peoples, governments, and lands as in ruinous decline. Through O'Brien's fourteen-month captivity diary and Cathcart's many journals, totaling about 283 handwritten pages, the chapter exposes how these non-elite citizens' self-interested framing of their captivity through masculinity, Othering, and Orientalism, in a uniquely American context, exhibits their conscious awareness and development upon preexisting political-literary trends within America that viewed North Africa through an Orientalist rather than an Other lens.

In examining Cathcart's and O'Brien's epistolary styles and impact, chapter three shows that even beyond American shores, non-elite citizens were keenly aware of the emerging American notions of nationhood, liberty, and citizenship. Through their correspondence, the captives successfully penetrated diplomatic networks and the minds of sympathetic diplomats like David Humphreys (minister to Lisbon, minister plenipotentiary to Madrid, and negotiator to Algiers), who exploited the captives' plight to help his own long-standing campaign to foster a single national American identity. Cathcart and O'Brien similarly deployed the pragmatic skills and style of correspondence they learned as merchant sailors to self-interestedly weave their cause for liberty into the emerging national narrative and position themselves for future government employment. Despite being captured so soon after the Revolution and being held in distant Algiers while founding national principles were still in a state of flux, they astutely deployed the emerging language of republican sensibility and patriotic duty to immerse their plight in the project of American nation building.

Once ransomed, Cathcart and O'Brien returned to American shores, barely touching dry land before they were shipped back to North Africa as US consuls. Chapter four, a social history of early American consular diplomacy, charts O'Brien's post-captivity career as US consul general to Algiers (1797–1803) and Cathcart's longer diplomatic career as a colorful consul to Tripoli (1798–1801), as an attaché to a rowdy Tunisian delegation in the United States (1805–1806), and finally as a quiet consul in Madeira, Portugal (1807–1815), and Cadiz, Spain (1815–1816). Throughout this chapter frequent reference is also made to William Eaton, America's exuberant consul to Tunis, who served alongside Cathcart and O'Brien. In 1800 correspondence between the State Department and its consuls in North Africa took between two and eighteen months to arrive. Consuls were therefore granted a surprising amount of autonomy and control over policy. This chapter details the diverse interests and heated exchanges between Cathcart, O'Brien, and their fellow diplomats on matters of policy, personality, and business interests. Their official correspondence with each other and the State Department, their private diary entries, and their commercial exchanges often overlap to the point where they become indistinguishable. These records expose the nature of early American consulships, where isolation gifted consuls with extraordinary discretionary powers and where their personal conflicts and private business dealings caused diplomatic crises.

In 1815, as Cathcart's diplomatic career drew to a close and O'Brien enjoyed his active retirement in a Pennsylvania market town, Riley's merchant brig *Commerce* hurtled onto the same rocks off the northwest African coast that had been snaring sailors for centuries. His crew was quickly enslaved and marched across the Sahara by nomadic tribesmen. Although Riley's captivity lasted less than three months, the details of his captivity floated across the Atlantic and made him a household name even before his return to American shores in 1816. Within a year he turned his comprehensive captivity journal of ethnographic and geographic observations into America's bestselling nonfiction account of Barbary captivity. His *Authentic Narrative of the Loss of the American Brig* Commerce went through at least twenty-five editions between 1817 and 1965 and introduced generations of Americans to North African tribal culture and a slave system with white slaves and African masters.[14] In spite of the narrative's recurring publication for over a century, chapter five joins historian Donald Ratcliffe in refuting the exaggerated claims of its commercial and cultural influence. It also interprets the text through its uncommon success in embracing and subverting the centuries-old practice of using captivity as a vehicle for literary-ethnography. Traditionally, captives seized the opportunity of their captivity to chart the history, ethnography, and geography of exotic regions in a way that highlighted the virtues of their own race, religion, and nation above those of their captors. Riley, however, used the medium to deconstruct monolithic stereotypes about Islam, individual and cultural traits of North Africans, and the commercial and agricultural potential of the region. In addition to analyzing the manuscript, the first published edition, and the heavily edited versions that were later included in anthologies, this chapter also traces the dissemination and readership of Riley's captivity, including both the published narrative and newspaper articles that preceded the book. The evolution of the narrative through its various editions, the public response, and the themes that each anthologist chose to excise or emphasize cumulatively provide a rich resource for the study of education, race, slavery, the distribution of literature, and captivity narratives in the nineteenth century.

The final chapter follows O'Brien, Cathcart, and Riley beyond where other historians have stopped, through their final years in the United States. This chapter touches on frontier towns, land speculation, state politics, and the American Colonization Society, but it is driven by Riley's, Cathcart's, and O'Brien's shared experience of taming the American interior. This cherished feature of national memory and identity builds on the broader sense of national identity that these three sailors and ex-captives had already helped forge by giving Americans a context of their nation in an increasingly globalized world. During their later years, O'Brien served as an unimpressive single-term legislator in the Pennsylvania General Assembly and tended a farm in Carlisle, Pennsylvania, a town at the crossroads of the western frontier and the urban centers of the Atlantic seaboard. Cathcart continued his furious pursuit of status and financial reimbursement and offered cunning political and commercial advice to his children in Indiana on how to successfully navigate the Jacksonian era in a frontier state. In 1818–1819, when employed as a government surveyor to cruise the Mississippi River and Louisiana bayous, the verbose Cathcart refused to follow instructions and merely count live oak and red cedar. Instead, he bestowed the government with an extraordinary report—virtually untouched since its submission—which extensively documents the region's environmental history, immigration, development, economics, and ill treatment of slaves and Native Americans.

By this time, Riley's *Narrative* and widely circulated newspaper articles had launched him into the national spotlight. Politicians and socialites courted him in Washington, DC. There he was briefly employed as agent for the US consul at Tangier, who was seeking reimbursements from the government. In 1819 the sailor's wanderlust again took hold and he, like Cathcart, became a government surveyor on the Indiana and Ohio frontiers, where in his words, "the forests bow before the axe of the *redeemed Captive*."[15] A year later he founded the town of Willshire in western Ohio, named after William Willshire, the British consul in Morocco who ransomed Riley and most of his crew. Like O'Brien, Riley served a single unimpressive term in his state assembly, and he explicitly invoked his experiences of slavery to campaign against the Missouri Compromise. He ultimately returned to the maritime frontier, establishing American trade with Morocco, before dying at sea while planning to bring Willshire, his impoverished redeemer and trading partner, back to the United States.

Through their contributions in print and a colorful parade of professions, the trio became purveyors of what historian David Jaffee calls the "Village Enlightenment." Jaffee defines the Village Enlightenment as "the formation of a market for cultural commodities in the printed form" that were produced by ordinary citizens, signifying the "erosion of a hierarchical structure of authority, in which cultural controls were held by a clerical or college-trained elite," and pointing to the "emergence of a social organization of knowledge suitable to the requirements of rural folk in the rising republic."[16] From the late eighteenth century onwards, non-specialist authors and booksellers who produced a broad range of publications that built virtue and developed practical skills came to "short-circuit the hierarchical flow of information."[17] These booksellers were in the commercial "'business' of Enlightenment" by making a living through democratizing both the production and consumption of knowledge.[18] This non-specialist knowledge, like the wholly new information articulated in Riley's *Narrative*, along with the political intelligence forwarded by O'Brien and Cathcart from Barbary, and their later writings about commerce, science, and surveying, all reflect the "practical information and personal insight" of Village Enlightenment texts.[19] In law, medicine, and religion, it was non-elite citizens who disrupted established knowledge of the era. With the proliferation of newspapers, journals, and scientific literature, non-elite citizens now had the tools to set agendas and "overthrow coercive and authoritarian structures" throughout the professional class.[20] Jaffee coined the term *Village Enlightenment* in 1990, during the earliest days of the internet. He could not have imagined that two centuries after the early republic a nascent computer network would similarly short-circuit the production of knowledge. Today, the democratized internet is rightfully critiqued for enabling conspiracy theorists and "fake news" to thrive by circumventing traditional gatekeepers. But, much like the Village Enlightenment, the bulk of new content is produced by ordinary people aspiring to be beneficial or benign, such as personal reviews of experiences, products, and places. As in earlier centuries, non-specialist authors often publish inaccurate data, but these are typically mistakes and misunderstandings, rarely reflecting true malice.

The lives of O'Brien, Cathcart, and Riley highlight how non-elite citizens cannily manipulated developing concepts of liberty, masculinity, and nationhood and exploited ongoing local and foreign affairs to self-interestedly maneuver through the various phases of their lives. These "victims of American Independence" repeatedly found opportunities in adversity. They turned the Revolution to their advantage by serving as privateers and capitalized on their captivity by writing bestselling narratives and using their ordeal as a qualification for employment in the consular service. Once back in the United States they used their modest fame to secure election to state legislatures and receive further government appointments to survey the nation's territorial expansions in the South and West. This successful self-interested pursuit of the opportunities provided by the expanding American empire could be termed *the invisible hand of American nation building*. The letters, diaries, captivity narratives, government reports, and political activism penned by O'Brien, Cathcart, and Riley were far more than purely self-serving. They truly made these self-made men agents of the Village Enlightenment.

CHAPTER ONE

Farmers, Privateers, and Prisoners of the Revolution

Come all you young fellows of Courage so Bold
Come Enter on Board and we will Cloth you with gold.
Recruiting song for the privateer Montgomery's
second voyage, 1782

Barnabas Downs was a Cape Cod farmer before and during the Revolution's early years. He survived three campaigns as a soldier before following tens of thousands of his countrymen in seeking fortune as a privateer. Life at sea was far less forgiving than on land and, if lucky, sailors were rewarded accordingly. One Massachusetts privateer, the *Montgomery*, made its crew rich on its very first voyage, netting each of its ordinary sailors £200 ($35,000 in 2018 US dollars) and the captain a staggering £1450 ($256,000). That was an enviable haul for just a few weeks of work. Instead of enjoying such a floating fortune, Downs's ship *Bunker Hill* was captured and the crew was imprisoned in Halifax a mere six days after setting sail. Downs contracted smallpox and then a fever, "which brought me to the very borders of eternity!"[1] Once restored to health and returned home in a prisoner exchange, he "could not resist the inclination I had to try once more what Providence would do for me."[2] Ignoring the evidence from his previous voyages, hoping Providence intended him riches rather than death, he sought to improve on his last voyage by joining a larger privateer, the *General Arnold*. Downs was still not dissuaded from the sea when, in a small boat transporting crew to the *General Arnold* in New York harbor, he was caught in bad weather, nearly drowned, and was driven aground on Governors Island, where he was stranded for twenty-four hours. Soon after, the *General Arnold* was hit by such a severe storm off Plymouth that, "death appeared inevitable, and we waited every moment for its appearance. Even now, when I recollect my feelings it is difficult to steady my pen!"[3] Two days later, when the storm subsided, only 60 of the original 120-man crew had survived. When rescuers from shore reached the stricken ship, they thought Downs too had perished, "but seeing one of my eye-lids move they took me up and laying me in the boat carried me ashore," force-feeding him until he regained consciousness.[4] Ultimately, 88 men died on the ship or as a result of their injuries. Downs lost both of his feet. Despite the physical impairment, within just six years he had married and raised five children. He lived "comfortably and respectably" on land, tending to his own household upkeep, and had a small business making spoons and inkstands, which financially sustained him when supplemented with an annual church collection.[5]

Despite his physical disability and initially framing himself as a victim of the Revolution, Downs built upon skills he learned during the Revolution to provide employment throughout his life and drew on public sympathy of his disability to supplement his income with charity from the local community.[6] Like Downs, fellow sailors—including Richard O'Brien, James Cathcart, and James Riley—found lessons rather than fortune in adversity, and each sailor successfully leveraged those early lessons to secure compensation and employment. O'Brien's, Cathcart's, and Riley's strategies and approaches to self-advocacy helped them transition from captives to consuls, then to authors, politicians, and bureaucrats.

For some sailors, like Downs, the Revolution was the most agonizing, glorious, and formative experience of their lives. Or at least that is what they chose to write in their correspondence at the time and to recount in their memoirs and pension applications decades later. Yet there is little by way of a paper trail for most participants in, and those born during, the Revolution. O'Brien, later a reliable correspondent during twenty years of captivity and government service, seems never to have penned a syllable about his Revolutionary adventures. Cathcart, a prolific correspondent from the age of 18 until his death, waited until he was 66 years old to sketch his Revolutionary service in just a few paragraphs of correspondence to family and patrons and once more under oath before a judge to bolster his pension application. Riley, an equally prolific correspondent and author, never documented his earliest memories, which would have been of the final years of the Revolution. Nor did he later reflect on how his family, his youth, and his life were shaped by the Revolution, life under the Articles of Confederation, the outcome of the Constitutional Convention, or the repercussions of the Jay Treaty. Given this silence in the sources, it is necessary to draw upon other sailors, such as Downs, to serve as surrogates to supplement the scarce records left by O'Brien, Cathcart, and Riley.

With their Irish lineage and scant connections to the colonies, both O'Brien and Cathcart eagerly pursued the profitable gray area between privateering and legitimate naval service, floating between privateers, state navies, and the Continental Navy. During this drifting they, and later Riley, learned to adapt to circumstances and craft their public personas of self-making and self-sacrifice in aid of self-interested ends. Take, for example, Cathcart's unverifiable claims of service in the Continental Navy and his equally dubious account of his imprisonment, where the motives of sailors' service were tested and from which Cathcart claims to have escaped. Yet in reality he defected to the Royal Navy. The curated public persona of self-sacrifice is similarly exemplified in subsequent pension applications. There Cathcart's records dovetail with O'Brien's and their contemporaries' memoirs in highlighting the role of selective and strategic memory and self-interest in 1820s and 1830s recollections of the Revolutionary War. Wanderlust, fortune-seeking, and mild patriotism were the primary motives that lured young men to undertake their Revolutionary War service at sea, and financial self-interest similarly drew their comrades to the Continental Army. But these initial inspirations faded from public (and apparently also private) memory with each decade.[7] Too young to take part in the Revolution, Riley nonetheless found his life at sea remarkably similar to that of sailors of the late colonial and Revolutionary eras.

The trio's hard lessons in self-making and adaptation during the Revolution and Napoleonic Wars positioned them to later capitalize on their Barbary captivity to secure government service. Furthermore, the generations of seafarers who kept records between 1750 and 1815 documented a maritime experience with the same risks, maritime culture, and politicized cosmopolitanism that O'Brien, Cathcart, and Riley experienced. They took the Revolution in stride. Though some sailors made overt declarations of patriotism in correspondence at the time, and especially in their later memoirs, some social historians overgeneralize these declarations into a form of Revolutionary exceptionalism. Scholars such as Jesse Lemisch, Peter Linebaugh, and Marcus Rediker depict sailors' experiences of the Revolution as representing the crescendo of sailors' intellectual and organizational influence on various transatlantic causes. The accumulation of racial, labor, economic, and ideological causes that these scholars allege sailors saw embodied in the Revolutionary struggle is equaled only by the alleged purity of sailors' motives and the exceptional nature of their wartime experiences, compared to the decades and conflicts before and after.[8] True, the scale of conflict and number of sailors who endured hardship during the Revolution was greater than decades before or after, because the colonies were one of the principal parties to that conflict, rather than being peripheral players in other struggles. But the nature of that hardship was entirely unexceptional for seafarers between 1750 and 1815, as were sailors' interpretations of and responses to these circumstances.

From the late colonial period to the end of the Napoleonic Wars (1750 to 1815), taking to sea was advertised as an opportunity for adventure and riches. In reality, optimistic farm boys like Downs and Riley ended up finding it to be a daily gamble with life, liberty, and property. Sailors risked disease, enslavement to corsairs, impressment into forced service in the Royal Navy, or imprisonment and seizure of their goods by privateers. They took to sea at ages as young as 8 or 12, like James Cathcart, or 13, like John Paul Jones.[9] But the overwhelming majority of sailors were clustered in the 20-to-24-year-old age bracket, with this group accounting for ten times as many sailors as the 30-to-34-year-old age group. Some had quit the sea before rounding their thirtieth birthday, but more than twice the number who voluntarily quit had actually died at sea in their teens or twenties, by drowning, shipwreck, or disease.[10]

These pervasive risks, though real, skew the written history of life at sea and of sailors in general. Ships' logs offer a glimpse into daily working life that is unparalleled in any other occupation of the era, and the overwhelming majority of those daily entries merely record the weather. Occasionally a sail is spotted on the horizon and then typically evaded to avoid a potential enemy warship, unscrupulous privateer, or pirate.

In spite of this wealth of sources and (occasional) adventure at sea, North American sailors in the Revolutionary era are best remembered for their activities on shore: for their coarse political activism, for being dragged drunk out of taverns by press gangs, and for their prominent roles in the Boston Massacre and Tea Party. This land-based memory of an occupation that is defined by the sea is oddly appropriate. The sailors who manned merchant ships, privateers, and navies actually spent most of their career ashore, and that is where this chapter partly dwells: on farms, in prisons, and in admiralty courts.

By the time of the Revolution, O'Brien was already a veteran of the sea. It was there he received his informal education in industry, navigation, leadership, geopolitics, and commerce. His formal education, as he later confessed to Cathcart, consisted of "only the primer or spelling book[;] Esop's fables and Vorter's arithmetic; . . . the Bible and mariner's compass; [and] a few gazetta reading."[11] Born to Irish parents in Maine (then part of Massachusetts), he traveled to Ireland and traversed the Atlantic on merchant ships before returning to America as a teenager to serve in the Pennsylvania State Navy and maybe also

James Leander Cathcart. In James Cathcart, *The Captives: Eleven Years a Prisoner in Algiers* (La Porte, IN: Herald Print, 1899), frontispiece.

the Virginia State Navy. The only evidence of this service are the pension applications of his widow, first lodged fifty years after the war, and a single letter from a Philadelphia-based shipowner who employed O'Brien during and after the war.[12]

Cathcart's pre-Revolutionary days, like the rest of his life, are better documented than O'Brien's. Born in Ireland, Cathcart's childhood education was relatively comprehensive, teaching him of ancient Rome and instilling a thirst for knowledge that served as a sort of intellectual escape during his later captivity in Algiers and which lead his captors to presume he was schooled in alchemy. It is unclear where or how Cathcart received this education, since he claims he was just 2 years old when he was shipped to America under the care of his uncle, Captain John Cathcart, who spent much of his time at sea. A year after the outbreak of the Revolution, his uncle joined the fight as an officer on the Massachusetts State Navy ship *Tyrannicide*.[13] In exhaustive testimony as part of a pension application in 1833 and a "rough index of your father's services" penned to his son a month later, James Cathcart claims that he joined the Revolution, as a midshipman aboard the *Tyrannicide*, sometime before mid-1779 at the age of 12.[14] There is no independent record of James Cathcart's Revolutionary service, which is consistent with other sailors of his age. They were old enough to take to sea as apprentices with the assistance of their kinship networks yet were often left off muster rolls.

Neither Cathcart nor O'Brien ever discussed what initially drew them to the sea. For boys without familial maritime connections, the motive was often to visit strange and exotic lands.[15] But those who came from sailor stock, like Cathcart and O'Brien, typically sought steady employment in a profession that offered the (very rare) prospect of promotion to the lucrative rank of captain and let them pursue that goal among crews that were composed of their hometown friends and neighbors.[16]

As boys, George Washington and Benjamin Franklin felt the pull of the sea and adventure but were talked out of it.[17] Sailors and prospective sailors came from all walks of life, though there are some patterns.[18] Cathcart's and O'Brien's familial path to port, and their Irish origins, mirror the paths of many colonial-era sailors.[19] A comprehensive study of mid-eighteenth-century sailors in Salem, Massachusetts, found that about 60 percent who departed from the port town were born in Salem or a neighboring town, and half of them sailed out with a captain from the same part of town.[20] During this period over 50 percent of Salem's boys aged 15 to 24 years old took to sea at least once every fifteen months, with each voyage ranging from a few weeks to a few months. There was therefore a reasonable expectation of regular maritime employment for those in proximity who knew how to get it. Even Riley, whose parents were farmers, benefited from being raised on the banks of the Connecticut River, just twenty-five miles from the sea, and having uncles in the maritime world to facilitate introductions and early employment.[21]

Rather than simplifying the lives of American merchant sailors, the success of the Revolution now made them the targets of all nations, and the friends of none. Like his predecessors in the colonial era, Riley faced the same and greater dangers a generation later. As a boy, Riley benefited from a basic formal education until the age of 8 when, like many farm boys, he was sent to work and live on a neighboring farm.[22] But like many coastal farm boys, he also expected to spend part of his youth at sea. Some were following wanderlust, others driven by poor employment prospects. Many, like Riley, were driven by both push and pull factors: "having become tired of hard work on the land, I concluded that the best way to get rid of it, was to go to sea and visit foreign countries," where ample and interesting work was readily available.[23] At the age of 15, against his parents' wishes, he ventured to the West Indies, and by "the age of twenty years had passed through the grades of cabin boy, cook, ordinary seaman, second mate, and chief mate, on board different vessels," ultimately becoming a captain in 1797, just as O'Brien and Cathcart were being released from captivity in Algiers and returning to the United States.[24]

By the time of the Revolution, sailors and shipowners were forced to either dry dock their brigs, refit them as privateers, or become smugglers. Privateering swept through Atlantic port towns like a tsunami from the earliest days of the

Revolution. Andrew Sherburne epitomizes this "rage for privateering." Just 13 years old in 1799, Sherburne's parents convinced him to join the Continental Navy rather than the privateer that he preferred. He secured the more respectable, though less lucrative, position through family connections. Driven by more than pure patriotism, he remembered that his brother, a privateer, had recently captured thirteen ships, and young Andrew now "became more eager to try my fortune at sea."[25] Even with the paltry division of prizes mandated in the Continental Navy, Sherburne's time aboard the USS *Ranger* netted him a small fortune of "about one ton of sugar, from thirty to forty gallons of fourth proof Jamaica rum, about twenty pounds of cotton, and about the same quantity of ginger, logwood and allspice, about seven hundred dollars in paper money, equal to one hundred dollars in specie."[26] So prevalent was the economic pressure of taking to sea that, while walking the streets in his sailor attire, Sherburne was regularly accosted to join ships, with recruiters pitching, "Ha shipmate, don't you wish to take a short cruise in a fine schooner and make your fortune?"[27]

The Continental Congress foresaw lucrative privateering luring experienced sailors from the Continental and state navies, so the legislation that underpinned privateering also mandated that at least one-third of each crew should be landlubbers.[28] Thanks, in part, to this measure, and despite ever-increasing bond rates that privateers were forced to pay before setting sail, Benjamin Rush (physician and Founding Father) feared as early as 1776 that the diversion of personnel to privateering would soon also cripple the fighting capacity of the army. Writing to Richard Henry Lee (fellow Pennsylvanian and Founding Father), Rush calculated that "the four Eastern States will find great difficulty in raising their quota of men, owing to that excessive rage for privateering which now prevails among them. . . . As a moderate computation, there are now not less than ten thousand men belonging to New England on board privateers."[29] On the domestic front, Abigail Adams feared she would inherit a greater burden of harvesting duties, writing to her husband, "the rage for privateering is as great here as any where. Vast Numbers are employd in that way. If it is necessary to make any more draughts upon us the women must Reap the Harvests. I am willing to do my part. I believe I could gather Corn and Husk it, but I should make a poor figure at digging Potatoes."[30] In total, colonial privateering attracted up to 3000 ships and 70,000 sailors over the course of the war, totaling approximately 3 percent of the colonial population, including women and slaves.[31] One estimate has those privateers capturing around 600 British ships, including 16 men-of-war, totaling a value of $18 million (about $450 million in 2018 US dollars); or by another estimate, they captured as many as 3,176 British ships, with 893 of those vessels recaptured or sold back to the British.[32] Either estimate far exceeds the combined damage inflicted by the state navies and the 13-ship Continental Navy.

One measure to stem the flow of sailors to privateering gave sailors of all ranks in state navies and the Continental Navy a share of prizes they captured. The crews of both state navy and Continental Navy ships were entitled to 50 percent of their captured prize (the value of the captured ships and cargoes, including any slaves), divided according to rank, with the other half going to the state.[33] Even the privateer vessels outfitted by state navies (a distinct category from privateers that entirely equipped themselves) ceded two-thirds of their prizes to the state and held just one-third for the captors; however, if they captured an enemy warship, they were entitled to 50 percent of the prize.[34] Though that was extremely rare because privateers were only lightly armed and were highly risk averse, fleeing from any fight they were not confident of winning. They were profit-seeking endeavors, not bold military enterprises. O'Brien and Cathcart joined many others like Sherburne in serving in this gray area between privateering and traditional naval service, receiving salaries from the government and at the same time profiting from shares of captured vessels.

The scant record of O'Brien's Revolutionary service is revealed only in a single letter from Mathew Irwin, his employer during and after the Revolution, and in the persistent pension applications of his widow, Elizabeth Maria O'Brien, which were lodged decades later in the 1830s and 1850s.[35] Four years into O'Brien's captivity in Algiers, Irwin, the Philadelphia-based owner of O'Brien's captured merchant brig *Dauphin*, wrote to President Washington pleading for government action to secure O'Brien's release. Irwin confirmed that O'Brien "is a Man of the strictest veracity and honor, and in the worst of times was a staunch Friend to his Country, in the year 1780 he was first Leiutenant of the Ship *Congress* (of which Vessell I was a principal owner) when she Captured the *Savage* Sloop of War after a very obstinate engagement."[36] It is easy to verify Irwin as a part owner of the twenty-four-gun, two-hundred-man privateer *Congress*, with other part owners including General Nathanael Greene and his two assistant quartermasters.[37] But if O'Brien was truly a lieutenant on the ship in September 1781 when it captured the Royal Navy sloop *Savage*, this means he participated in one of the bloodiest battles of an American privateer during the war. The battle was so intense that the ships quickly lost all maneuverability when sails and ropes were shredded, and dozens were killed by cannon fire at such proximity that the flares from each ship scorched the men opposite. Adding to the reverence for the *Congress*'s crew was that the *Savage* had just plundered Washington's home at Mount Vernon, and it was rare for a privateer to challenge a Royal Navy ship of equal strength.[38] Yet O'Brien never wrote about this celebrated service in his own letters to Washington during a decade of captivity, nor did his family cite it in posthumous pension applications.

Instead, his family's pension claims list him as a lieutenant on the Virginia State Navy ship *Jefferson*.[39] There is no record of a fishing ship, brig, privateer, or state navy ship named the *Jefferson*, which is surprising for the small Virginian fleet. His family likely recalled his rank of lieutenant correctly, but they misremembered the name and state of the ship he served on. Alternatively, given the predilection for unnecessary exaggeration and outright lies in pension applications, it is also possible that O'Brien's family knew he never served in the Virginia State Navy, but was merely a privateer. As a privateer he would have been ineligible for a Revolutionary War pension until the pension reforms of 1832, eight years after his death. In their pension applications submitted from 1831 to 1851, O'Brien's widow, son, and lawyer, like many other applicants, may have believed their application would only be successful if O'Brien was presented as a patriotic state navy sailor rather than a mercenary privateer.[40] It is also telling that these applications do not include typical verifying information such as the names of additional ships he served on, the commanders of those ships, the dates of his service, or the names of any living sailors or their families who could corroborate O'Brien's service in the Virginia State Navy.

Cathcart's Revolutionary service, though slightly better documented, is even more fraught. He was just 8 years old when the war began in 1775. By 1779, aged 12, he claims to have been employed thanks to his uncle Captain John Cathcart, who was his only relative in the colonies and with whom he had sailed from Ireland a decade earlier. Like many boys and young men in colonial port cities, the younger Cathcart alleges this family connection helped him find Revolutionary work as a midshipman on the *Tyrannicide*, a fourteen-gun, seventy-five-man privateer, which his uncle John captained until it was destroyed in the Penobscot Expedition, the largest American naval expedition of the Revolution.[41] The Penobscot Expedition was meticulously planned to be a major strategic victory for the Continentals, with forty-four ships, including privateers, state navies, and the Continental Navy, working to best the unprepared Royal Army and Navy at a poorly defended island fort on what is now the central coast of Maine. Complementing naval forces were one hundred Continental artillerymen, led by none other than Paul Revere, supported by one thousand militiamen.[42] Due to an impressive series of strategic missteps by Continental officers, what should have been an easy conquest instead became a month-long siege-turned-retreat into the wilderness without guides or supplies. Many Continental ships, including the *Tyrannicide*, were lost, making this the greatest American naval disaster until Pearl Harbor.[43] Revere was soon placed under house arrest and fought for two years to clear his name.

Cathcart's Revolutionary endeavors prior to the Penobscot Expedition are sketchy. If he was aboard the *Tyrannicide* on June 16, 1779, as he claims, he would have aided in the capture at sea of thirty-four South Carolina slaves—men, women, and children—who had themselves been captured by a British privateer. By bringing these slaves back to Boston and claiming them as legitimate prizes, Captain Cathcart and the *Tyrannicide* instigated a spectacular four-year legal battle between Massachusetts and South Carolina that threatened the unity between the colonies during the Revolution and shaped constitutional discussions of slavery after the war. According to Emily Blanck, the first historian to unearth and detail the significance of the *Tyrannicide* affair to American legal history, the ensuing court cases to determine ownership or freedom of the slaves forced the American political elite to ask themselves how cooperation or long-term unity between colonies with such radically different ideas of liberty could be realistically maintained.[44]

The saga began in April 1779 when a British privateer raided South Carolina's Waccamaw Peninsula and captured the thirty-four slaves. Although Lord Dunmore's Proclamation offered freedom to slaves who joined the Loyalist cause, British privateers continued to capture slaves and sell them in the Caribbean islands. Blanck speculates this might have been the fate of the thirty-four South Carolinians if they did not then endure two months of changing hands at sea.[45] First, the British privateer was quickly bested by a Spanish ship, and the thirty-four slaves became Spanish property, only for that Spanish ship to then be taken by two other British privateers. Finally, on June 16, those British privateers were captured by the *Tyrannicide* and another American privateer, and the ships and slaves were transported to Boston, where the slaves were stowed on Castle Island fort until the courts could rule on their fate.[46] While they waited, ten of the slaves were hired out by Paul Revere, then commander of the troops stationed on Castle Island (before the Penobscot Expedition brought his military career to an inglorious end). John Hancock requested three slaves for his home on Beacon Hill, and even abolitionist Nathaniel Appleton petitioned for one servant.[47]

The drawn-out legal process reached a fever pitch in 1783 when South Carolina governor Benjamin Guerard wrote to Massachusetts governor John Hancock to complain about "the illegal Detention of the said Negroes, contrary to the Articles of Confederation, & as a gross Attack on the Dignity, Independence & Sovereignty of this State, & to demand peremptorily that they be forthwith restored to this State at the expense of the State of Massachusetts."[48] When the legal broadsides finally rang silent, the Massachusetts courts decided the slaves were indeed property, but since the slaves had not committed any crime, Massachusetts had no obligation to detain or extradite the slaves to

South Carolina.[49] Twenty of the slaves had already returned to South Carolina before this final decision, but the fourteen who remained in Massachusetts were protected by local black communities for the rest of their lives. In Blanck's words, "as a hybrid of Massachusetts and South Carolina, the *Tyrannicide* slaves found themselves legally enslaved but de facto emancipated."[50] Given the irony of the young James Cathcart's (possible) role in attempting to profit from slavery, only to become a slave himself six years later, it is unsurprising that he omitted the *Tyrannicide* affair from his scant recollections of Revolutionary service.

If Cathcart's actual Revolutionary activities before the Penobscot Expedition are sketchy, then his activities afterward are manifestly suspect. There is no record of him from soon after the *Tyrannicide*'s capture of the South Carolina slaves (mid-1779) until late 1782. Perhaps he was captured at Penobscot Bay, or perhaps he fled with his uncle. He claims to have joined the Continental Navy frigate *Confederacy* in October 1779, tasked with transporting French minister Count Gerard back to France and John Jay to Spain.[51] Many of the *Confederacy*'s crew were impressed sailors and delinquents captured along the Delaware River, where Cathcart claims he joined the crew. In 1779 the ship's officers even attempted to board and nearly opened fire on an American brig in the Delaware River that refused to surrender its crew.[52] This was not an isolated incident. Although colonialists bemoaned British impressment, they were also regular perpetrators, coercing captured British sailors and their own countrymen into service aboard privateers and in the Continental Navy. At least one British sailor, Thomas Haley, was captured and enlisted by an American privateer and then had to explain himself to British authorities when he was again captured and thrown in an English prison.[53] If pressed into service on the *Confederacy*, Cathcart's most patriotic act during the Revolution may have actually been against his will. In any case, there is no record of him joining the ship, being paid for his service, receiving shares for the three ships the *Confederacy* captured, or being imprisoned with its crew when they were captured by the Royal Navy just over two years after the frigate first launched.[54] He claims that less than a year after the crew was imprisoned on the infamous prison hulks in New York Harbor, *Jersey* and *Good Hope*, he successfully escaped with another prisoner, Benjamin Russell of Connecticut, and rejoined the fight in March 1782.[55] Yet there is no record of anyone named Benjamin Russell from Connecticut filing for a pension, and the name does not appear on any prisoner lists or in any prisoner memoirs from the New York prison hulks. If Cathcart fabricated his service on the *Confederacy*, it was likely to bolster his pension claim by linking himself to Continental service and the personal hardship of imprisonment on hulks that were notorious for their squalid conditions and prodigious death rates.

Prison hulk in New York Harbor. In Ebenezer Fox, *The Adventures of Ebenezer Fox in The Revolutionary War* (Boston: Charles Fox, 1847), 128.

Over twenty years of hyperbolically patriotic publications about sailors of the Revolution may have influenced Cathcart's own recollections of the war, which he did not pen until 1833. Though the pension reforms of 1832 invited applications from privateers and militias, Cathcart may still have hedged his bets by emphasizing or fabricating his imprisonment and Continental Navy service. Either scenario was unnecessary, since two shipmates on the *Tyrannicide* had already been awarded pensions, one acknowledging his profits from three prizes and the other unconvincingly describing the *Tyrannicide* as a "sloop of war." The reviewing government official saw through the vagueness, correcting in the margins, "privateer." Civil servants were clearly aware of how pension applicants routinely massaged language to most favorably shape their service, yet did not hold this against them, granting pensions to both.[56]

An alternative scenario, equally typical of Revolutionary-era sailors, is that Cathcart continued to serve under his uncle after the Penobscot Expedition rather than joining the crew of the *Confederacy*. If so, the younger Cathcart's movements would be perfectly traceable. Following the humiliation at Penobscot Bay, John Cathcart continued to captain ships primarily owned by a single maritime firm, Tracy, Jackson and Tracy. The Massachusetts firm was prominent before the Revolution and likely commissioned more than fifty privateers during the war.[57] Commanding the firm's troubled privateer *Essex* in November 1779, Cathcart captured a brig near Jamaica "with a valuable cargo of rum, sugar, coffee, cocoa, etc.," but sixteen of the *Essex* crew died of disease and malnutrition en route to Massachusetts to officially claim their prize.[58] Their fate was all too common. After all, the single greatest cause of sailors leaving the profession was through death at sea, mostly from disease, which accounted for 30 percent of those who stopped sailing.[59]

Six months later the *Essex* was hunting for prizes off the Irish coast with two more American privateers, the *Pilgrim* and *Defense*. Captain Cathcart showed no hesitation in preying upon Irish merchant ships, despite only recently making his home in the colonies, after having been born and raised in Ireland where his family still lived. One morning in June 1781, the trio of privateers spotted a sail on the horizon and pursued it into the afternoon, when the *Essex* noticed another sail in the distance and left the other American privateers to chase this new prize. Unfortunately, the *Essex* learned too late that it was pursuing the Royal Navy frigate *Queen Charlotte*, which easily overpowered the *Essex* while the other two American privateers fled. Rather than the crew of the *Essex* being consigned to a long stay in in an English prison, as was the norm, Captain Cathcart somehow appeared free in Boston within six months, likely the result of a fortuitous prisoner exchange. From there, he captained the Massachusetts State Navy ship *Tartar* for merely a matter of days before returning to Boston Harbor to hide from a ship he prematurely thought was a British fifty-gun frigate, but embarrassingly turned out to be just an eighteen-gun British privateer. The newspapers promptly shamed him for cowardice.[60] Although similar mistakes by other American privateers did not become public knowledge and fodder for newspapers, all privateers were similarly risk averse. Cathcart made up for the public shaming by going on to take several prizes. Two years later when the Massachusetts State Navy sold the *Tartar* as a privateer, the new owners retained Cathcart as captain, but in early 1783, within just five weeks of setting sail, the *Tartar* was captured.[61] This was the last action Captain Cathcart saw of the Revolutionary War and would also have been the last for young James had he indeed stayed with his uncle.

Whether James Cathcart was a prisoner-turned-British-sailor or a Continental-sailor-turned-lying-pension-seeker, he and his uncle were clearly adaptable. And they were both victims and financial beneficiaries of the Revolution. The pair likely enjoyed greater benefits than O'Brien, who was probably promoted to merchant captain at the close of the Revolution thanks to his service during the war but did not receive an obvious monetary benefit from his service since his widow filed for a Revolutionary War pension eight years after his death.

None of the muster rolls or surviving documents of the *Confederacy* validate Cathcart's claim that, as a teenager serving on the Continental frigate, he was captured, held on the prison ships *Jersey* and *Good Hope*, or escaped in 1782. Nor is he mentioned in the handful of memoirs written by American prisoners who were on the *Jersey* and *Good Hope* or in the British-produced lists of prisoners. It is unclear whether the *Confederacy's* crew was imprisoned in the New York prison hulks or in England. According to what might be a misreading of a letter from the *Confederacy's* captain Seth Harding, one historian argues that the captured sailors were sent to England, whereas the New York–based Loyalist newspaper *Rivington's Royal Gazette*, and the pension application of *Confederacy* sailor Francis Clarydge, claim the crew was sent to the *Jersey*.[62]

Irrespective of where Cathcart was initially imprisoned, he soon joined the Royal Navy, where he appears as an ordinary seaman on the muster roll for the *Enterprize* in November 1782 and then the Royal Navy frigate *Leander* in June 1783.[63] It's possible he defected to the Royal Navy before even entering prison. In reporting the *Confederacy's* capture, the *Rivington's Royal Gazette* notes that among "near 300 men on board her [the *Confederacy*] were found a number of British seamen who had been forced into the enemy's service thro' the harshest treatment in their [colonial] gaols, these with great alacrity immediately entered into [the service] of their native country."[64] Many of the *Confederacy's* crew were indeed impressed British and colonial sailors. As an Irishman, Cathcart may have immediately opted to join them in Royal Naval service rather than suffer the high chance of disease and death in the prison hulks before his sixteenth birthday.

The imprisonment of Revolutionary sailors, their subsequent service in the Royal Navy, and the unverifiable claims in pension applications all highlight the difficulties in researching imprisoned sailors and their negotiable loyalties over the course of the war. Whereas fewer than eight thousand colonials were killed in battle during the Revolution, up to twelve thousand died in the more than twenty New York prison ships that were reserved for sailors from late 1777 onward, and up to eighteen thousand more sailors were held in prisons in Britain.[65] None was considered a prisoner of war because Britain retained its claim of sovereignty over the colonies; instead, they were classified as civil prisoners and charged with treason.

The colonial prisoners held in Britain were typically sailors and, as such, can serve as an additional pool to help illuminate O'Brien's, and especially Cathcart's, unresolved issues of identity, loyalty, and escape claims. These British-based prisoners enjoyed a far-lower mortality rate than their comrades in New York, although they were still highly motivated to escape or defect. According to analysis by historian Paul Gilje, when imprisoned sailors are divided by rank, colonial captains held in British prisons accounted for more than half of successful prison escapees, compared to over one-third of all junior officers, one-fifth of petty officers, and less than 5 percent of ordinary seamen.[66] More revealing is the breakdown of defections by birthplace, which Gilje found exposes distinct differences in allegiances between American-born and foreign-born prisoners. Of those sailors serving among colonial forces who were held in British prisons, almost 60 percent of foreign-born prisoners joined the Royal Navy in exchange for a pardon, whereas just 12 percent of American-born prisoners enlisted.[67] Cathcart's Irish birth therefore places him in this comfortable majority of foreign-born prisoners who tacked their allegiances to the prevailing breeze and joined the Royal Navy to avoid prison.

Approximately the same 8 to 12 percent of prisoners in both New York prison hulks and British prisons opted to receive pardons by shipping out with the Royal Navy.[68] Superficially, this suggests the conditions and location of imprisonment had no bearing on the probability of a prisoner's defection. However, this does not take into account the process of defection. According to Charles Herbert, held at Mill Prison in Plymouth, fellow prisoners often learned of a comrade's impending defection before they slipped away and harassed the traitor for amusement and to discourage future defections. On the evening of October 4, 1778, a group of defectors raucously celebrating their impending freedom incurred the ire of their fellow prisoners, who, according to Herbert, decided that, "as they would not let us sleep the first part of the night, we would not let them sleep the latter; accordingly, we all turned out and had an Indian Pow-wow, and as solid as the prison is, we made it shake. In this manner we spent the night."[69] Though there are no reported murders of defectors in the spacious British prisons, the toxic confinement of the prison hulks offered far fewer opportunities for prisoners to covertly offer their services in exchange for a pardon, and word of any offer would have spread like the pox among the closely confined and disease-ridden prisoners.

Another option, taken by John Green from Mill Prison, was to while away the hours by writing hundreds of letters to former business partners and friends in Britain, France, and the North American colonies. The letters are both sentimental and guilt inducing, full of apologies to owners of ships and cargoes that were captured with him, along with details of his "miserable" and "almost naked" circumstances and his requests to exert pressure on British officials for better treatment, parole, or a prisoner exchange.[70] This approach of sailors in distress tapping into their existing business networks was commonly exercised throughout the colonial, Revolutionary, and post-Revolutionary eras, and it was enthusiastically pursued by both Cathcart and O'Brien when they were held in Algiers years later.

If Cathcart, as he claims, was sent to and successfully escaped from the *Jersey* there is some precedent.[71] During a three-month period, up to two hundred prisoners escaped from the *Jersey*, and most former prisoners who wrote memoirs recount attempted and successful escapes.[72] They had ample reason to escape, with patient neglect and cramped quarters causing disease to spread at an alarming rate. Up to eight corpses were thrown over the side of the *Jersey* each day.[73] Conditions on the ship, aptly nicknamed *Hell*, led the colonial captives to surprise their British captors by establishing their own code of governing bylaws.[74] Imprisoned officers served as judges to try those who violated regulations ranging from smoking, to hygiene, to bad language. By establishing this form of self-government, the prisoners were engaging in subtle resistance against their forsaken circumstances and the absolute authority of their British and Loyalist guards. The prisoners were also demonstrating to themselves and their captors that if they could effectively exercise self-government in squalid conditions then they were certainly qualified to practice independent self-government on a grander scale. The model was especially apt, as the imprisoned sailors did not behave anarchically or install ordinary sailors in positions of authority over the officers, as some more moderate patriots, such as John Adams, feared they might.[75]

Prison reminiscences, like most non-elite citizens' recollections of the Revolution, were penned decades after the fact and are replete with innocent errors, exaggerations, and outright fabrications. Some prisoners even plagiarized each other's diary entries during captivity. For example, the diaries of Jonathan Carpenter and Timothy Connor, both in Forton Prison, share numerous suspiciously similar entries and even contain blatantly retrospective ones.[76] In an entry dated July 4, 1776, Carpenter celebrated that "the thirteen United States were Declared free and Independent."[77] This and other entries must have been written after the fact since it is impossible the news reached England on the same day the Declaration of Independence was printed in North America. Such errors and suspicious circumstances compound with time. It is telling that the publication of imprisoned sailors' memoirs mainly occurred after the pension act reforms of 1818 that, for the first time, invited applications from servicemen who had not been disabled in the line of duty. Further memoirs and applications came in the wake of the 1832 reforms, which expanded the pension to veterans who served with state navies, privateers, and militias. The pension applications themselves were typically minimalist, requiring applicants just to list the location, rank, and other details of their service, along with the names of officers under whom they served. The memoirs, however, gushingly tapped into 1820's and 1830's nostalgia for the dying Revolutionary generation. Mention of privateers was entirely absent from these memoirs, and sailors emphasized or fabricated more reputable service. In pension applications, veterans also downplayed or neglected their captivity during the war, whereas in their memoirs their ill treatment at the hands of the British was a central theme.[78] One historian speculates that this curious absence of veterans' compelling captivity sagas in pension applications points to a culture that celebrated wartime heroics and made prisoners feel like failures.[79] Yet triumph over adversity and British abuse was integral to Revolutionary heroism and played out at great length in memoirs. A more likely scenario is that veterans did not mention their captivity in pension applications because sailors of the era were accustomed to spending part of their career in captivity, whether due to impressment by the British, imprisonment at the hands of privateers or state militaries in Europe, or captivity in the Barbary States. The risk was so commonplace that it hardly warranted mention in a brief government document that asked explicitly for services rendered, not for hardships endured. This reality remained constant for the following decades, when Robert Forbes, future opium trader and dynasty builder, recounted being captured at sea three times while traversing the Atlantic as a child in the early nineteenth century. As testimony to the expected regularity of this sort of hardship, these childhood experiences did not discourage Forbes from becoming a lifelong sailor.[80]

Soon after being promoted in his early twenties to captain of a merchant brig, James Riley grew bored of his regular route from the Connecticut River to the West Indies. To make his travels more lucrative, interesting, and dangerous, he secured employment as master of the New York–based brig *The Two Marys*, repeatedly traversing the Atlantic between 1800 and 1807. Between transatlantic voyages Riley married Phebe Miller, a Connecticut native and daughter of a Revolutionary War veteran. By the time Riley was shipwrecked in North Africa in 1815 the couple had five children. From the time Riley first took to sea, and long after he returned from North Africa, Phebe and the children, like many seafaring families, lived with and were supported by their extended family and the local maritime community.

   Since Cathcart's and O'Brien's time as merchant sailors, the improved design of ships steadily transformed the practice of seafaring, allowing smaller crews to man ever-larger ships and skillfully discharge ever-expanding duties. The ratio of a ship's tonnage per crewman is the traditional method of measuring ships. This ratio increased from just seven to ten tons per man shortly before the Revolution to fifteen tons per man in 1786, when O'Brien and Cathcart had finished their Revolutionary service and reentered the merchant trade. This ratio again increased to more than eighteen tons per man in 1806. By the time of Riley's death at sea in 1840, further design improvements increased the average ship size to five hundred tons, which required fewer than sixteen crew and represented a staggering ratio of thirty-one tons per man.[81]

   While transoceanic merchant ships of the early eighteenth century were already complex floating factories that enabled global commerce, those factories grew exponentially larger and more sophisticated during the Industrial Revolution and in the decades before and after, requiring new skills and specialization from ever-fewer operators.[82] The ages of sail and steam are separated in historiography and popular imagination as if the modes of transport within each era were homogenous and there was a clear delineation between the two periods.

But based on the tons-per-crewman ratios, advances within the age of sail were clearly as significant to the practice and volume of labor and commerce as advancements between the ages of sail and steam. In fact, coal-powered ships in the early "age of steam" were also equipped with sails. And many had to be followed by sail ships that carried their coal supply.

Cruising the Atlantic, or even the distant South Pacific, during the first decade of the nineteenth century, a time of notional peace for the early republic, was still no safer for seafarers than it was during the Revolution. Both the major maritime powers, Britain and France, continued to harass American sailors. The British continued to impress American seamen, taking as many as ten thousand sailors between 1793 and the first shots of the War of 1812, while the French used flimsy pretexts to imprison sailors and seize their cargoes.[83] French privateers and officials had at least some legitimate cause for confusion, which they were more than happy to exploit. The Revolution upended what historian Nathan Perl-Rosenthal calls the "common sense of nationality." This was an informal system during the eighteenth century that assigned mariners' nationality based on superficial factors such as their dress, speech, and ship design. These features were confusingly shared by both American and British seamen, and they became an even greater liability in the 1790s when the British Admiralty and Foreign Ministry declared that any English-speaking sailors, even those on American-flagged ships, could be assumed British.[84] American shipping became even riskier during the 1798–1800 Quasi-War with France, when between eighteen hundred and twenty-three hundred American merchant ships were captured and insurance rates soared by over 500 percent.[85] Captain John Green Jr. and his lightly armed merchant ship *Pegou* were typical victims, taken by French frigates after merely "appearing suspect." Whatever that meant. The crew languished in prison in Lorient for three months before the *Pegou* was deemed a legitimate prize.[86]

Captain Ebenezer Hill Corey of the brig *Eliza*, owned by the prominent Providence firm Brown & Ives, might hold a record for falling victim to the greatest number of calamities in a single voyage. His 1807–1808 journey from Providence to South America, then to New Holland (Australia) and Canton, China, should have been uneventful and profitable. Instead, his stop in South America coincided with a British attempt to capture Buenos Aires from Spanish control. Corey was impressed by the Royal Navy for three weeks to serve as their pilot up the Río de la Plata for the ultimately failed attack. After returning to the *Eliza* to find much of his cargo damaged or eaten by mice, Corey limped to New Holland. Then, while en route to Canton, he struck a reef off Nairai Island in the Fijian archipelago. The *Eliza* was lost, some of the crew drowned, and others spent four days in longboats searching the islands for another Western brig to hitch a ride home. Unfortunately, Corey found the Boston merchant

Captain James Riley. In James Riley, *An Authentic Narrative of the Loss of the American Brig* Commerce: *Wrecked on the Western Coast of Africa, in the Month of August, 1815* (New York: T. & W. Mercein, 1817), frontispiece.

ship *Jenny*. He quickly clashed with its drunken and manipulative captain, who stole the thousands of dollars that Corey saved from the wrecked *Eliza* and soon made Corey his prisoner after discovering that Corey had been recording unflattering impressions of the *Jenny*'s officers and crew. While in the Marianas, the *Jenny*'s captain took the opportunity to (falsely) inform the Spanish authorities that Corey had voluntarily worn a British uniform to serve as a paid pilot for the British fleet in their attack on Buenos Aires. Corey now became a Spanish prisoner and was hauled to Manila for trial.[87] He cleared his name but died of disease before returning to Providence. Adding an even darker legacy to the *Eliza*'s fateful journey is that their wreck in Fiji resulted in their cache of firearms being taken ashore and reportedly used for the first time in inter-tribal warfare by one of the *Eliza*'s crew and other Western mercenaries on behalf of native Fijians.[88]

Riley's self-described first "lessons in the school of adversity" came almost simultaneously at the hands of the French during the Napoleonic Wars.[89] In late December 1807, *The Two Marys*, now partly owned by Riley, sailed for Nantes, a once-bustling port city now well into a half-century economic lull. En route, British warships twice boarded *The Two Marys* and wrote in the brig's various official documents that she was forbidden from entering any French port.[90] Instead of finding sanctuary upon reaching Belle Isle, an island near the mouth of the Loire River, the local French Commissary of the Marine spotted the notations made by the British officers who boarded *The Two Marys*. These notes by overzealous British officers were sufficient for the Commissary to promptly deem *The Two Marys* a legitimate prize and imprison her crew, despite neither the ship nor cargo being British.[91] After his short imprisonment and release, Riley spent almost two years traversing the French countryside, unsuccessfully looking for work and an amenable bureaucrat to take up his cause and return *The Two Marys* and its cargo to its rightful owners. He continued to petition for restitution over the next twenty years, buoyed by President Andrew Jackson's calls for the French to make amends in his second and third annual messages to Congress. Ultimately, Riley was reimbursed just 25 percent of his losses.[92]

Riley was not an outlier. His was just one of at least five hundred American ships swept up by French privateers between 1803 and 1810, when there was little difference on the Atlantic between a neutral flag and an enemy's.[93] In a naïve attempt to protect American sailors and hurt the European economies that targeted them, and just one day before *The Two Marys* set sail, President Thomas Jefferson signed the Embargo Act of 1807, which made illegal all trade between the United States and foreign ports. Just days earlier Napoleon had issued the Milan Decree, which stated that merchant ships of any neutral nation were legitimate prizes if they sailed from a British port, had been searched at sea by a British warship, or did not carry a certified document listing all crewman and their nationalities in the precise form dictated by the Franco-American Treaty of 1778. Riley had almost certainly not heard of the decree until it was used to seize his ship. Despite the sweeping nature of the Milan Decree, its strict bureaucratic demands were actually an asset for attentive American sailors who increasingly found that French prize courts were beginning to trust the authority and authenticity of a ship's paperwork, even if it conflicted with the testimony of the crew. Perhaps Riley's ship would never have been seized if he had kept a clean set of *The Two Mary*'s documents that had not been marked by the Royal Navy. Or if the French Commissary he met was as sympathetic to neutral shipping as was the Guadeloupe prize court, which routinely returned American ships and cargoes when their paperwork was in order and even forced the offending French privateers to pay court costs and damages.[94]

By the time Riley returned to Connecticut in late 1809, Jefferson's Embargo Act of 1807 and Non-Intercourse Act of 1809 had crippled American foreign trade. Riley described it as leaving "commerce languishing and restricted; many mercantile houses ruined; and individual capital, credit, and resources, quite exhausted or paralyzed by the continued hostility of the powers at war."[95] Within a series of dueling parodies between pro- and anti-embargo songwriters, one staunch Federalist penned a catchy ditty mourning the impact of the embargo on sailors: "Our ships, all in motion. / Once whitened the ocean, / They sail'd and return'd with a cargo; / Now doom'd to decay / They have fallen a prey /

To Jefferson, worms, and Embargo."⁹⁶ Years of financial gains evaporated for sailors, shipowners, mercantile houses, and businesses in port towns that were secondary beneficiaries of a once-thriving seafaring trade. Deprived of opportunity, Riley remained in the United States, serving uneventfully as a civil defense volunteer during the War of 1812 before fatefully returning to sea on the soon-to-be-shipwrecked brig *Commerce* in 1815.⁹⁷

Prosperity for sailors depended upon individual luck and adaptability to circumstances. Their commercial interests did not need a world at peace. During the Revolution, fishing fleets in the colonies sat in dry dock, but their crews were not similarly left to rot. Instead, they found opportunities in privateering, smuggling, and naval service. Larger merchant brigs were likewise fitted out with cannons and redeployed for a new purpose.⁹⁸ Unlike these predecessors, Riley's early years at sea were marred by his unremitting bad luck and his inability to navigate politically treacherous waters. This was despite years of US neutrality, lucrative smuggling opportunities during the Embargo Act, and failed applications during the War of 1812 to secure higher station and bind himself to this "second American Revolution." Far from discouraging the young sailor, Riley acknowledged these failures as an unavoidable part of seafaring, and they served as educational experiences that improved his later responses to captivity and financial ruin.

Despite the image of sailors as ragged, drunken, and lustful louts, throughout the eighteenth century there was little to distinguish Jack Tar (the common term for a sailor) from a landlubber or an English sailor from an American one. A sailor was simply a landman who took to sea and soon returned to life on the land if he wasn't buried deep beneath the waves. Though Riley came from a farming background and O'Brien and Cathcart from seafaring stock, the more significant difference is that Riley did not have the opportunity to pursue privateering or attach himself to a nation-building conflict before his captivity in North Africa. Both Cathcart and O'Brien, in contrast, enjoyed the opportunity (if not the reality) of profit-making and aligning themselves with a virtuous cause to call on during captivity. To compensate for this absence, Riley's petitions to Congress eagerly emphasized his victimhood to the French and British navies, prison, and financial hardship at the hands of his own government's self-imposed embargo.

For each of these sailors, before, during, and after the Revolution, taking to sea was an exercise in juggling multiple selves. In port towns they joined multiracial and multinational communities, and on ships they almost certainly, and slyly, carried the flags and papers of many nations to disguise themselves and evade capture and seizure of cargoes.⁹⁹ Given this cosmopolitan experience and the strategic misrepresentation of their ships' home ports, it is therefore unsurprising that O'Brien's, Cathcart's, and Riley's early years at sea taught them how to market their roles in nation-building and tug at specific national heartstrings when framing their hardships as virtuous sacrifices. Between voyages, the trio likely worked on farms and in port towns. They switched between merchant shipping, privateers, and navies depending on the available opportunities, and they used those experiences to position themselves for future employment in other fields. These early lessons served them well during their later captivity in North Africa, when their diaries and correspondence became sources of aggressive lobbying and identity formation.

CHAPTER TWO

Diaries of Barbary Orientalism and American Masculinity in Algiers

This day wind at West, no arrivals. Last night 2 Spanish Oraners
had a dispute & fought with their knives. One struck the other
with his knife in the belly & let his guts come completely out. . . .
A slave was bastinadoed [beaten on the feet] 450 strokes for information being made against him [to] the Guardian of Bagnio
Byelique [one of Algiers's slave prisons] [regarding the prison's pet]
lions & tigers on account that it was said he defrauded the lions
of their grub.

> Richard O'Brien, Remarks and Observations in Algiers, *1790*

The greatest inconvenience in this prison [Bagnio Byelique] are in
consequence of the lions and tygers being kept there which creates
an insufferable stench. . . . They frequently break loose and have
killed several of the slaves as they dare not destroy them even
in their own defence. . . . The offals from their dens serve to
maintain an enormous number of rats, the largest I ever saw,
which frequently serve to satisfy the craving appetite of some of
the poor slaves.

> James Cathcart, "Account of Captivity"

In the first decades of the American republic the new nation and her citizens
faced persistent internal and external threats to their sovereignty. There was the
civil unrest of Shays' Rebellion and the Whiskey Rebellion, impressment of
American sailors by the major seafaring powers, murder or capture by Native
Americans, naval war with France, and an averted war with Britain. For merchant sailors in the Mediterranean, the centuries-old specter of Barbary corsairs from Morocco, Tunis, Tripoli, and Algiers were an added threat.

The crews of the *Maria* and *Dauphin* were among the first post-Revolutionary North Americans to be held as captives, or "white slaves," in these North African "Barbary States." Richard O'Brien was captaining the Philadelphia-based merchant ship *Dauphin* when on July 30, 1785, Algerian corsairs captured the ship and crew 240 miles off the Rock of Lisbon, now known as Cabo da Roca, the westernmost point of Portugal. O'Brien's rank afforded him several perks in captivity and was largely responsible for his becoming the leader and spokesman of the American captives, which is explored at greater length in chapter three. James Cathcart was an 18-year-old common sailor when his Boston merchant ship the *Maria* was captured by corsairs three miles off Cape St. Vincent, the southwesternmost point of Portugal, on July 25, 1785, just days before O'Brien's capture. Although Cathcart lacked O'Brien's rank, through hard work, luck, and knowing which palms to grease, he won favor with influential Algerians and fellow captives and amassed sufficient wealth to spend his captivity in comparative comfort.

Existing literature in the fields of American Orientalism and masculinity largely focus on elites, and it is dominated by how domestic American audiences interpreted Barbary captivity. Rather than study how emerging concepts of American Orientalism and masculinity were applied to the captives' plight from American or European shores, much can be learned by exploring how the captives themselves understood these concepts and learned to deploy them, as chronicled in their diaries, into a broader national narrative. Within their semi-public captivity diaries, O'Brien's and Cathcart's commentaries on Algiers and their interpretation of their circumstances of captivity demonstrate an awareness of nuances in American masculinity and Orientalism that cultural elites were still developing during these years. Furthermore, these two non-elite citizens strategically anticipated and appropriated this elite framing of Barbary Orientalism and American masculinity to produce narratives likely to find sympathy amongst the social and political elite—who were the only readers of O'Brien's and Cathcart's diaries and represented the captives' greatest chance of securing freedom.

Mirroring the atypical nature of their captivity, their narratives were also unlike the traditional single-volume Native American captivity narratives or later African American slave narratives. One scholar astutely describes Cathcart's detailed (if occasionally selective) journals as a stylistic fusion of diplomatic correspondence and captivity narrative, authored with a select audience firmly in mind.[1] While a captive, he sent the diary to successive American diplomats, and, when free, he delivered the journal to President John Adams. O'Brien's diary was likewise a fusion of several genres, interspersed with copies of his correspondence, and forwarded to American agents.

The two entries from O'Brien's and Cathcart's diaries that lead this chapter are representative of each author's favored style and content. The selected entries highlight the plight of common sailors held captive in Algiers as well as the exotic image of North Africa, replete with lions, with whom captives competed for food at great risk. Differences in the language and structure of these two entries illustrate the pair's different approaches to writing their captivity narratives and the broader complexities and approaches of early American developments in Orientalism and masculinity that distinguished a new nation from the Old World. The format, content, and style of these passages also reflect Cathcart's and O'Brien's very different positions at the time of captivity, their different circumstances of captivity, and their different agendas.

O'Brien's only surviving diary, lasting just fourteen months of his ten-year captivity, was kept as if it was a ship's logbook. Additionally, he sent approximately ninety-six letters during his ten years in Algiers—some went to Cathcart within Algiers and some, of particular significance, were transcribed in his diary. In the style of a ship's logbook, O'Brien's diary entries typically begin with a weather report and contain largely dispassionate commentary on the commercial and diplomatic comings and goings of Algiers. Even when discussing the torture, death, or sexual conquests of fellow slaves, O'Brien's prose remains unsentimental and terse. Conversely, Cathcart's multiple journals totaling 283 handwritten pages contain lengthy entries that contrast Algiers's wholesale barbarism with the author's interpretation of infant America's enlightened ideas of governance, manners, religious tolerance, and "manly fortitude." The language, content, and framing of O'Brien's and Cathcart's musings and their everyday experiences clearly exhibit an "American awareness of the Arab or Islamic Orient," which Edward Said erroneously claimed did not exist until after World War II.[2]

For captives in Barbary at this time, the symbolism of slavery, Orientalism, and masculinity were potent and inseparable in how they chose to record their ordeal. The captives' characterization of these themes in a uniquely American context was self-interested and paralleled an emerging political-literary trend within America that framed North Africa in an Orientalist rather than an Other lens. With purpose and alternating impassioned and dispassionate prose, Cathcart's and O'Brien's diaries catalog their encounters and ethnographic observations of the culture, government, commerce, interracial dynamics, geology, and climate of Algiers. Captive sailors typically interpreted their ordeal through the experiences of their predecessors, whose narratives were popular within the sailing community, and so they reproduced narratives with highly similar structures, themes, and goals. The American captives of 1785, however, took noticeable departures from the prescribed form to more closely align themselves with the values of the new nation, and in doing so helped establish a framework for American masculinity and Orientalism.

Enslaved Europeans in Barbary. In Pierre Dan, *Historie van Barbaryen, en des zelfs zee-roovers*
. . . *in 't Nederduitsch gebracht door G. v. Broekhuizen* (Amsterdam: Jan ten Hoorn, 1684).

Americans generally interpreted the Muslim world in 1770–1820 as a benign and exotic Other, supported by popular tales such as *One Thousand and One Nights*, first published in English in 1706. The Barbary States, however, were singled out in literature and political discourse as a barbarous site of Orientalism and political, social, and even agricultural degradation. Magazines, newspaper reports, plays, novels, and nonfiction captivity narratives provided Americans with volumes of information on the shades of cultural diversity between North Africa, Persia, Arabia, and Turkey.[3] For North Americans, the Muslim world was not a stereotyped whole. The distinct Orientalism of North Africa evolved during America's period of conflict with Barbary and influenced how captives perceived and wrote about their captivity. This in turn validated and reinforced the use of North Africa as a site for early American Orientalism and a testing ground for American virtues of governance and masculinity.[4]

Just as there was an American awareness of cultural diversity within the Orient, there was a diversity of masculinities within North America.[5] The weight of scholarship on masculinity in the early republic rests on the elite and their framing of masculinity during and after the Revolution as inextricably linked to the necessary political traits of an emerging nation, such as civic virtue, self-restraint, ambition, and stoicism.[6] Overtly gendered, masculine language was common in political discourse from the Declaration of Independence to soapbox speeches. The concept of liberty, for example, operated as masculine both at the level of the individual and the state. One highly visible example of the intersection of these two levels is in the Declaration of Independence, which charges that, "the present King of Great Britain . . . has dissolved Representative Houses repeatedly, for opposing with *manly firmness* his invasions on the rights of the people."[7] To deprive an individual or state of liberty, by oppression or burdensome taxation, was to deny them the "manly" natural right to self-rule.[8] Conversely, the conduct of individual men was also assessed in the language of politics, such as the irrational *ungoverned man*. The political display of masculinity was also strategic for non-politicians, such as merchants and sailors, whose professional success depended upon securing and holding the trust of other men.[9] This phenomenon is doubly true in the calculated displays of masculinity and loyalty in letter writing, which is catalogued in chapter three. Yet sailors' tactical exploitation of masculine language to engender trust under adverse circumstances is similarly evident in their semipublic diaries.

Straddling three continents and harboring empires, the Mediterranean is most remembered for its centuries-long roaring trade in slaves, ransom, and tribute, despite its more wholesome enterprises that rivaled those of the Atlantic. In the early eighteenth century the British fleet was ordered to protect the crucial supply of grain from North Africa, which included seven to eight thousand tons shipped to England from the port of Oran alone. By the end of the century the number of British ships in the Mediterranean equaled those in the Atlantic.[10] During the years preceding the American Revolution the Thirteen Colonies built a strong trade network into Southern Europe using their own ships and crew to increase their profits on cargos of grain, fish, and wood products.[11] Though the colonies' Mediterranean trade plummeted during the Revolution, by the early 1790s it had recovered to its prewar levels, representing approximately 15 percent of all US exports.[12] In this final decade of the eighteen century, European Mediterranean ports received 100 American merchant ships annually, while those same ports received an annual fleet of approximately 170 ships from Algiers that carried agricultural goods from land that Philadelphia publisher and economist Mathew Carey praised for producing "such a profusion of the most delicious fruits, rice, roots, and grain of every species, that the inhabitants enjoy annually two, and frequently three crops."[13] According to a report prepared by then secretary of state Thomas Jefferson, American trade in the Mediterranean in 1790 employed twelve hundred sailors and, as a proportion of American exports, accounted for 25 percent of preserved fish and 16 percent of wheat and flour.[14] This trade increased exponentially over the next two decades in spite of the risk posed by Barbary corsairs. The number of American merchant ships making repeat trips to the Mediterranean grew threefold between the years 1804 and 1807.[15] By the 1830s American merchant sailors were so active in the Mediterranean that diplomat and travel writer John Lloyd Stephens skipped the region entirely, deciding, "I need not attempt to interest you in Smyrna," an ancient city on the Western coast of modern-day Turkey, "it is too everyday a place; every Cape Cod sailor knows it better than I do."[16] It is in this context of modest commercial and cultural familiarity with the Mediterranean and Muslim worlds, but little actual depth of knowledge of them, that Cathcart and O'Brien were held in Algiers and used their semipublic diaries to make both ethnographic observations for the education of diplomats and statesmen who received the diaries and Orientalist critiques for the benefit of their own posterity and the still-forming American principles of governance and masculinity.

Native American captivity dominates the primary and secondary literature on Othering in the genre of captivity narratives in colonial and early America. Yet the first Barbary captivity narrative penned by a North American—Abraham Browne in 1655—predates that of Mary Rowlandson's infamous captivity among Native Americans by twenty-seven years.[17] In contrast to the typical captivity narrative, a single-volume text published within the captive's lifetime, O'Brien's and Cathcart's diaries were offered only to American officials as a sort of background briefing to help smooth American-Algerian negotiations. Cathcart's narrative was eventually compiled from his journals, edited by his granddaughter, and published as *The Captives* in 1899, fifty-six years after his death. The atypical format of these captivity narratives distinguishes them from both Native American captivity narratives and African American slave narratives, and it appropriately reflects the atypical nature of the authors' captivity under the especially peculiar institution of Ottoman–North African slavery.[18] Under this system some of the slaves, like some African American slaves in the United States, were permitted to hire themselves out and earn money. Yet these systems of slavery significantly differed in that North African masters provided opportunities for a captive's upward mobility, opportunities for captives to buy their way out of labor in exchange for a monthly fee, the opportunity to be ransomed home, and different treatment according to a captive's social status prior to captivity. Importantly, once slaves in North Africa converted to the religion of their masters they were released, but it meant they would no longer be ransomed by their Christian homelands or welcomed home. Cathcart and O'Brien were repeatedly encouraged to convert to Islam, to "turn Turk," with promises of wealth, horses, and politically connected wives.

   Like the hundreds of thousands of sailors who arrived on tens of thousands of ships before them, when the crews of the *Maria* and *Dauphin* arrived in Algiers they were met and fed by some of the city's empathetic slave population, who explained the local slave system and, as Cathcart remembered, "informed them of many particulars very pleasing to people in their situation."[19] The officers, Captain O'Brien of the *Dauphin*, Captain Isaac Stephens of the *Maria*, and Captain Zaccheus Coffin, a passenger on the *Dauphin*, were separated from their crews and housed with the British consul Charles Logie. In Algiers the captive officers were typically given *papaluna* status, a sort of parole, whereby captives paid a modest monthly fee to be granted release from the slave prisons.[20] Papalunas were allowed to roam the city, and when forced to work, their duties were light. This privileged status owed to the twin facts that officers attracted twice the ransom of ordinary sailors and, once housed by European consuls, the captive officers no longer cost the Algerian government room and board. O'Brien spent his entire captivity as a papaluna, first with consul Logie and then with the Spanish consul Miguel D'Expilly, during which time he was occasionally assigned to help build and maintain the Algerian corsair fleet. For the most part, however, he acted as the captives' spokesman, writing to American officials on the captives' behalf and distributing information and funds from the government.

Compared to the languid pace and limited dangers that O'Brien faced in captivity, Cathcart's decade in Algiers was marked by well-documented drama and extraordinary social mobility. After a yearlong assignment to the palace garden, which was a lucky first posting that came with a light workload and cash tips, he was reassigned and used his tips to bribe his way into the Bagnio de Gallera slave prison. This prison housed the wealthiest and best-connected slaves who held posts in the Algerian bureaucracy.[21] Cathcart's investment in networking with the slave elite quickly paid off. By chance, before leaving Boston on the *Maria*, he met a Leghornese sailor, Giovanni de la Cruz, who was captured by Algerian corsairs a year after Cathcart and was also held in the Bagnio Gallera. De la Cruz served as clerk of the Algerian marine, a high-ranking administrative post from which he likely recommended in 1787 that Cathcart be named the coffee server to the vicklehadge, the secretary of the marine. This position also came with cash tips in addition to increasing Cathcart's network of influential slaves, and it even made him supervisor of half a dozen other slaves.

In 1797 Cathcart's friend de la Cruz contracted the plague that swept through Algiers each year and was especially fatal for the slaves held in Bagnio Gallera, where both Cathcart and de la Cruz lived. After seeing fellow slaves carried from his prison home at first sight of illness, only to be buried a mere twelve hours later, Cathcart sensibly hypothesized that the unusual virulence and high mortality rate of the plague in Bagnio Gallera had something to do with its sharing a sewer system with a neighboring hospital.[22] Whatever the source of the plague, Cathcart became its beneficiary by taking on the responsibilities of clerk of the marine when de la Cruz first fell ill, and then formally replacing him when he died. He lasted just ten months in the job before the minister of the marine was forced to remove Cathcart from the position when Cathcart discovered the financial discrepancies of a Turkish superior. In turn the Turk accused Cathcart of negligence and left the minister of the marine, Hassan Ali, to mediate. Ali could not side with a Christian over a fellow Muslim, irrespective of the evidence. Cathcart's luck soon returned when the king of Naples ransomed three hundred of his subjects, "many of them being employed in the

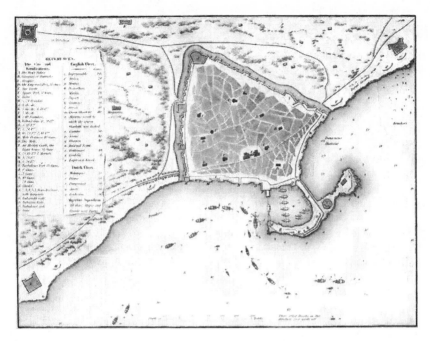

Plan of the city and fortifications of Algiers. In Filippo Pananti, *Narrative of a Residence in Algiers: Comprising a Geographical and Historical Account of the Regency* [. . .] (London: Henry Colburn, 1818), 393.

most eligible situations, [and] many vacancies remained to be filled by those unfortunate men who remained."[23] Cathcart was promoted to clerk, or chief administrator, of Bagnio Gallera, a position he held from 1788 to 1791, but only after three successive clerks died of the plague within a single month.[24]

Finally, in 1794, a year before the successful American negotiation with Algiers, Cathcart rose to the position of chief Christian clerk to the dey (who was selected by the city's civilian, religious, and military leaders to rule Algiers for his lifetime). Cathcart owed this elevation to the highest position a Christian could hold in Algiers to Hassan Ali, his former master and minister of the marine, who became dey in 1791 and remembered Cathcart's aptitude from years earlier. The new dey even lent Cathcart half the customary fee required to secure the position.[25] The chief Christian clerk advised the dey on relations with Christian nations and acted as an intermediary between the dey and Christian ambassadors. The position also came with regular cash tips from visiting dignitaries, cushy living quarters, and management of a tavern in one of the city's slave prisons, which came in addition to the two taverns that Cathcart already operated. All these perks helped him accumulate a personal wealth he valued at $10,000 (relative to the income and wealth of other Americans, this equates to $7 million in 2018 US dollars).[26] Though he was never a papaluna, his status, wealth, and influence within Algiers far exceeded that of any captive officer. In fact, while serving as chief Christian clerk, an American captain captured in 1793 asked Cathcart to use his influence to have the captain relieved from work at the marine and made a papaluna.[27] Years earlier Cathcart was even permitted to recreationally join a slave working party to the interior of the country and play the tourist as his fellow captives toiled in a leech-infested swamp.[28]

Though Cathcart's and O'Brien's diaries are markedly different in their prose, content, and length, this was not due to the authors having particularly different backgrounds prior to captivity. Neither was actively religious, both were merchant sailors prior to and after the Revolution, both served in national or state navies during the Revolution, neither received a comprehensive formal education, one was born in Ireland while the other spent his youth there, and both were captured by Algerian corsairs within a week of each other. The greatest points of difference at their time of capture was their rank and their personality type. O'Brien's seasoned officer status produced a diary that mimicked a ship's log in form and content; its concise entries were almost exclusively descriptive and shied away from emotive commentary. Even the title of his diary, *Remarks and Observations*, was the typical title given to merchant and naval ships' logs and was also often used as the heading for individual log entries of the era. In contrast, Cathcart's verbose journal entries dripped with passion, venom, and purple prose.

Etymologically, the word *Barbary* bespeaks Othering. One derivation is from the Greek *barbaros* or the Latin *barbarus*, meaning non-Greek or non-Roman and therefore uncivilized. An alternative derivation is from the Arabic *berbera*, a reference to North African tribes who spoke incomprehensible languages and shunned trade and communication.[29] Less believable origins include *bar*, meaning desert, which was also the name of the son of an Egyptian king.[30] Even the word *corsair* derives from the Latin word *cursarius*, meaning "plunder."[31]

Despite this appearance of the West's belief in an inherent malevolence of North Africans, there is a notable, often misunderstood, distinction between Othering and Orientalism. According to Edward Said, the late eighteenth century was a "very roughly defined starting point" of Orientalism. For the first time, American literature of the East, in this case North Africa, exceeded simple Othering, whereby authors and captives without malice constructed their own and their nation's identity by contrasting themselves and their nation's (or religion's) values with those of their exotic and romanticized captors. Instead, in the late eighteenth century, they now engaged in the recognizable early stages of Orientalism by portraying Algerians, Barbary governance, and even North

African architecture and landscape as in a state of steadfast regression, adding prejudice to the political, cultural, and physical divide between the New and Old Worlds. This shift built on preexisting trends in European travel litera-ture, such as works by Emanuel d'Aranda, Pierre Dan, Francis Knight, and Jo-seph Morgan, as well as the Abbe Constantin de Chassebouef Volney's *Travels Through Egypt and Syria* and *The Ruins, or A Survey of the Revolution of Empires*, though both these texts were not translated and published in the United States until well after the *Maria* and *Dauphin* were captured in 1785.

In spite of this existing literary trend, there was a distinctly American and republican flavor to the nation's reportage of the Islamic world during the early republic, and within that world, North Africa, the only site of American con-flict, reserved a special place. The nation's early flirtation with Orientalism began a process that was refined and clarified until the mid-twentieth century when Said claimed that "the specifically American contribution to the history of Orientalism" was "its conversion from a fundamentally philosophical disci-pline and a vaguely general apprehension of the Orient into a social science specialty."[32] Though Cathcart and O'Brien were far from qualified social scien-tists, it is flippant of Said to suggest that, "leaving aside the campaigns against the Barbary pirates in 1801 and 1815, let us consider the founding of the Amer-ican Oriental Society in 1842" as the beginning of American Orientalism.[33] Said offers no explanation for why we should leave aside this earlier engagement with North Africa. In demonstrating early Americans' regionally specific atti-tudes towards the Islamic Orient, the historically significant writings of Cath-cart, O'Brien, and later James Riley, represent an inconvenient anomaly in Said's timeline for Orientalism and are therefore casually dismissed. Said writes dismissively of "occasional diplomatic and military encounters with Barbary pi-rates and the like." These encounters, however, provided a fertile middle ground of Orientalism, whereby captives met Said's own criteria of "support[ing] the caricatures propagated in the popular culture" and applying fundamental prin-ciples of the social sciences to critique both America and Algiers.[34]

Due to the political crisis of American captives being held in Algiers, Amer-ican public discourse around Barbary in the 1780s and 1790s was distinct from discussion of the rest of the Muslim world. Far from a uniform accusation that the whole Muslim world was barbaric, fictional and nonfictional literature in the early American republic exhibits diversity, nuance, and carefully distin-guished views of the geographic regions. Beginning with a few bland informa-tive articles in 1786 that were inspired by the capture of the *Maria* and *Dau-phin*, American magazine articles on the Muslim world had, by the 1790s, blossomed into hundreds of ethnographic travel accounts, poems, and exotic Oriental tales. Though American magazines did not publish Oriental tales set in North Africa until after the captives' release, the captivity diaries, correspondence, and plays available before this date certainly contributed to a program of "localized Orientalism" within the broader "blurry Other" of portrayals of the Muslim world.[35]

From the moment of their capture, Cathcart and O'Brien reflected this diverse and nuanced engagement with Orientalism and Othering of the Muslim world. The pair's diaries include the dispassionate information that characterized American magazine articles about Barbary in addition to wholly unromantic tales of torture, corruption, and superstition in Algiers, which constitute a more bigoted, ideological contribution to the program of localized Orientalism. O'Brien began his brief captivity diary as he meant to continue it, with accounts of the diplomatic affairs of the British, French, and Spanish consuls and the details of their correspondence that had become public knowledge.[36] The earliest sign of personal commentary on these affairs is his inoffensive observation that "of course Logie," the British consul, "& the Spaniard will never be friends," and that was even before Logie drunkenly claimed that he could build a better frigate than the Spanish-born chief shipbuilder in Algiers.[37] Even O'Brien's single mention of superstition in Algiers was innocuous compared to the ridicule-laden texts of most other captives and travel writers. Following a four-hour lunar eclipse, there were a "variety of conjectures & superstitious notions respecting the eclipse which they suppose to denote to them the death of the present Dey—or an earthquake."[38]

Cathcart likewise began his own captivity journal with six dispassionate pages of recent history between the Barbary States and Christian nations.[39] He detailed the fraught relationship between Spain and Algiers and the "fear and respect" that Algiers held for Britain's "superiority at sea & her garrisons in the Mediterranean during the war which concluded in acknowledging the independence of the United States."[40] These dispassionate entries continue, noting that after the *Maria*'s capture, Cathcart and his fellow crewmen spent nine days at sea before, "being private property," they arrived in Algiers on the eve of the feast that marked the end of Ramadan. They were given old clothes "swarming with myriads of vermin" and were paraded throughout the city in scenes reminiscent of slave auctions throughout Europe and North America.[41] Algerian locals "were curious to see Americans, having supposed us to be the aborigines of the country . . . and were much surprised to see us so fair or, as they expressed themselves, so much like Englishmen."[42]

Rather than seizing upon these initial experiences of captivity to make a political statement about slavery or Algerian assumptions about the New World, Cathcart chose to highlight small favors and surprising camaraderie. From his first drink of clean water from a magnificent fountain that "made so permanent an impression on my mind that I shall remember [it] to the last hour of my existence" to the "Christian slaves of all denominations . . . who could afford it brought us the fruits of the season, wine, bread, and everything that was cooked, or could be eaten without cooking."[43] His observations of locals and their customs soon turned to ridicule however. Cathcart mocked one of his early master's interests in alchemy and was astonished that "in all this Regency was not a man, in my time, who could calculate an eclipse of the sun or moon." And he sweepingly disregarded the entire city of Algiers: "There is very little in the city of Algiers which attracts the notice of strangers, the streets are narrow and dark, especially the Jews' quarter."[44]

As Cathcart, rather than O'Brien, was the more prolific chronicler of inner thoughts and intimate dialogue while in captivity, it is his journals that most explicitly build on literature that framed North Africa as in a state of decay due to its leaders, its religion, and its decadence. In contrast to this decay, the cooler, enlightened, republican heads of the American captives reflected their (and their nation's) prospects for long-term prosperity. American narrators, from captive sailors to the cultured elite, collectively borrowed from their European predecessors in constructing North Africa as retrogressive.[45] Cathcart described the farmers he saw outside of Algiers as "an inoffensive race of beings and such as we would suppose the first cultivators of the earth were" and ultimately decided that "if this country was blessed with a good government which would promote the welfare of its subjects and encourage agriculture, arts and manufactures, it would become in a very few years a perfect paradise."[46] Judging the region's individual, civic, and religious life, the American captives aligned with Western elites in concluding that a backwards religion had enabled bad government that decoupled Barbary and its people from the steady march of industry and civilization.[47] The captives' commentary on the poisonous nature of Algiers's government was likely borne out of both a frustration at serving such (from their perspective) inferior masters and also a not-so-subtle jab at the allegedly superior American government, whose inaction was responsible for their continued captivity.

In the budding fictional and nonfictional literature by American authors about Barbary, the counterpoints of manly fortitude and ungoverned passions were inextricably linked to the construction of Barbary Orientalism. In their own ways, Cathcart's and O'Brien's diaries followed suit. Yet with just two dozen sailors on American-flagged ships held captive from 1785 to 1793, and at most seven hundred American captives during the entire thirty-year conflict, are these captives anomalous in the development of American masculinity? On the contrary, Myra Glenn found in her research on sailors who led particularly perilous lives that the masculine traits non-elite sailors chose to emphasize after shipwreck, captivity, or bankruptcy reflect how society defined codes of masculinity.[48] Scholars of masculinity in the early republic and Revolutionary era largely focus on civic-centered concepts of masculinity, as propagated by the political and religious elite.[49] These scholars broadly agree that a man simply needed to control his life and defend his freedom.[50] Men simultaneously channeled their impulses and were risk-takers for political principle.[51] The idea of the self-made man was not popularized until the mid-nineteenth century, but self-making had several precursors that pervade post-Revolutionary captivity narratives, such as individualizing the principle espoused during the Revolution that freedom was an earned rather than an innate right.

Incapable of physically resisting slavery, the American captives in Algiers lacked the common means whereby men could prove their masculine virtue. Instead, they reframed masculine attributes of control and freedom to suit their circumstances. Control over one's life instead became manly fortitude in the face of their captors' ungoverned passions, and freedom became resistance to efforts by their captors to induce religious conversion. How the captives depicted their fortitude reflects their broader approach to diary keeping, as influenced by their station prior to captivity and their personality. For example, O'Brien never dwelled on the rare occasions when he was taken from his residence with the British or Spanish consuls and put to hard labor constructing ships or sails for Algerian corsairs. He fleetingly referred to these days in his diary as "employed making the 2nd mainsail," and was "busily employed" a few months later "in laying the ways in the water for launching the new frigate."[52] A month later, in December 1790, he was "employed making sails & [mooring] the cruisers" and "at sundry—public jobs at the marine."[53] In closing an entry on the fifth anniversary of his arrival in Algiers, he succinctly recorded that he and his fellow sailmakers were threatened by their overseer for inattentive work. The overseer warned, "are you not all slaves? Why do you not work, infidels? I will give you all 100 bastinados each [100 strokes with a cane on the soles of their feet]."[54] O'Brien merely reported the dialogue. He did not take the opportunity to chastise the overseer for his cruelty or highlight his religiously tinged language. His reports on the weather and arrivals at the docks represent the same proportion of these entries as his passing references to hard labor and threats of beatings.

It was Cathcart who expressed outrage at O'Brien's forced labor and credited himself with alleviating it. Though O'Brien never mentioned being put to work in the British consul's garden upon arriving in Algiers, Cathcart was outraged enough for the both of them at finding O'Brien and the other American officers digging holes, hauling manure, and feeding livestock. Cathcart claims he shared a little money with them and allegedly "could not refrain from tears at viewing their humiliating situation which affected us more as they suffered this indignity from a person (the British Consul) who ranked among Christians and gentlemen, was of the same religion and spoke the same language, and from

The manner of bastinading (the caning of the soles of a captive's feet). In James Wilson Stevens, *An Historical and Geographical Account of Algiers* (Philadelphia: Hogan & M'Elroy, 1797), frontispiece.

whom a more humane treatment might naturally have been expected."[55] Among his occasional stints at hard labor, O'Brien spent a few weeks cleaning mold off a corsair, a particularly unenviable task which he never mentioned in his diary or correspondence and which Cathcart relished in recording that he helped improve by giving O'Brien a bottle of wine and dinner each day, which Cathcart sourced from one of the three taverns he operated.[56] For O'Brien, fortitude meant remaining silent about his personal ordeals. He reserved the explicit invocation of fortitude for descriptions of others' circumstances. Just once, in April 1790, he privately invoked the sentiment without referring to another specific captive, noting that, "we must bare [news of congressional inaction] with that manly fortitude that has characterized the unfortunate remnant of Americans in Algiers. Fortitude under afflictions is a Christian & manly virtue."[57]

Cathcart, in contrast, trumpeted his manly fortitude, and what Christine Sears sarcastically dubs his "benevolent self-sacrifice," at every opportunity. This aggressive approach, unparalleled by other American captives, owed to his personality, his need as a lowly common sailor to establish his credentials, and the greater narrative structure of his captivity diary. Importantly, this approach also owed to his Irish birth and his service in the Royal Navy during the Revolution. Referring to narratives written by sailors who were impressed by the British decades later, Myra Glenn could have been writing about Cathcart in observing that sailors who were naturalized citizens were notorious for using their narratives to establish their new American identity and to elicit sympathy, money, and political support from their adopted countrymen.[58] At least 27 percent of sailors captured on American-flagged ships and freed in the American-Algerian treaty of 1795–1796 were similarly not born in any of the Thirteen Colonies and had a pressing need to legitimize their American identity.[59]

From the beginning of Cathcart's captivity he bemoaned being "doomed to labor in the palace garden," though he immediately confessed that the work was light, with the exception of "taking care of two lions, two tigers and two antelopes."[60] His intellectual curiosity and alliance with cultured civilization were highlighted repeatedly when his guards prevented him from reading and writing, which he claims profoundly affected him both mentally and physically.[61] No ordeal was too small to warrant mentioning. Though he never contracted the plague, the third time he was exposed he wrote O'Brien a melancholy letter addressed from "Deaths Door," in which he told O'Brien that he was "on the verge of Eternity" and was "doom'd to be a Victim to this Contagion."[62] He even complained that when freed from the slave prison to live and earn money working with a European resident, a rare luxury among captives, he endured a series of indignities that included being offered cold coffee *without sugar*.[63]

To bolster the captives' self-classification as embodiments of American masculine virtue, their actions and even their inaction (that is, their fortitude) were framed in contrast to their captors' wanton violence and ungoverned passions. During the Revolution the Founding Fathers linked the "taming of passions" to the language of masculinity as part of a campaign to reign in the male mob's more disorderly and violent democratic desires. The free exercise of a man's passions was the antithesis of the values of the new nation and an impediment to forming a responsible government. These passions could manifest in the actions of both the individual and the state, which intersected in the popular phrase *ungoverned passions*. Although rarely referred to as such in the narratives of American captives, ungoverned passions were evoked in day-to-day accounts of captors' unchecked cruelty and irrational behavior. In November 1790, O'Brien recorded a story forwarded from Tunis of a French trader and father of six from Marseilles who refused to remove his shoes while in a Moor's home during prayer. Initially the "mob was for burning him but had not patience [so they] cut him to pieces" with the consent of the ruling bey of Tunis.[64] A few months later O'Brien wrote that "a slave was unmercifully flogged at the Marine. He received full 2000 bastinados on his feet & hind parts."[65] During the intervening months O'Brien detailed the cases of a Christian slave who was killed by a mob of drunken Turks, and a slave who attempted to escape and was punished with a staggering "1000 bastinados on the feet & 1000 on the backside" as another unsuccessful escapee watched in horror and begged to be decapitated instead.[66] During these months he also made a candid assessment of the Algerian justice system, remarking that when "two Moorish concubines have been murdered—one cut to pieces by a Turk, the other drowned in a cistern," the suspected murderers, "two young men of good families[,] . . . will be tried [in] the Algerine fashion: if poor & no friends, they will be hung, if they have money, they will bribe & get off."[67] Four months into his own captivity Cathcart recounted the arbitrary tyranny of his masters in the palace gardens, who amused themselves by giving bastinados to the palace slaves, allegedly resulting in Cathcart's loss of four toenails.[68]

It was not until America's successful treaty, negotiated in September 1795 by Joseph Donaldson, that Cathcart employed a variation on the phrase *ungoverned passions*. At the time of this negotiation, Cathcart served as the dey's chief advisor on affairs with Christian nations and acted an intermediary between Donaldson and the dey. All of Cathcart's uses of the word *passion* were leveled at the dey during and in the wake of the treaty negotiation, which likely reflects his own heightened emotional state more than representing an objective assessment of the Algerian leader, with whom he had been on intimate terms and about whom he had written for many years.[69] During the negotiation, Cathcart diagnosed the dey as "a man wholly governed by his passions," with these passions so ungoverned that they came out in his facial hair. Cathcart could tell that he was "not in a bad humor, as his whiskers did not curl neither did his beard stand erect."[70] In identifying the dey's physical appearance as a mirror unto his mood, Cathcart was perpetuating a century-old trope that when a Barbary man is consumed by his "passions," he physically transforms to appear "just as he is."[71]

From the early 1790s the captives' ambiguous use of the term *liberty*, in both a literal and an abstract political sense, represented a distinct break from how sailors perceived the concept and used the term during the Revolution. This evolution for Cathcart and O'Brien began to reflect the usage of political elites like Jefferson who assigned liberty to both individuals and the movement of goods: "The liberation of our citizens has an intimate connexion with the liberation of our commerce in the Mediterranean."[72] Just ten years earlier for sailors of the Revolution, liberty was a practical rather than an abstract concept, meaning the individual sovereignty to act freely in the moment.[73] Cathcart employed this day-to-day usage early in his captivity, remarking that captives assigned to the palace kitchen were worked harder but had "more liberty" than other captives, while later in his captivity he also applied the term to an individual's more abstract state of being.[74] O'Brien regularly invoked the term on an individual level that was both philosophical and patriotic, referring to individual captives seeking to secure their liberty, and more philosophically, referring to "the unfortunate remnant of Americans in captivity" as "unfortunate remnants to Liberty."[75] That Cathcart's and O'Brien's use of "liberty" a decade after the Revolution straddles the immediate interpretation of Revolutionary-era sailors *and* the abstract political meaning of elites further suggests that it was during captivity that the pair were developing an increasingly sophisticated awareness of American-specific rhetoric and were framing their identity and captivity through that rhetoric.

Throughout the Revolutionary and early republic eras, the concepts of liberty and slavery were not a natural dichotomy. They were not binary opposites, with citizens or nations either entirely free or entirely slave with nothing between. Rather, these concepts existed on a fuzzy continuum. For instance, on the national stage and denoting more than mere national independence, the "meaning of freedom enshrined by America's revolutionary and nationalist ideologies also lay in humans' *agency*: their ability to alter circumstances, to change the environment, to reform government, and above all to resist oppression. . . . Freedom and slavery thus became linked to virtue, understood as the will to resist tyranny. . . . Continued enslavement thus signified a choice to submit."[76] Yet on an individual level, Cathcart and O'Brien did not have the option to choose liberty by resisting their captivity—to escape by land or sea was essentially impossible and would put those who remained behind at greater risk. According to Nicholas Wood, Americans in Barbary broadly accepted the paradigm of liberty that was established by American elites during the Revolution, whereby one's liberty was directly proportional to their resistance of tyranny. The captives, however, operated according to adapted criteria: "While Barbary narratives uniformly stress the individual's obligation to resist conversion to Islam, physical resistance to slavery itself was extremely rare. . . . Americans in Barbary had no moral duty to virtuously choose liberty or death over slavery but simply to survive enslavement, resist any pressure to convert to Islam, and patiently await the government's intervention on behalf of its citizens."[77] Or, as O'Brien remarked, it was the obligation of the nation to "show those people the English, Spaniards & Portuguese that we are not a dastardly effeminate race, but is necessitated to arm to maintain the honour & dignity of the United States."[78] Since the pair could not fight or flee to secure their freedom they would *earn* it.

Their diary entries therefore emphasize their disgust for those who "turned Turk" and show how they seized upon everyday opportunities to act in the interest of their countrymen by improving their conditions while working towards their ultimate freedom. O'Brien, in correspondence forwarded to several American diplomats, remarked that he "would be happy in being hangman for all these dogs" that turned Turk "& many others of their damned dispositions."[79] Cathcart shared this disdain over five pages of his diary that made much of his brush with forced conversion in July 1793.[80] His eloquent and emphatic responses to religious conversion are prime examples of the self-conscious nature of sailors', especially Cathcart's, journals which must be interpreted as partially fictional or at least embellished. The incident began at a low personal moment when he decided to nurse his misery by drinking on an empty stomach at the tavern attached to the city's insane asylum. Challenging a local sheriff on his knowledge of Islam compounded his troubles. To the swelling crowd of tavern patrons this challenge was interpreted as an intention to convert. Cathcart "escaped the greatest danger I had ever been in since my captivity commenced" by the good humor of the dey, who refused to believe that Cathcart now aspired to turn Turk without any incentive.[81] The dey was sure of this because, years prior, he had been the minister of the marine and, according to Cathcart, had offered him a salary, command of a corsair, "a wife and a house and garden," and possible promotion to admiral if he converted. According to Cathcart's retelling, the minister-turned-dey saved him from this latest predicament by recalling that Cathcart "would deserve contempt if he should become an apostate from the religion of his forefathers merely to promote his worldly interests" and that Cathcart had previously declared, "do you suppose that I can not bear slavery with all its concomitants and degradations sooner than renounce the faith which I was taught to hold sacred by my mother, whom I hope yet to live to see and to thank more for her instructions than her nourishment."[82] Cathcart particularly loathed those who converted to Islam, even if necessary to spare their own lives. He labeled two Irish converts as "the most complicated villains in the regency," and as evidence of their character, the type that lacked fortitude and was susceptible to conversion, he gave a lengthy account of when the two were joined by an English captain at a local brothel. The Irishmen were arrested and banished to Smyrna, while the English captain was deported under armed escort, and their preferred prostitute was stripped naked and banished from the city.[83]

For centuries, immersion in the Orient, conflict with it, and potential corruption by it were underlying themes of European-Barbary captivity narratives. American narratives of the late eighteenth and early nineteenth centuries relied heavily upon stereotypes established by their predecessors. Much of this legacy is reflected in Cathcart's and O'Brien's diaries. True to the captivity narrative genre, O'Brien and Cathcart wrote of themselves and their fellow captives as embodiments of masculine virtue, contrasting themselves with their volatile captors. In their own ways, Cathcart and O'Brien internalized and reflected the West's long historical imagination of the Muslim world as an exotic Other. Yet their semipublic diaries also reflected and helped construct a uniquely American-Orientalist image of Barbary, brought to life through torturous, superstitious, and uneducated captors, whose ungoverned passions represented the antithesis of the enlightened American republic and her citizens. Similarly, the particular brand of masculinity that the captives touted was pitched as uniquely American:

from O'Brien's claims that "manly fortitude . . . has characterized the unfortunate remnant of Americans in Algiers" and "Patience & fortitude under afflictions is a Christian & manly virtue" to Cathcart's firm resolve to "wait with
fortitude becoming a Christian and an American."[84]

For Europeans of any nation a captor's barbarity and a captive's fortitude
were depicted and internalized almost exclusively through the lens of Christianity. This was the inevitable result of centuries of European captivity narratives using Barbary and Islam as favorite mediums for Othering. In particular,
historian Greta LaFleur identifies Western obsession with, and accusations of,
"sodomy" as a stand-in for any personal behavior or cultural trait deemed "un-
Christian." Even benign sleeping and eating practices in the Ottoman Empire
were considered evidence of sodomy since they were different from European
Christian eating and sleeping habits. The absence of sex was irrelevant. The
mere fact of a cultural difference made it un-Christian, and being un-Christian
made it sodomy.[85]

It is no coincidence that the preceding extracts by Cathcart and O'Brien,
which show that they identified themselves and their brand of masculine fortitude as both American and Christian, were penned precisely midway through
their captivity. In time, this interpretation of and referencing to themselves as
Christians almost ceased as they increasingly identified themselves, and their
greatest chance for freedom, with the US government rather than divine intervention. Through this subtle change in rhetoric they sought to distinguish
themselves and their responses to captivity from those of the Old World. Specifically, as explored in the next chapter, they honed and pitched their ordeal
to correspondents as an ongoing struggle of republican sensibility and national
duty.

CHAPTER THREE

Captivity by Correspondence

It is the duty of our country to redeem us on the best terms they
can. Our unfortunate crews are employed on the most laborious
work. We are not prisoners of war—we are slaves.
                    Richard O'Brien to John Adams, February 13, 1787

Seventy years before the United States began slowly professionalizing its diplomatic corps, Richard O'Brien, James Cathcart, and other enterprising captives
in Algiers used their isolation and local insights to become accidental diplomats. These captives leveraged their personal and business networks to become
diplomatic activists as a means of influencing formal diplomacy. Though they
had mixed success, the style and substance of their advocacy offers rare insights
into how non-elites engaged in political networking and the self-interested construction of national identity from abroad. Focusing on the style of O'Brien's
and Cathcart's correspondence, and how this correspondence was informed
by their mercantile backgrounds, reveals non-elite citizens' nuanced awareness
of the development of United States nationhood and citizenship at the turn of
the nineteenth century—even as these non-elite citizens were held captive in
the backwater of Algiers. Focusing on these two captives also shows how these
citizens exploited their existing mercantile skill set and commercial networks

to strategically insert themselves into the emerging national narrative, and how they were adept at incorporating that knowledge into their quest for freedom or at least better conditions in captivity. They achieved this feat by combining a businesslike writing style with patriotic content to win the trust and sympathy of their audience. The extent of their success is exemplified in their relationship with one diplomat in particular, David Humphreys, who variously served between 1791 and 1801 as US minister to Spain and Portugal and negotiator to Algiers.

As members of the highly mobile Atlantic and Mediterranean maritime labor force, Cathcart and O'Brien were accustomed to juggling a plurality of loyalties, identities, and motives at any given moment. The cosmopolitan mariner's identity and loyalty were divided between his nation of origin, his often multinational and interracial crew, and his immediate economic and political interests (such as release from Barbary captivity or imprisonment in Europe). O'Brien pursued his multiple goals of establishing credibility, providing intelligence, and eliciting government and public support through his savvy use of public, private, sentimental, and formal epistolary genres. Cathcart, even more dramatically, pledged allegiance to the United States, Britain, and Algiers at one point or another throughout his captivity, all the while framing himself as a martyr for, and paragon of, American independence.

During almost eleven years of captivity in Algiers, Cathcart and O'Brien were allowed to correspond with businessmen, family, military officers, and diplomats, including Thomas Jefferson. They even wrote to President George Washington. Writing and receiving correspondence and newspapers through friendly European consuls was a common feature of the particularly peculiar institution of Ottoman slavery. Captives were typically freed upon payment of a ransom, so captors encouraged their slaves to correspond with families, business partners, and governments to elicit speedy payments. Access to a broad range of contacts is also unsurprising given Cathcart's and O'Brien's backgrounds in maritime trade and quasi-military service. Those professions offered introductions to the etiquette and networks of business and government.

Between 1784 and 1815 the fledging American diplomatic service was slow to build reliable networks in North Africa to provide diplomatic intelligence. It fell to the captive sailors to build them, from the deck up. This period also includes two better-known nation-building conflicts: the Quasi-War (1798–1800) and the War of 1812 (1812–1815). In both of these conflicts the American public and government relied on diplomatic intelligence from existing formal diplomatic networks or informal networks of trusted informants, such as the family and friends of government officials in London, Paris, and other European capitals.[1] No such networks existed in North Africa to help initiate negotiations in the 1780s.

O'Brien and Cathcart took advantage of this diplomatic vacuum to position themselves at the center of the flow of intelligence between the United States and Barbary. As sailors and veterans of the Revolution, their approach to correspondence, like their approach to diary keeping, was a blend of objective commercial reporting and patriotic humanitarianism. Between dispassionate passages on Algerian military defenses and maritime trade, they appealed to Americanized virtues of sensibility, including "honor" and "the flame of liberty." They also repeatedly referred to the nation's commercial interest and to their own service in the Revolution, framing their captivity as the first post-Revolutionary test of America's principles and military prowess against a non-European power.

In Algiers the pair carved out positions for themselves at the intersection of formal and informal diplomatic networks. O'Brien, one of the first captains to be captured, and Cathcart, one of the most resourceful common sailors, rose from among their "brother captives" to become accidental diplomats or "diplomats without portfolio."[2] Characteristics of both the formal and informal featured in their correspondence with American and European government officials and also in their networking strategies with businessmen, consuls, and officials within Algiers. Unlike formal diplomats, the captives were not named to represent or act autonomously on behalf of a specific nation. Their diplomatic contacts therefore regarded them as useful informants rather than government agents with established reputations in political circles and formal lines of communication to the State Department. So when they wrote to Jefferson or William Carmichael (US chargé d'affaires to Madrid), they accessed the formal network in an informal capacity, as ordinary citizens in extraordinary circumstances.

First coined in the fifteenth century and popularized in the sixteenth and seventeenth centuries, the phrase *Republic of Letters* referred to educated men who formed a loose international network that circulated the latest knowledge in science, philosophy, and any other field of interest.[3] Much like the crew of a merchant ship, this loose network transcended the religious, national, and political allegiances that marred stationary physical venues of public discourse. Complementing this network of elites was what historian Lawrence Peskin shrewdly calls the "second class citizens of the Republic of Letters," who spread correspondence and news within the United States and across the seas. From the pages of newspapers in Dedham, Massachusetts, and Cooperstown, New York, and Middlebury, Vermont, these second-class citizens read and spread the petitions and letters penned by O'Brien and the other captives. Marked as second class thanks to their social status, gender, race, or perceived illiteracy, they were barred from fully participating in the political-literary-scientific discourse that was dominated by elite white men.[4]

Although sailors boasted higher literacy rates than the general population, by virtue of their lowly social status as sailors, captives-turned-quasi-diplomats like O'Brien and Cathcart struggled to escape their second-class status. In the realm of political, scientific, and literary discourse, an American sailor's connection to the Republic of Letters was typically as a mere courier. They were conduits of information—which was precisely how most senior government officials saw sailors like O'Brien and Cathcart when they were captives in Algiers. Given the ambiguous nature of the captives' relationship with government officials, scholars are understandably wary of emphatically labeling O'Brien and Cathcart as either subjugated slaves or quasi-diplomatic agents. Nevertheless, in the dying years of the Republic of Letters, from the mid-eighteenth century onward, highly literate American sailors began to embrace a more sophisticated role in the flow of information, and in this new role they shaped the development of republican sensibility and American national identity. Historians differ on whether this increasing engagement in social and political discourse was primarily motivated by sailors' "idealistic" or "mercenary" interests.[5] But surely there was some of both at work, with the weighting of each interest changing for each sailor in response to their circumstances at a given moment. Whichever the dominant motive, it was an assertive role that veterans of the Revolution like Cathcart and O'Brien clearly continued in their journals and correspondence from captivity.

Both the substance and targets of O'Brien's and Cathcart's lobbying efforts reflect the differences in their career status and in their approaches to self-advocacy. They also highlight how commercial networks, professional training, and status informed diplomacy during the early republic. No single letter incorporates all of Cathcart's or O'Brien's epistolary styles, since the style and content of each letter was tailored to the author's immediate goal and recipient. The following letters are just two examples that illustrate elements the captives regularly included in their correspondence:

Cathcart to O'Brien, date unknown:

> The first Six months of my residence in his [British surgeon Dr. Werner's] house I coppied all his Accompts from the time of his commencing Shop keeper and carried them on untill he settled with his correspondence. I then made out his Accompts current and Balanced them much to his advantage, as Consull Logie can Certify they having pass'd through the British Chancery Office. . . . In short Sir the whole weight of his Business was depending on me he being entirely Ignorant in the mercantile line. He may be a good Surgeon for what I know but his education in other points I assure you is very Superficial.[6]

O'Brien to Humphreys, November 12, 1793:

> *Algerine Maritime Force, the 12th Nov. 1793:*
> One frigate of 44 guns, built in Algiers by Spanish King's constructor.
> One frigate of 22 guns, English built.
> One frigate of 24 guns, French built.
> One frigate of 24 guns, Levant built, at sea.
> One polacre of 18 guns, Genoa built, at sea.
> One brig of 20 guns, built by Spanish constructor, at sea.
> One xebeck of 20 guns, built by Spanish constructor.
> One xebeck of 12 guns, built on the coast.
> One xebeck of 14 guns, built on the coast.
> One xebeck of 12 guns, built in Spain.
> One brig on the stocks, pierced for twenty guns, will be launched and ready
> for sea in thirty days.
> N.B. They carry, each corsair, at the rate of 12 men to each gun, fully.
>
> The corsairs of Algiers and Tunis combined may make a formidable fleet of
> sea robbers; and as the Algerines have become masters of the Western Ocean,
> the Tunisians will do the same; and if they meet no success they will go into
> the English Channel, and on to the coasts of the United States. Then, hon-
> ored sir, what will be the alarm! I am afraid they will in this their second
> expedition take 8 or 10 more of American vessels. The enemies of the United
> States tells the Dey much is to be got by being at war.[7]

By the time O'Brien was captured in 1785, he had been at sea for about the
average length of an American sailor's entire career and had spent at least four
years as an officer on merchant ships and privateers. It was a life that exposed
him to the protocols of government, military, and commercial networks throughout the Atlantic. In the early republic, the success and safety of sailors could be
measured by their familiarity with these multiple, overlapping networks. This
was a period when commercial and national interests happily intertwined and
access to up-to-date intelligence was a vital commodity.[8] In reading O'Brien's
and Cathcart's journals and correspondence from captivity, their practice of
cataloguing, manipulating, and pitching information was clearly informed by
their existing mercantile skill set. Like commercial traders, they kept detailed
financial accounts, logs of events, records of wind direction, and arrivals and
departures at Algerian docks.[9]

As advised by mercantile textbooks of the period, Cathcart later created lists
and tables that converted North African measurements of weight, distance,
currency, and time.[10] He also kept the financial accounts of foreign nationals,
consuls, and Algerian officials. As mentioned in the letter quoted above, for six

months he kept the books of Dr. Philip Werner, the doctor to the British consul and the only free British subject in Algiers. He later catalogued the expenditures of the Swedish consul and the consul's brother, listing the price of each purchase in sequins, pounds, and *manboobs*, the currency of Algiers. Cathcart similarly included the cost of each item in multiple currencies when he was later tasked with cataloguing the dey's long lists of expenditures and tribute demands.[11] Taken together, these documents are a treasure trove of authoritative historical information on the mercantile roots of non-elite quasi-diplomatic communication from a surprising source: captive merchant sailors. Beyond the distracting drama of the authors' captivity, these documents provide a remarkably detailed record that combines commercial information with political and cultural insights that serve as an underexplored window into the strategies and techniques of distant citizens participating in political-commercial discourse in this turbulent time in the republic's history.

The significant differences in O'Brien's and Cathcart's educational backgrounds and status at the time of captivity are reflected in their unique approaches. O'Brien applied his mercantile education in corresponding almost exclusively with European and American diplomats and businessmen. His diary is largely dedicated to reporting and reflecting on the affairs of consuls, who, along with American officials, were his primary correspondents. He also wrote to the Philadelphia owners of his ill-fated ship "by Every Convenient opportunity." Eight letters penned by O'Brien from captivity were published in American newspapers. They were addressed equally to his government and to his business contacts. Irrespective of their addressee, the letters were circulated throughout mercantile networks and forwarded to newspaper publishers even before ultimately reaching their intended recipients.[12] This lifecycle of O'Brien's correspondence, in which letters were published in newspapers before they reached their addressees, is a telling example of how non-elite news bearers, including their family and friends, served as second-class citizens of the Republic of Letters.[13]

Cathcart was nine years younger than O'Brien and was captured long before grasping O'Brien's level of experience or access to professional transnational networks. Being of lower occupational status, comparatively unconnected, and just 18 years old, Cathcart was forced to build his own local network of influential European slaves and Algerian officials—while at the same time relentlessly trying to convince O'Brien and O'Brien's regular diplomatic contacts that he, too, was a valuable asset worthy of inclusion in the more formal international network. To make his mark, as mentioned in chapter two, Cathcart sent his unsolicited journal and correspondence to diplomats such as Humphreys and Joseph Donaldson and, when he briefly returned to Philadelphia following his release from captivity, he even sent the journal to President Adams just one day before they were scheduled to meet.[14]

Cathcart wrote twenty-seven surviving letters during his decade of captivity in Algiers. They chart his rise through the ranks of the slave community, from his beginnings evading beatings in the palace garden, to his graduating to the Bagnio de Gallera, and eventually to his managing three lucrative taverns and, even more lucratively, becoming chief Christian clerk to the dey. He was a "self-made slave."[15] However locally prominent he became in Algiers, none of his correspondence was published in American newspapers as eight O'Brien's letters were.[16] Conversely, despite O'Brien's status as the captives' leader and spokesman, he never met privately with or heavily lobbied either of the deys who Cathcart served and knew intimately. For most of his captivity, O'Brien believed the captives' greatest chance to secure freedom and avoid the capture of even more Americans was instead to inform and help shape American government efforts rather than stir public sentiment or seek private ransom.

Deploying these styles of correspondence and networking strategies, O'Brien and Cathcart used their status as the points of origin in the flow of diplomatic intelligence to advance their agendas, specifically to secure comfort in captivity and ultimately win their own freedom. And in the longer term, to establish themselves as credible local agents for diplomatic and commercial enterprises. The intelligence they supplied served at least one of three goals: (1) to supply information that built credibility, (2) to make policy suggestions based on that information, and (3) to reference virtues they calculated would resonate with American officials and elicit responses to their requests for aid and ransom.

It is no coincidence that these three features figure prominently in a lengthy letter from O'Brien to Jefferson that was selected to be the first primary document in the official six-volume US government collection of correspondence, accounts, treaties, and petitions of the Barbary conflict.[17] This letter of June 1786 serves as a primer on the mercantile influence, networking strategy, and formulaic correspondence of the captive who supplied the government with most of its intelligence and analysis from Barbary. In it O'Brien combines dispassionate information—such as an inventory of Algerian corsairs and the months they cruised the Mediterranean—with policy advice that said the United States could not become commercially competitive until this foreign crisis was resolved. The latter insight is unsurprising, since sailors lived the politics of international finance. O'Brien knew that it was the heavy insurance rates on American shipping due to the risk of corsairs, rather than the actual costs inflicted by the corsairs, that forced Americans to leave the profitable Mediterranean market to larger seafaring nations, "particularly the English, French & Spanish," who, O'Brien wrote, happily "reap such benefits in being the carriers of our commerce." He argued that the cost of a treaty would be rapidly offset by revenue from Mediterranean trade and that the government would realize "in a short time the great insurance we pay would obtain us a peace."[18] Similarly, insurers, European banks, and governments closely watched American management of the Algerian crisis to gauge the nascent nation's financial savvy and its ability to repay old debts and secure new credit.[19] From the beginning of his captivity, O'Brien's reflective engagement with this commercial aspect of the crisis served well the first two aims of his correspondence, supplying both data and informed advice from within Algiers and, more generally, showing the potential value of a mercantile education at work.

O'Brien's final set of concerns almost became palpable through his impassioned contrast of the righteous captives with the American merchant John Lamb, who, according to O'Brien, was an affront to republican virtues, had violated diplomatic protocol, and had ignored basic eighteenth-century gentlemanly etiquette. From March to April 1786, Lamb negotiated on behalf of the US government to ransom its citizens. Jefferson, then minister to France, acknowledged that Lamb's "manners and appearance are not promising," but he was optimistic that, as a merchant with some experience in the region, Lamb "seems to possess some talents which may be proper in a matter of bargain."[20] But when Lamb reached Algiers, O'Brien reported that, as the first official American diplomat in the regency, Lamb's "ungentleman like behavior[;] . . . unguarded expressions[;] his hints, threats & despising the French & Spaniards[;] . . . vulgar language[;] . . . & the cloth he wore" had damaged America's reputation in Barbary. The most severe damage was caused by Lamb exceeding the maximum ransom of $200 per captive that was approved by Congress and lying that he would return with the unauthorized sum within four months. Lamb failed to mention this deal to the US government. This gaffe caused O'Brien to "hope never to see him in Algiers on any business for the United States except to chuse mules and Barbary horses." Citing Lamb's ignorance of local diplomatic etiquette as a clear impediment to successful negotiation, O'Brien turned this failure into an opportunity to seize a more active role in the negotiation for his own liberty: "I believe they [Algiers] are inclinable to a peace with the Americans but should for political views be negociated very private, particularly by the [captive] Americans."[21]

Formal diplomats of the period already had established reputations in political circles and formal lines of communication to people like Jefferson. They did not need to build credibility or cite republican virtues to spur government action. Their advice was already trusted. So the substance and underlying goals of their correspondence were notably different to those of O'Brien and the other captive sailors. Letters from Nathaniel Cutting (consul to Le Harve, France), Michael Murphy (consul to Malaga, Spain), and Joel Barlow provided the government with much objective intelligence regarding the diplomatic and commercial comings and goings of their posts and occasionally offered policy advice based on that information.[22] This intelligence and advice was never bookended with emotive pleas and professions of national loyalty from authors who were determined to prove their worth, as was the correspondence from the captives.

Jefferson's reports to Congress as secretary of state suggest that O'Brien's multifaceted approach to self-advocacy was successful, even as O'Brien's ultimate goal of redemption remained elusive. He quickly established himself as a credible source of information and the primary intermediary between the captives and the United States. The reports to Congress referred to O'Brien as "a very sensible man, and to whom we are indebted for very minute information."[23] Jefferson later advised Humphreys, then minister to Portugal, to correspond with O'Brien above all the other captives, as he "is a sensible man, and whose conduct since he has been there [in Algiers] has been particularly meritorious."[24] Jefferson did not specify what had been particularly meritorious about his conduct. As explored in the preceding chapter, unlike his captured crewmen, O'Brien and the other officers rarely endured hard labor and did not share plague-infested prisons with up to twenty seven of the dey's—occasionally man-eating—pet lions and tigers. Nor did he engage in tireless station-climbing like Cathcart. The only meritorious conduct which Jefferson could be referring to was O'Brien's default leadership of the captives and his crafted communications with US officials.

When President Washington appointed John Paul Jones to negotiate a treaty and ransom with Algiers in June 1792, Jefferson's instructions to Jones included passages of advice and intelligence from O'Brien's correspondence with the then secretary of state. Jefferson further suggested that, upon arrival, Jones should defer to O'Brien's knowledge of local diplomatic protocols and contacts.[25] Unfortunately, Jones died in Paris before he could take up the post. This advice was passed on to his successor, Thomas Barclay, who got as far as Lisbon and was preparing to depart for Algiers when he, too, died in January 1793. Finally, in July 1794, Humphreys was empowered to negotiate a treaty with Algiers and ransom the American captives, perhaps because he was already in the region and the administration did not want to tempt fate by sending yet another diplomat on the perilous voyage.[26]

More than mere vehicles for diplomatic intelligence, O'Brien and Cathcart used their correspondence to strategically frame themselves as "victims of [the same] American independence" they had fought for and which their fellow citizens were then enjoying. "Victims," because they would not have been captured and held in Algiers for over a decade if the United States had remained a British colony, protected by the Royal Navy and its costly treaties with the Barbary States.[27]

In linking their ordeal to the Revolution, O'Brien and Cathcart were trying to elicit from strangers both sympathy and a sense of shared suffering. This campaign based on images of shared suffering and sympathetic osmosis chimes with historian and philosopher Ernest Renan's observation almost a century later that, in nation building, "more valuable by far than common customs posts and frontiers conforming to strategic ideas is the fact of sharing, in the past, a glorious heritage and regrets . . . [and] of having suffered, enjoyed, and hoped together." And he stressed that "suffering in common unifies more than joy does."[28]

After seven years in Algiers, O'Brien broadcast in a letter, later published in the *Providence Gazette and Country Journal*, that he and his fellow captives "appear to be the living victims of American independence . . . at a time when a great part of the world are enlightened by the flame of liberty."[29] Three months later, he again deployed the "victim of Independence" trope in a private letter to Humphreys. However, in the intervening months the seasonal return of the plague darkened O'Brien's outlook. He became less optimistic about remaining a "living" victim and cautioned that the captives "are on the verge of eternity, and to all appearances are destined to be the victims of American independence."[30]

Cathcart marked his eighth anniversary of captivity by employing the trope in a much-quoted journal entry that lamented the perceived neglect the US government was showing its citizens in Algiers: "O! America, could you see the miserable situation of your citizens in captivity, who have shed their blood to secure you the liberty you now possess and enjoy . . . and we, the very men who have assisted in all your laudable enterprises, are now cast off because we have been unfortunate; are denied the rights of our common country. . . . It seems that we are doomed to be the only victims of American Independence."[31] Cathcart again referred to his fellow captives as "the only Victims of American Independency" in a 1794 letter to Humphreys.[32]

The origin of the term *victims of independence* cannot be definitively attributed to either captive. Within just two years of O'Brien's and Cathcart's capture, and well before their own deployment of the term, the sentiment was already center stage at benefit concerts held throughout New England for the Barbary captives. Some invoked the captives' Revolutionary War service as a call to arms—or rather a call for citizens to empty their purses and "repay the debt" to the captive veterans. Jefferson's personal scrapbook of newspaper clippings includes a poem read at one such benefit in Philadelphia that was timed to exert influence on delegates to the 1787 Grand Convention that ended up drafting the new Constitution. The benefit was billed as being "for the relief of our fellow citizens enslaved at Algiers," and it pleaded for contributions on behalf of the veterans being held in captivity: "Those veterans perhaps, whose patriot toil, / Gave independence to their native soil, / Lost in the sad vicissitudes of fate, / Call on their country to repay the debt."[33]

Remarkably, it took more than seven years of captivity before O'Brien and Cathcart classified themselves victims of independence. Why the delay? And what finally inspired their embrace of the label? Their initial use of the term was unlikely an attempt to win support from the idealistic Humphreys, as it began shortly *before* he took on the well-worn mantle of Algiers negotiator; he was still minister to Portugal and powerless to help them. Did it simply take the captives seven years to learn what the organizers of New England charitable benefits already knew and realize the value in fully tying their cause to the revered Revolution? Alternatively, having read American newspapers and diplomatic correspondence throughout seven years of captivity, did they perceive that only after seven years nostalgia for the Revolution had begun to take hold of the American popular imagination? And it was only then that the captives saw it as advantageous to reframe their captivity in relation to their role in the Revolution? We are left guessing, since O'Brien and Cathcart left only sparse sources to cross-reference their thoughts.

The captives clearly understood the emerging narrative of national identity and sensed how to weave their past experiences and present circumstances into that narrative. But they were also well-schooled in rank opportunism from their maritime days on the Revolutionary-era Atlantic, where sailors were often more mercenary than idealistic and more loyal to their crews than to their country. Like the young Republic's strategic alliances and betrayals in the wake of independence, Revolutionary-era sailors also held multiple allegiances and shifted their loyalties with the breeze.[34]

Cathcart's fluctuating identification as a British subject and declarations of loyalty to the United States bear stark testimony to this tradition of sailors' negotiable loyalties and nonlinear path to embracing American, or any, citizenship. His wavering allegiances also highlight how the American Revolution disrupted the "common sense of nationality." Since common identifying features were shared by both American and British seamen, American sailors enjoyed a brief window immediately after the Revolution, coinciding with Cathcart's captivity, when they could simply opt into American citizenship by declaring it. Given the diverse international composition of the crews on captured American-flagged ships, captives knew that establishing their national credentials were essential to stirring government action. The majority of the thirteen American ships captured by Algiers between 1785 and 1796 had at least one foreign crewman. Approximately 27 percent of the sixty-two captives freed by the US treaty of 1796 were foreigners. Cathcart's ship, the *Maria*, was a rarity in that all crew had at least a tenuous claim to US citizenship. Even in this case, Cathcart and other British-born crewmen of the *Maria* took full advantage of the not-so-common sense of nationality in the post-Revolutionary decades to initially invoke their British subjecthood to petition for assistance from King George III.[35]

In December 1785, Irish-born Cathcart first raised his colors when he joined this petition of eleven captives from the *Maria* and *Dauphin* who claimed British nationality and pleaded for the king to secure their freedom. A few, including Cathcart, even cited their service in the Royal Navy.[36] In citing their military service to the Crown, much like the Revolutionary veterans' self-description as victims of independence, the captives implied that liberty was a just reward for those who had proven their national loyalty through military service. This was a longstanding approach by Western captives in Barbary. French captives wrote similar pleas to King Louis XIII as early as December 1622.[37]

Cathcart then changed tack in 1791 when he told Dr. Werner, the doctor to the British consul, that he never consented to his name being added to a subsequent list of British captives who were seeking ransom through the donations of British subjects. Cathcart reasoned after "much deliberation" that it was impossible to expect "the declining Empire of Great Britain would wish to have rescued from Slavery the Citizens of a power which promises fair to be her greatest rival at a period not far distant."[38] If sincere, he would have been absurdly optimistic to see the United States as soon becoming a global rival to the British Empire. Instead, this was far more likely a dispassionate calculation that severing ties with Britain and declaring his citizenship and loyalty to the United States would yield the greatest chance of liberty. His renewed declaration of loyalty to the United States was fortified with the requisite invocation of manly American fortitude and the acknowledgement that liberty was an *earned*, not an *innate*, right: "[I] am firmly resolved to wait with the fortitude be coming a christian and an American until my captivity expires by honorable redemption and by my perseverance will endeavor to merit the attention of that worthy country my adopted Patria."[39]

Yet three years later, in January 1794, Cathcart's rejected patria, "the declining Empire," returned to the forefront of his mind when he once again changed tack to seek out British assistance. He now implored William Wilberforce to "endeavour to finish the charitable work you have so humanely commenced" and raise a £675 ransom "which I am certain might be raised in eight days in the City of Dublin alone." Cathcart does not try to elicit sympathy by explicitly linking his captivity to Wilberforce's broader antislavery work. Although Cathcart's diary and other correspondence regularly frame his captivity as "miserable slavery," the word *slave* is strangely mentioned just once in passing in his letter to Wilberforce. And "the horrors" of his circumstances in captivity are

fleetingly mentioned as "easier to imagine than describe." Rather than emphasize his status as a slave, Cathcart played up his Irish birth and British subjecthood. True, the reference in Cathcart's letter to "the charitable work you have so
humanely commenced" might have alluded to Wilberforce's antislavery work.
But equally, it might have merely been a reminder that Wilberforce had pledged
assistance in an earlier correspondence on October 1, 1791, which unfortunately has not survived. In any case, Cathcart claimed to have finally settled on
identifying himself and his cause as British, confidently assuring Wilberforce
that his childhood connection to Ireland was sufficient to raise his ransom, and
"if every other means miscarries I intend to write petitions to all the great Men
in Office in Ireland imploring their assistance to raise a subscription for my
redemption." Wilberforce did not respond, and Cathcart did not fulfill his
alleged intention to petition "all the great Men in Office in Ireland."[40]

This brief flirtation with Britain's leading abolitionist was likely prompted
by a string of disasters in November 1793, rather than a sign of Cathcart's enduring allegiance to a country that he left as an 8-year-old and had since fought
both for and against. Two months earlier, Algiers and Portugal finalized a treaty
that freed Algerian corsairs to roam the Mediterranean and Atlantic without
fear of assault from the troublesome Portuguese Navy. By November the corsairs returned to Algiers with 110 crew from ten American merchant ships. At
the time of this mass-capture, only 10 of the original 21 Americans taken in
1785 were still in Algiers. This new wave of captures inspired O'Brien to break
with his placid tone and try to galvanize Humphreys. O'Brien called it diplomatic negligence to have ignored his two-year-old warning of precisely this outcome if Portugal beat the United States to signing a treaty with Algiers.[41] Cathcart also knew foreign relations in Barbary were a zero-sum game. If a treaty
was made with one nation, war must be declared on another. If Algiers was at
peace with all seafaring nations, its treasury would be full with tribute but its
slave-labor force would dwindle and its fleet of unemployed corsairs would turn
mutinous. Therefore, the treaty with Portugal scuttled hopes of an American
truce for the foreseeable future, leading Cathcart once again to switch loyalties
and feel out an alternative route to redemption through Wilberforce and his
twice-rejected patria.

After hearing nothing from Wilberforce, Cathcart expunged all traces of
their correspondence from his records. He shifted his loyalty back to his adopted
patria and sought to earn his freedom and "merit the attention" of the US government through a (heavily padded) record of personal risk and sacrifice. By
Cathcart's own account, much of this national service and sacrifice occurred
when he rose to the position of chief Christian clerk to the dey in 1794. Cathcart's authority and access to the dey increased exponentially. Yet he waited
almost a year before consistently lobbying the dey to resume negotiations with

the United States. To maintain the appearance of loyalty during this year of apparent neglect, Cathcart correspondingly increased references to self-sacrifice on behalf of his fellow American captives. Like a mantra, he repeated phrases such as "if by your Captivity you render your Country service—scorn Liberty and glory in your Chains." His increased access to power was only matched by his increased complaints at mistreatment: "For this some time past I have led a miserable life, the Dey has no one to spit his Venom at but me, I may be call'd his American Spiteometer." But as a paid public official who also received income from three taverns, on top of bribes and lucrative international trade, Cathcart had the rare luxury to "glory" in his chains, unlike his "brother captives" who found no glory in plague-infested prisons or at hard labor.[42]

During this period Cathcart received informal solicitations for assistance from American consuls in the Mediterranean and captive officers in Algiers who typically ignored their socially inferior captive countrymen. Robert Montgomery, the US consul to Alicante, Spain, asked Cathcart to exploit his position to ship a breeding bull from Algiers to a friend in Ireland.[43] A month later, Montgomery received word that the United States and Algiers had finally struck a treaty and had agreed on a ransom for the captives. He now congratulated Cathcart on his "happy deliverance" from a decade of captivity and took the opportunity again to request "the breeding bull . . . by first opportunity," for which he would reimburse Cathcart and provide a recommendation for future employment.[44] A fellow captive, Captain Timothy Newman, similarly asked Cathcart to "use your interest to endeavor to get me leave from [hard labor in] the Marine, for which I shall ever feel myself under the greatest obligation." Cathcart notes that he "immediately applied to the Dey & got him [Newman] from the works to be a papaluna, that is to go where he pleased in the town & pay half a sequin each lunar month for this privilege."[45]

Until now the tidal shifts in Cathcart's loyalties flowed between the shores of the United States and Britain. When made chief Christian clerk, he gained yet another loyalty: to Algiers. His status was both that of an employee and a captive. As a trusted and high-ranking confidante of the dey, he was expected to put the interests of Algiers above those of himself and his homeland—be that homeland the United States or Britain. This new conflict of loyalties was tested in September 1795 when Cathcart, O'Brien, and the Swedish consul in Algiers assisted Joseph Donaldson in America's belated, and ultimately successful, treaty negotiation. According to Cathcart's account, simply negotiating a passport to allow Donaldson to embark for Algiers was a high-risk ordeal worthy of commendation. The dey was convinced the US government was not taking the crisis seriously; after all, they had waited a decade to send a negotiator to make realistic overtures to Algiers, only to have two negotiators die en route, Lamb exacerbate the crisis, and Humphreys remain in Lisbon while proposing to send Donaldson, his deputy. It fell to Cathcart to personally accept responsibility for Donaldson's arrival and to vouch for the sincerity of his mission.[46] On the surface, this acceptance of responsibility gives the impression of Cathcart's selfless devotion to an American treaty. It is an impression that Cathcart went to great pains to highlight in his journal entries from this period. He was less forthright in acknowledging that another perk of the chief Christian clerk was to be counted among the ransomed captives of any nation that signed a treaty during the clerk's tenure, whatever the clerk's actual nationality. So bringing any representative of a nation at war with Algiers, including Donaldson, one step closer to a treaty also brought Cathcart one step closer to his own freedom. From the perspective of a captive seeking liberty, it was irrelevant and a mere coincidence that the United States was the nation for which he lobbied.

The active roles of Cathcart and O'Brien as advisers, and Cathcart as the primary intermediary between Donaldson and the dey, were featured in a sixty-four-page stand-alone section of Cathcart's semi-official journal. The journal details a series of incidents that illustrate the role of personality in the dynamics and outcome of remote diplomatic negotiations, including an account of Cathcart's loathing for Donaldson, which nearly caused Cathcart to sabotage the US negotiation out of spite. When Cathcart hesitated to transmit an imprudent message from Donaldson to the dey that would likely have Cathcart beaten, Donaldson assured Cathcart that he "would have the consolation of having received it for having endeavored to promote the interest of my country."[47] In a retort that was surprisingly included in Cathcart's posthumous captivity narrative, he confessed that, "in order to mortify Donaldson for his ill-timed obstinacy, I told him that I would endeavor to reverse the tables on him; that I had property enough to pay my ransom or would be redeemed by Portugal, if I thought proper to espouse their cause; and that I would place him in a position to receive [a beating] which he thought so light about, and that he might console himself by knowing that it was an excellent cure for the gout."[48] This contrasts starkly with Cathcart's repeated pledge of self-sacrifice on behalf of his American "brother captives." As a further sign of the sailor's pragmatism that contrasts with his claims of patriotism and self-congratulatory benevolence, Cathcart kept a "Statement of Charges" that included "compensation for his services in effecting a negotiation with the regency of Algiers from Oct 1794 to Feb 7, 1797."[49] Thus, in addition to already being paid by Algiers to perform a job that would secure the redemption of himself and his fellow captives, Cathcart also sought financial reimbursement from the US government for his services to the Algerian government while in captivity.

O'Brien's and Cathcart's rich correspondence with senior merchants and government officials reveals a degree of autonomy that is uncommon in other systems of slavery. Yet the extent of their actual influence is suspect. To Jefferson, the captives were passive observers and informants, not autonomous agents. A decade of O'Brien's petitions and reports failed to instigate any change in Jefferson's Algerian policy. Rather, Jefferson periodically pointed to the captives as timely examples that reaffirmed his broader foreign policy strategy: to secure access to international trade through the most cost-effective means and, when necessary, deploy military assets to maintain that commercial access.[50] Although the public were highly impassioned and informed about the captives' plight and embraced it as a nationalistic struggle, this success in public relations did not translate into government action.

Humphreys, the new negotiator, was another matter. He embodied the Revolutionary-era ideal of a multitalented, romantic, idealistic, and industrious man of learning. He was a Yale graduate, an aide-de-camp to Washington during the Revolution, a junior diplomat and secretary to Jefferson in Paris, and a member of a federalist group of satirists called the Connecticut Wits. Later, he helped establish America's wool industry by importing merino sheep from Spain, where he was minister plenipotentiary, having already served as the first US minister to Portugal.[51] Despite his refined origins, in one important respect Humphreys was an everyman: his susceptibilities to patriotic pleas from captives and his interest in fostering nationalism to assure the long-term viability of the United States were commonplace. For other citizens, these susceptibilities manifested in Fourth of July toasts and newspaper articles that referenced American values of liberty, humanity, and the impossibility of a vigorous national response to crises under the Articles of Confederation.[52] Humphreys therefore makes an ideal subject through which to gauge the penetration of the captives' plight into nationalistic discourse.

Since his days as a Connecticut Wit in the 1780s and 1790s, Humphreys had written about the American captives in Algiers. They were first mentioned in his epic poem *On the Happiness of America* published in October 1786, just a year after O'Brien's and Cathcart's capture. In this poem, Humphreys shared Jefferson's and O'Brien's opinion that Barbary threatened the freedom of American commerce and the young nation's hope to become a benevolent "empire of liberty":

Then wake, Columbia! daughter of the skies,
Awake to glory, and to greatness rise!
Arise and spread thy virgin charms abroad,
Thou last, thou fairest offspring of a God;
Extend thy view where future blessings lie,
And ope new prospects for th' enraptur'd eye!
See a new era on this globe begun,

And circling years in brighter orbits run;
See the fair dawn of universal peace,
When hell-born discord through the world shall cease!
Commerce the task assign'd by heaven's decree,
From pirate rage to vindicate the sea![53]

He wrote of them again two years later in *A Poem on the Future Glory of the United States of America*, which coincided with the first wave of the captives' correspondence to appear in American newspapers and began to stir public sympathy for the captives as a project in republican sensibility:

Oh ye great pow'rs, who passports basely Crave
From Afric's lords, to sail the midland wave
Great fallen pow'rs, whose gems and golden bribes
Buy paltry passports from these savage tribes!
Ye, whose fine purples, silks, and stuffs of gold,
(An annual tribute) their dark limbs infold
Ye, whose mean policy for them equips,
To plague mankind, the predatory ships—[54]

Humphreys still shared the view—reflecting established European policy and Jefferson's personal opinion—that paying tribute was dishonorable, that it enabled future captures and impeded commerce in and around the Mediterranean. This was an eighteenth-century version of "we don't negotiate with terrorists." The passion that Humphreys showed for the captives in this later poem, however, foreshadowed his future departure from Jefferson's policy that government officials should feign disinterest in the captives in order to lower Algerian ransom and tribute demands. Thanks to direct appeals from captives and their families in the late 1780s and early 1790s, the captives became more than abstract policy dilemmas. They became symbols of American military and commercial impotence and the romantic victims of an unfinished struggle for liberty. Humphreys's evolving interest in their cause predated the broader public's changing perception of the crisis.[55] This evolving interest was reflected in his impatient and sentimental plea for action in *A Poem on the Future Glory of the United States of America*:

How long shall widows weep their sons in vain,
The prop of years, in slav'ry's iron chain?
How long the love-sick maid, unheeded, rove
The sounding shore, and call her absent love;
With wasting fears and sighs his lot bewail,
And seem to see him in each coming sail?
How long the merchant turn his failing eyes,

In desperation, on the seas and skies,
And ask his captur'd ships, his ravish'd goods,
With frantic ravings, of the heav'ns and floods?
How long, Columbians dear! will ye complain
Of wrongs unpunish'd on the midland main?
In timid sloth shall injur'd brav'ry sleep?
Awake! awake! avengers of the deep!
Revenge! revenge! the voice of nature cries;
Awake to glory, and to vengeance rise![56]

Although fiercely patriotic, Humphreys was not a natural ally of the captives or of sailors in general. His allegiance to the elite over ordinary citizens and sailors was clear since 1786/1787, when he joined future Barbary negotiator Joel Barlow and the rest of the Connecticut Wits in publishing their most celebrated satirical poem, *The Anarchiad*. This lengthy poem was a response to Shays' Rebellion and earlier incidents of civil unrest in the 1760s and 1770s. The authors shared the fears of James Madison and John Adams that mobs like "the mighty *Jacktar* guid[ing] the helm of state" would fracture the nation and lead to "the young Democracy of *hell*." According to Humphreys and the Wits, the fact that the sailor was "nurs'd on the waves, in blust'ring tempests bred, / His heart of marble, and his brain of lead" explained why he "enjoys the storm" of anarchy and revolution.[57]

The internal challenges to the nation that inspired *The Anarchiad* persisted a year later when Humphreys published his sentimental *Poem on the Future Glory of the United States of America*. And those challenges remained in late 1793, in the midst of the Whiskey Rebellion, even as his poetry and official correspondence show a softening position on sailors' and citizens' roles as legitimate actors in leading and shaping political debates. This change occurred just as he was officially empowered to negotiate with Algiers. He subsequently wrote to Washington advocating that the president declare a national day of fasting and prayer on behalf of the captives. He also recommended the construction of a navy and the start of a swift war against Algiers to help earn the respect of Europe and build a single *national* American identity.

With the continued partisanship and violent rebellions within the former colonies that motivated *The Anarchiad*, Humphreys's surprising evolution to support the captive sailors is attributable to various factors, alone or in combination. Maybe the captives succeeded in taming the diplomat through their use of Revolutionary rhetoric and sentimental appeals to patriotism. More likely, Humphreys's support for the captive sailors was reached dispassionately and was entirely consistent with the chief concern of *The Anarchiad*: that internal disputes and the absence of a national identity threatened the continued existence of the *United* States. Since his time as an aide de camp to Washington, Humphreys had pursued a campaign of using republican rhetoric to transcend and thwart the bitter partisanship that threatened the integrity of the young nation. In the captives, who had no allegiance to party or region, Humphreys found an ideal cause to aid his decade-old campaign of using republican rhetoric to construct a national American identity. He exposed a Machiavellian commitment to this campaign in advocating the sociopolitical benefits of declaring war against Algiers, telling Washington that "the *whole Nation* ought, from every sentiment of patriotism, liberty & humanity, be roused into exertion, as one Man."[58] Unlike Britain and France, against which America had waged domestically divisive wars, Algiers received no sympathy from any section of the population and was the ideal Other to facilitate Humphreys's campaign.

Whatever the cause or causes of Humphreys's growing support for the captives, it culminated in his remarkable decision to abandon his post and return to the United States to lobby personally for the captives and to pen an unauthorized address to the American people. The address fundamentally conflicted with the administration's steadfast approach, which, as Jefferson put it, was "to wear the appearance of neglecting them [the captives]." Humphreys's address suggested the government conduct a lottery to raise ransom money, and, as O'Brien had often counseled, he disputed the government's position that they must first negotiate a national treaty before the captives could be ransomed. The address also emphasized the patriotic and humanitarian duty of freeing "our brave fellow citizens whom," like Cathcart and O'Brien, "fought the battles which established our Independence [and] are literally in chains." Humphreys did not use the phrase *victims of American independence*, but he was clearly affected by the argument and thought it sufficiently compelling to himself redeploy. He wrote the address as if he were an informed private citizen using his pen to influence policy through public discourse. It reads like a departing British ambassador's candid valedictory dispatch, or a contemporary op-ed. The byline identifies Humphreys as the "Late Commissioner Plenipotentiary from the United States of America to the Dey and Regency of Algiers." But the public knew him to still be employed as minister to Portugal and part of Washington's inner circle. The public and newspaper editors were left unsure if this address signaled a welcome change in policy or an inappropriate and unauthorized personal declaration by a still-public official. So the address was reprinted in newspapers, mainly in New York and Massachusetts, before Secretary of State Edmund Randolph quashed it—but not before Humphreys's suggestion of a national lottery sparked a series of citizen-driven donation drives and theatre benefits in late 1794 in cities and towns from Philadelphia to Charleston and Baltimore to Augusta, Georgia.[59]

Despite their best efforts, O'Brien and Cathcart were unable to convince

Jefferson to change government policy and quickly strike a treaty with Algiers, or even to ransom the captives separately outside a national treaty. Likewise, despite the captives' apparent taming of Humphreys, the diplomat's intensified rhetorical support and unsanctioned actions on behalf of the captives could equally be attributed to his own long-standing interest in fostering American national unity. Yet these shortcomings should not overshadow the sophisticated means by which relatively unexceptional and politically unconnected citizens, isolated in Algiers, acted out of self-interest to participate in the construction of American identity through both private correspondence and national public appeals. Participation in this construction of national identity was often a secondary objective, when a conscious objective at all, of these ordinary citizens for whom the rhetoric of national identity often served as a mere vehicle to achieve their more immediate goals.

Foreign conflicts and encounters abroad often play a role in founding myths and the formation of national identity. But the resulting discourse typically occurs in the domestic realm: in newspapers, taverns, and political speeches. The participants themselves are made into passive vehicles for a narrative that is applied to *their* experiences. Indeed, the Algerian crisis was used by different domestic interests to highlight America's military impotence, to castigate its ineffective federal government, and to draw attention to the hypocrisy of its own slavery. Yet while in captivity O'Brien and Cathcart actively shirked their role as passive vehicles. They were keenly aware of domestic affairs and actively guided the narrative of their captivity to secure their redemption and to position themselves for future government employment. Despite being captured so soon after the Revolution and being held in distant Algiers while founding national principles were still in a state of flux, they astutely deployed the language of republicanism and patriotic duty to immerse their plight in the project of American nation building. But the captives were not necessarily patriotic idealists like Humphreys. Like many non-elites of the period, their loyalties and sense of citizenship could be auctioned to satisfy their immediate needs. Black Loyalists during the Revolution and War of 1812 shared a similar predilection for selling their loyalty to any nation that offered them liberty. Meanwhile, non-elite citizen-insurgents within America, such as participants in Shays' Rebellion in Massachusetts, deployed similar rhetoric as the captives with the goal of highlighting the contrast between Revolutionary ideals and their present economic hardships. In each case, in Barbary and Massachusetts, their anxieties and senses of national identity reflected their own unique circumstances and self-interest. Thus, although Barbary captives and Massachusetts insurgents used the same Revolutionary rhetoric to advance their causes, they did so to very different ends. The anxieties over tax collectors felt by the participants in

Shays' Rebellion were not shared by the captives in Algiers, whose ransoms depended upon the government's ability to collect taxes.

Ultimately, the lessons in self-aggrandizement and incessant networking that O'Brien and Cathcart learned as merchant sailors and honed in Algiers were just early chapters in their, and Barbary's, role in American nation building. Soon after their release, as explored in the next chapter, O'Brien became the US consul general to Algiers and Cathcart the US consul to Tripoli. In his new post, O'Brien was accused of tarnishing America's national honor by permitting the first American frigate to visit Constantinople to sail under the Algerian flag and to transport tribute from Algiers to the Grand Porte. Meanwhile in Tripoli, Cathcart's lousy relationship with the ruling bashaw arguably hastened the First Barbary War. There he also plotted America's first attempted foreign regime change with William Eaton, whose march "to the shores of Tripoli" was immortalized in the "Marines' Hymn."

CHAPTER FOUR

From Captives to Consuls and Coup-Makers

One article ought to be added to our constitution: no person shall
be eligible to be a candidate for the Presidency of the US before
they reside six months in each of the Barbary States.

James Cathcart to William Eaton, March 15, 1801

Consul, noun. In American politics, a person who having failed
to secure an office from the people is given one by the Administration on condition that he leave the country.

Ambrose Bierce, The Devil's Dictionary, *1911*

Consuls in the early American republic served in the historical shadow of more
publicly eminent men and more consequential diplomatic events. From the
Revolution to the early republic, politically connected "ministers," such as Benjamin Franklin, Thomas Jefferson, John Jay, and John Adams, were appointed
to the most important foreign courts to manage intergovernmental relations.
They are dutifully honored in historical literature and the popular imagination
for helping forge a uniquely American identity on the world stage, for securing
the financing for the Revolution, and for avoiding a war with Britain in the
1790s. However, between 1781 and 1820, the number of these high-ranking

ministers or ambassadors increased from just two to seven, while the number of consuls leapt from three to eighty-three.[1]

Unlike the high-ranking ministers appointed to exalted posts in Britain and France, these more numerous consuls were appointed to second-tier nations such as China, Mexico, and the Barbary States. They were mostly business-savvy ships' captains, merchants, and international traders, as well as former Barbary captives—such as James Cathcart and Richard O'Brien. They often lived outside the nations with which they were to conduct relations and were not even required to be American citizens. Between 1790 and 1799, approximately half of America's consuls were foreigners.[2] These consuls are rarely, if ever, included in the annals of American diplomatic history. Nor are they routinely included in literature on the nation's developing identity or its place in the world. Admittedly, it did not inspire confidence in the early US government that the nation's very first consul, William Palfrey, died en route to his post in France, where he was succeeded by Thomas Barclay, who later died in 1793 en route to Algiers to negotiate for the freedom of O'Brien, Cathcart, and their fellow 120 American captives. Thus the consular service was born of death and uncertainty.[3] Yet, American consuls, much like American captives, helped define national identity through the haphazard and ill-defined nature of their occupation, which forced them to both represent "Americanness" and determine who qualified as American.[4]

Consuls to the Barbary States were physically closer to the United States than their colleagues in China, but they shared the same feeling of isolation. Samuel Shaw, the first US consul to Canton, China (1786–1794), was the most distant and most ignored of the merchant-consul class. He received no compensation from the government and was rarely roused to exercise his official responsibilities. The US government did not closely monitor the affairs of these distant consuls, so the ill-instructed, commercially oriented officials sent the State Department mercantile intelligence that had little diplomatic value.[5]

The first five years of Cathcart's, Eaton's, and O'Brien's tenures as consuls appear at first glance quiet and unremarkable, especially compared to the preceding decade, when over one hundred Americans were held as slaves in Algiers, or the First Barbary War that soon defined their new careers. Yet even this lull between conflicts offers significant contributions to our understanding of the practice of American consular diplomacy in the early republic. These years reveal that the interplay between consuls' professional agency, private business activities, and personal relationships did not merely arise during conflict—when consuls naturally sought to leverage relationships for political gain. Rather, these overlapping networks and relationships were the norm in North Africa, with their benefits and/or consequences merely exacerbated during conflict. Indeed, many of these conflicts may not have occurred if clearer lines of communication had tightened consuls' discretionary powers, if instructions had been reiterated to prevent consuls engaging in private trade, and if consuls had been more frequent and forthright in their communications to each other to prevent suspicion and mistrust from festering.

O'Brien's entire vocabulary seemed stitched together by maritime metaphors, and according to one of these many metaphors, "O'Brien, Eaton & Cathcart might be compare'd unto 3 light houses erected on 3 dangerous shoals, and light houses erected to prevent Valuable commerce running thereon."[6] He was named US consul general to Algiers in December 1797 (serving to 1803), while Eaton served as consul to Tunis (1798–1803) before commanding American land forces in Tripoli (1804), and Cathcart became consul to Tripoli (1798–1801); then to Funchal, the capital city of the Portuguese archipelago of Madeira (1807–1815); and then to Cadiz, Spain (1815–1816).[7] Between consulships in Tripoli and Funchal, Cathcart was a long-suffering State Department attaché to a colorful Tunisian delegation (1805–1806) that wreaked havoc throughout its tour of America's northeast.[8] During this period of O'Brien's, Cathcart's, and Eaton's diplomatic service, the US government employed between fifty-two and eighty-three active consuls.[9]

Cathcart, O'Brien, and Eaton were outliers in the early American consular service in a number of ways. Their postings to Barbary made them the nation's only salaried consuls, they spent more time warding off war than they spent aiding seamen or facilitating commerce, and they even planned and attempted a coup d'état. Through these few consuls we can gain an uncommon and comprehensive insight into the principles and practices of the early American consular service and the diplomatic corps more broadly.

As consuls rather than captives, a major feature of Cathcart's and O'Brien's correspondence was now its relative scarcity. With correspondence between the United States and North Africa taking between two to eighteen months to reach its destination, consuls were given wide-ranging discretionary powers to act on their own initiative if immediate action was deemed necessary to advance the national interest or prevent disaster.[10] With the former captives now part of the diplomatic establishment, or what little of an establishment existed at the turn of the nineteenth century, their letters to the State Department were no longer an exercise in "informal diplomacy." Rather, the new form of informal diplomacy in their new careers was the interplay between private enterprise and public diplomacy. This was a period when consular colleagues were also business partners, commercial networks provided diplomatic intelligence, and bad business deals led to diplomatic crises and vice versa.[11] To this mix is added the role of personality as a factor in a consul's ultimate successes or failures.

Consuls Eaton, Cathcart, and O'Brien each impeded and advanced American policy through their private businesses and personal relationships with locals and their fellow consuls. Meanwhile, their autonomy caused incidents of national embarrassment, hastened the First Barbary War, and was ultimately a vital asset in Eaton's march "to the shores of Tripoli," memorialized in the "Marines' Hymn." In isolation, neither the consuls' private enterprises, interpersonal relationships, nor the tyranny of distance can account for the breakdown in relations and crises that the consuls faced. Their autonomy, private businesses, and interpersonal relationships are inextricably linked and must be read in tandem. This reveals a need to reevaluate the role and practice of consulships in the early republic, especially in North Africa, where the existing environment of political uncertainty was compounded by American consuls being given powers above their official title and salaries below their needs.

Throughout their correspondence and semipublic diaries from captivity, both Cathcart and O'Brien displayed the qualities and language they thought necessary to advance their immediate goals. Initially those goals were merely securing the attention and acknowledgement of their government, but over time they turned to considerations of future employment. During their later years of captivity the pair began to look beyond their still-distant freedom and toward career prospects in government service or other positions that friends in politics could help secure. Transparent lobbying and maneuvering toward careers in government service emerge in the way each boasted of their instrumental role in securing the 1795 Treaty of Peace and Amity with Algiers. Although O'Brien was uninterested in returning to the city, both he and Cathcart suggested they had strong cases for a future working relationship with the government of Algiers. It was essential they portray their captivity as an exercise in political education and relationship-building, since they both had effectively been unemployed during their decade of captivity. O'Brien's framing of his captivity as "nine years experience and study" in Barbary affairs proved to be his undoing when he, rather than the eager Cathcart, was persuaded to accept the post of consul general to Algiers. This was the same city that he and Cathcart had alternately described as "hell" and "the city of bondage" in the address lines of their correspondence.[12]

The pair also directly solicited all-purpose letters of recommendation from merchants, sailors, fellow captives, government officials, and foreign consuls with whom they had contact during the course of their captivity. O'Brien advertised that he had earned the unreserved trust and respect from his captive countrymen, such that they hoped the government would redeem him, if only him, so that he could help inform government policy or tour America and drum up support for the captives' cause.[13] The brother of the Swedish consul in Algiers, who was empowered to act on behalf of the United States, suggested to David Humphreys that "you must have a capable man for consul here, and a man who merits the confidence to have full powers, and a public credit considerable, always open for the cases absolutely necessary for the good of his country. I know among the present slaves here only Captain O'Brien, who possesses the requisite qualities to fill such a place."[14] When Joel Barlow discovered that Cathcart was making overtures for the position of consul general to Algiers, he did not need any encouragement to thwart Cathcart's bid, advising the secretary of state that Cathcart "has neither the talents or the dignity of character necessary for that purpose."[15]

Ultimately, it was O'Brien who was offered, and reluctantly accepted, the position of consul general to Algiers in December 1797 with an annual salary of $2,400 ($49,000 in 2018 US dollars) and a further $1,600 ($32,600) for official expenses. Meanwhile, Cathcart was appointed consul to Tripoli a year later with a salary and "contingent expenses" of about $2,200.[16] Cathcart felt himself the obvious choice to become America's new consul general, given his prior service as chief Christian clerk to the dey and his familiarity with Algerian governance and its influential personalities. The rejection greatly wounded his pride, dented his tireless ambition for self-advancement, and caused his first fissure with O'Brien. Perhaps Cathcart was passed over because his former position was perceived to compromise his loyalty to the United States, despite his protestations of loyalty. Perhaps it was because prior to captivity he was a mere common sailor, whereas O'Brien was a captain. Perhaps it was because O'Brien was the primary intermediary between the captives and American officials. Or perhaps it was due to the negative comments about him in his recommendations. Given Cathcart's palpable eagerness and O'Brien's reluctance to take up the post, it is likely that the rejection reflected a combination of all the above. Thus the conferral of their consular appointments launched the pair into their new careers—and for Cathcart began a series of perceived betrayals by O'Brien, which resulted in an increasingly hostile and occasionally paranoid working relationship that defined their tenure as American agents in Barbary. While their lobbying efforts to achieve freedom from captivity were slow to be rewarded, their success in securing government employment, and many subsequent such appointments, proved the pair to be accomplished job-seekers.

When the bulk of the American captives finally returned to Philadelphia on February 8, 1797, hundreds of citizens boisterously celebrated their return at a local tavern. Summaries of the celebration and the circumstances of their captivity circulated as far as Charleston.[17] For O'Brien and Cathcart, their return to American shores was just a long-planned stopover en route to something grander. The pair shared the entrepreneurial spirit and self-made prospects of many American men at the turn of the nineteenth century, including a young Daniel Webster. Five years after O'Brien's and Cathcart's sojourn in America,

Webster wrote that "the world is nothing but a contra-dance, and every one, *volens, nolens*, has a part in it. Some are sinking, others rising, others balancing, some gradually ascending towards the top, others flamingly leading down. Some cast off from Fame and Fortune, and some again in a comfortable *allemande* with both."[18]

For men of ambition, ten years in Algiers was certainly akin to "sinking" or "flamingly leading down." As captives they were unemployed, impoverished, enslaved, emasculated, and dependent on the charity of others, hence their persistent protestations of manliness outlined in chapter two. Now free, they planned to "gradually ascend towards the top."

But to the top of what competition? Cathcart was arguably more Algerian than American. Arriving in North America at the age of 8, he spent just ten years in the colonies (and much of that at sea on merchant ships, in the Continental Navy, or in the Royal Navy) before he was captured and held in Algiers for almost eleven years. With roots in Ireland, his formative years in Algiers, and his heart allegedly in the United States, Cathcart clearly had a need to persuade both himself and others of his credentials as an American if he were to achieve his ambitions.

While in the United States, both he and O'Brien learned they would return to Barbary—this time as consuls, not captives. During this stopover the dey assigned O'Brien (interestingly, not Cathcart) with overseeing the construction in Portsmouth of a brig and two cruisers that the dey had purchased from the United States "according to the choice and taste of Captain O'Brien."[19] O'Brien was also tasked with overseeing the construction of the thirty-four-gun frigate *Crescent* that was included, with much humiliation, as a "gift" from the US government under the terms of their peace treaty with Algiers. Cathcart had also lobbied for this job of construction overseer, but was again passed over—this time by his former master the dey, who appeared to have greater faith in O'Brien.[20] Cathcart's perennial competitor attended to this unpaid duty despite the 1795 treaty making him a free man and after being named consul general to Algiers. Much like Cathcart's multiple loyalties while chief Christian clerk, O'Brien was now serving multiple masters: he had duties to himself as a freeman; to his former master, the dey, as a construction overseer; and to the United States as a named consul. Unlike Cathcart, O'Brien (who had lived longer in the American colonies than had Cathcart) never felt the need to justify or explain these multiple duties-cum-loyalties or to litter his correspondence or diary with patriotic posturing to confirm that his primary loyalty was to America. In January 1798 the *Crescent* was completed and loaded with naval stores, which were also part of America's tribute commitment. O'Brien boarded and arrived in Algiers a month later.

Meanwhile in Philadelphia, Cathcart's priorities were clear: find a wife from a respectable, well-connected family, and make a triumphant return to Barbary. Following a determined courtship campaign launched in July 1797, and taking less than a year, Cathcart married Jane Bancker Woodside, who was born to a well-connected Philadelphia family of Irish stock. The courtship included a lot of insufferable poetry from Cathcart, which appeared to have little impact on Jane Woodside:

> When Janey smiled her lovely look
> My wandering heart a prisoner took
> And bound it with so strong a chain
> I ne'er expect it back again
>
> Then Janey treat a captive true
> With gentle usage 'tis its due
> It pants for thee alone
> Then take it kindly to thy breast
> And give the weary wanderer rest
> And keep it near thy own
>
> For Janey thus my heart has moved
> Accept it lovely fair
> I have like before but never loved
> Then let me not despair.[21]

Just as in captivity Cathcart again lobbied influential advisors, this time calling on his future bride's parents throughout the courtship to alleviate "Janey's" doubts of his sincerity.[22] As in captivity where he courted multiple nations in the hope that one would provide freedom, so too back in Philadelphia he simultaneously courted multiple women in the hope that one would become his wife. Woodside, who "like lightning she darts thro' each throbbing vein," was not his first choice. Her doubts were spurred by Cathcart's own reckless confession of his pursuit of another: "You said my dearest when I had the pleasure of walking with you that you did not believe I loved you, & that you had heard me declare my sentiments to another on the same subject. . . . My conduct it is true deserves censure, your good sense is shown in observing it, & your candour in declaring it, but consider my love that there is no person infallible, & that perfection is not to be found on this side the grave."[23] It is understandable why Eaton would later say that it was "unhappy for his friends that he [Cathcart] finished his education in Barbary!"[24]

This cynical interpretation of Cathcart's courtship strategy may be unjust. The diaries of bachelors in the early republic show it was common to simultaneously court multiple women and engage in premarital sex.[25] And according

Jane B. Cathcart. In James Cathcart, *The Captives: Eleven Years a Prisoner in Algiers* (La Porte, IN: Herald Print, 1899), frontispiece.

to one analysis of sailors' typical approaches to women, Jack Tar presumed the fairer sex was always more than happy to serve in his preferred role of wife or wench.[26] By comparison, Cathcart's courtship seems genuinely romantic.

However romantic it began, the licentious sailor in Cathcart soon resurfaced when he, his new bride, and Eaton embarked for Barbary on January 4, 1799, from Delaware Bay. While in Philadelphia, Cathcart hired an English maid, Betsy Robinson, to assist his bride in domestic responsibilities and to keep her company in Tripoli, where Cathcart knew few would speak English or be fit to associate with "decent society." In the course of the thirty-six-day journey between the United States and Algiers, there was an unclear falling-out between Cathcart and Robinson. According to Cathcart, he "had seen enough of her on the passage to cause me to form no very favorable opinion of her." As a fellow passenger, Eaton suggested that Cathcart unsuccessfully tried to seduce Robinson, remarking that "he deluded her into a persuasion that his family and manners must have been at least civilized if not refined."[27] Whatever happened en route, Robinson fled to O'Brien's protection as soon as the ship docked in Algiers.

Robinson did not take the first ship back to the United States, as she had initially intended and which would have left Cathcart to happily forget the incident. Instead, she fell in love with her protector, O'Brien. The pair was married by Cathcart's old acquaintance from captivity, the Swedish consul Matthias Skjoldebrand, on March 25, 1799, just six weeks after Robinson arrived in Algiers. Eaton congratulated O'Brien, writing that "the manna from heaven to the famishing children of promise could not be more timely and miraculously given than is this goodly woman to my good friend. The Lord give you many days and <u>nights</u> of happiness, and may you see the fruits of your labors until the seventh generation. I have dispatched an express with the news to Cathcart and his Lady. Alas, poor devils, how they will be chafed on the occasion. But be assured it gives great joy to Eaton."[28]

Cathcart was closer to fuming than chafed. It is a telling sign of his character and his belief in the severity of this incident that he made a full complaint to Secretary of State Timothy Pickering after receiving word that O'Brien and Robinson were married. Cathcart remained entirely silent about Robinson between the time of their arrival in North Africa and her marriage to O'Brien. He could tolerate a private rejection but could not endure this public humiliation. He confided to Pickering that "when Mr. O'Brien wished to take her to the table I objected, as I did not consider her a fit person to be on intimate terms with my wife; especially in a place where there is no other female society." Surely Robinson and Mrs. Cathcart would have been on intimate terms if she had remained the Cathcarts' maid in Tripoli, where English-speaking society was even more limited than it was in Algiers.[29] Several months later he spun the saga further in a private complaint to Eaton, who had witnessed the affair in its entirety. Cathcart now claimed that, rather than Robinson fleeing to O'Brien's protection, O'Brien "took every means to entice her from the service of a young creature [Mrs. Cathcart] in a barbarous community, when it was impossible to procure another female attendant."[30]

Following O'Brien's selection for the post of Algiers ahead of Cathcart, this second incident marked a tipping point, when Cathcart's sense of betrayal and mild distrust of O'Brien now became deeply intensified and personal. This personal dislike soon affected their working relationship and resulted in Cathcart refusing to forward diplomatic intelligence to O'Brien. It also gave rise to Cathcart sending unprofessional criticisms of O'Brien's character in official correspondence to State Department officials.

The "three lighthouses"—O'Brien, Eaton, and Cathcart—were appointed to their new roles on the heels of the Consular Act of 1792. This was the first legislative attempt to define the authority and responsibilities of American consuls.[31] Subsequent legislation soon refined it, but for over one hundred years the act remained the legislative core of the consular service.[32] It instructed consuls to receive the official protests and declarations of citizens, specifically "captains, masters, crews, passengers, and merchants"; it instructed them to aid stranded sailors; to temporarily manage citizens' estates if they died while abroad; and specified the fees consuls may collect for providing these services. For authenticating protests or declarations, a consul was entitled to two dollars, while settling a deceased citizen's estate entitled him to 5 percent of the gross amount of the estate. The act further specified that of all US consuls, only those in Barbary would be given a salary, "not exceeding two thousand dollars," since these consuls would be too busy preventing hostilities between nations to earn a living through private trade and fee collection. This unique provision of a salary for America's consuls in Barbary did not dissuade each of them from dabbling in private trade, which greatly contributed to diplomatic crises and growing distrust between the consuls and locals.

It was common European practice to appoint merchants as consuls and allow them to supplement their meager wages by dabbling in international trade and local business dealings. However, these side-businesses were not expected to take up much of their time and were certainly not expected to cause conflicts of interest with their positions as consuls. British consuls performed similar services for their nation's subjects as American consuls were instructed to do under the 1792 act. In Algiers, these consuls were typically merchants or business-savvy military officers. Like a chamber of commerce, they called meetings of British merchants to discuss stranded or captive sailors and determine the levies to be imposed on traders.[33] These responsibilities had similarly been the core business of the Marseille Chamber of Commerce since it was formed in 1599.[34] Following instructions from Louis XIV, however, the French consuls in Barbary became notable exceptions to this practice. They were salaried and explicitly prohibited from conducting private trade—and as prerequisites they had to be over the age of thirty and required over three years prior service as a vice consul.[35]

For new consuls dispatched on behalf of the young American republic, the practicalities of life as an unsalaried merchant-consul were problematic. Their European counterparts had decades-old (if not centuries-old) private trade networks and established lines of credit, whereas novice American consuls were forced to spend much of their time establishing trade networks and building their private purse. Having to depend upon fees, having comparatively limited access to established private trade networks, and the scarcity of high quality consuls all contributed to a string of corruption scandals and a generally low opinion of the early American diplomatic corps.[36] Aside from the salaried Barbary consuls, a consular posting was an honorary and honorific role. Appointments were sought and accepted because they conferred respectability and officialdom. Such status helped consuls rise above other merchants to secure more credit and better business deals from local traders.[37] Through the networks they formed as consuls, they each positioned themselves for future employment opportunities either within America or abroad or within government or the private sector.

Diplomacy in Barbary was a tricky and haphazard affair, when it occurred at all. Without a professional diplomatic corps, it was difficult to convince eminent (or even merely capable) citizens to leave their families, civilized society, and business opportunities to take instead a post in North Africa. Joel Barlow, a Yale graduate, lawyer, newspaper publisher, and poet, is a notable exception. Most American representatives to second-tier nations were therefore international traders, like the ignoble Algiers negotiators John Lamb and Joseph Donaldson, although typically they exhibited more cosmopolitanism and polish. Some of Cathcart's, O'Brien's, and Eaton's troubles may be attributed to the fact that these three were qualified consuls but were given posts which exclusively dealt with affairs of state, and therefore, they should have been handled by more seasoned ministers. As Cathcart himself noted, "that these offices partakes very little of the duties of consuls which strictly considered relate only to commercial affairs, whereas the duties of consuls in the Barbary States are chiefly political they are in fact rather Ministers than Consuls. Now sir if we do the duty of Ministers why should we not enjoy the rights and emoluments annexed to the office? Ought not the reward bear some proportion to the service we render our country?"[38]

More frustrating than the "barbarous" nature of governance in North Africa and the lack of civilized society in which the consuls and their families could mingle was that the functions of consuls were constantly impeded by the delay of correspondence between the United States and North Africa. This crippling delay ranged from two to eighteen months. Even within the Barbary States, correspondence took an average of six weeks to travel between the regencies.[39] To avoid the potentially catastrophic consequences of this time lag in a turbulent diplomatic, military, and political environment, consuls were granted a surprising amount of autonomy in determining how they conducted affairs ranging from minor matters of protocol to major initiatives.

The success of diplomacy in isolated outposts such as Algiers had always relied on interpersonal dynamics and the abilities of agents who were "on the spot," as they were called in commercial parlance, to act autonomously. British consuls in Barbary were permitted to conduct "diplomatic policy on the hoof" for three reasons that applied equally to the American consuls in North Africa: (1) the distance involved was not conducive to asking and receiving timely instructions, (2) consuls were expected to be more knowledgeable about local political affairs than their superiors in London or Washington, and (3) consuls were exposed to physical danger and political volatility that might demand immediate action.[40] President John Adams affirmed this degree of discretionary power and the importance of a consul's commercial connections and personal integrity in 1797:

> It also appears to be of importance to place at Algiers a person, as consul, in whose integrity and ability much confidence may be placed, to whom a considerable latitude of discretion should be allowed, for the interest of the United States in relation to their commerce. That country is so remote, as to render it impracticable for the consul to ask and receive instructions in sudden emergencies. He may sometimes find it necessary to make instant engagements for money, or its equivalent, to prevent greater expenses or more serious evils. For these reasons, it appears to me to be expedient to vest the consul at Algiers with a degree of discretionary power, which can be requisite in no other situation.[41]

Nine years later, in response to an attempted coup in Tripoli that was inspired by Cathcart and executed by Eaton with little government input, President Jefferson cautiously reiterated Adams's position on the necessity of consuls' discretionary powers:

> In operations at such a distance, it becomes necessary to leave much to the discretion of the agents employed; but events may still turn up beyond the limits of that discretion. Unable in such a case to consult his Government, a zealous citizen will act as he believes that [the government] would direct him, were it apprised of the circumstances, and will take on himself the responsibility. In all these cases, the purity and patriotism of the motives should shield the agent from blame, and even secure a sanction, where the error is not too injurious.[42]

Here Jefferson is retroactively, though reluctantly, sanctioning Eaton's and Cathcart's staging of a military coup to install an American-friendly government in Tripoli, which makes it difficult to imagine the point at which a consul's discretion would therefore qualify as "too injurious." Irrespective of differences in the power and influence of nations and the specific instructions given to consuls, the basic mechanics of how Western nations conducted diplomatic affairs in Algiers, Tripoli, and Tunis in the late eighteenth and early nineteenth centuries were relatively standardized.

Between O'Brien's arrival in Algiers in February 1798 and the close of 1800, he wrote one hundred letters to his superiors in the State Department.[43] Cathcart arrived in Barbary a year later but by the end of 1800 still managed to send well over fifty letters to Washington. These were the quiet years for Americans in North Africa, although the "quiet" was only relative compared to the decade-long Algerian crisis that preceded this interlude and the First Barbary War that soon followed it. Through bad luck, bad timing, and bad decisions, Cathcart and O'Brien found themselves at the epicenter of each of these phases of America's relationship with Barbary.

When Eaton, the Cathcarts, and Betsy Robinson arrived in Barbary after their salacious voyage, they met O'Brien in Algiers, where he had just exercised his discretionary powers in a cunning maneuver that both subdued Algerian posturing toward the United States and also saved the American government tens of thousands of dollars in the bargain. By 1799 the former dey, who had built a decade of awkward rapport with his former American captives, had died and his successor was now impatient with the perpetual delays of US tribute stipulated in the 1795 treaty—the same treaty that O'Brien himself had been freed from captivity to deliver. The debt incurred during the Revolution had chronically delayed this payment of cash and naval stores, and an outbreak of smallpox further delayed construction of ships being built in America for the dey. To alleviate the dey's concern and prevent a nullification of the hard-negotiated treaty, O'Brien used his initiative to offer the dey the three American-built ships he had overseen construction of, in addition to the frigate *Crescent*, all free of charge in lieu of other tribute. He successfully cleared all outstanding American debts by drastically inflating the cost of constructing the ships and took advantage of the fact that neither the new dey nor the prime minister knew the particulars of the treaty, which stipulated that all tribute must be paid in cash or naval stores. To give the deal a veneer of sincerity, O'Brien convinced the Algerians that the deal would be met with the wrath of the US government, and he was only advocating it because at that time America and Algiers shared a common enemy, the French, against whom America was fighting the Quasi-War.[44] This was precisely the sort of maneuver that Jefferson had in mind a decade earlier when writing that he hoped having a mercantile background would cause Lamb to "possess some talents which may be proper in a matter of bargain."[45]

Cathcart's start in Tripoli was less auspicious. He had just sailed from Algiers, arriving on April 5. While still aboard his ship, Bryan McDonogh, agent for the British, Swedes, and Americans in Tripoli, drew up alongside in a boat from port and informed Cathcart that the bashaw, the ruler of Tripoli, "would not receive me as consul for the United States of America, as I had not brought the stores and brig promised by Capt. O'Brien two years ago" when O'Brien made a preliminary treaty with Tripoli. Furthermore, "he would give us forty days from the time of our departure before he would order his cruisers to capture American vessels; that he would then order the American flag to be hauled down and openly declare war against the United States of America, and by that act let the world see that the Bashaw of Tripoli was an independent Prince, and would be respected as such in spite of Algiers, Tunis or even the Grand Signore."[46] With this shot over the bow even before touching shore, Cathcart became the untimely victim of the bashaw's need to make a global statement of independence and strength. With that statement made, Cathcart was accepted as consul on a probationary basis and spent his tenure trying to prevent war from a weak negotiating position. He regularly mocked O'Brien's frequent use of maritime metaphors, but Cathcart's position was akin to an isolated sailor helplessly watching a gathering storm on the horizon.

In a journal entry five days after his arrival, he proudly noted the cost-saving value in the American government appointing a former chief Christian clerk intimately familiar with the less honorable nuances of diplomatic transactions in the region. When a new consul arrived in Barbary, it was customary to offer the respective ruler a series of lavish gifts. Similarly, American consuls were later asked to give presents upon the rulers' birthdays, their sons' circumcisions, on George Washington's birthday, and even upon his death.[47] Cathcart brought gifts from the United States, but he "very fortunately had kept back a number of articles belonging to the presents, expecting a second demand," and thus he saved the American government the expense of purchasing these same gifts in Tripoli at exorbitant prices.[48]

O'Brien likewise rightly claimed that his captivity provided "nine years experience and study," though he hoped to apply those lessons *anywhere except* back in Barbary. Nevertheless, his early correspondence with Eaton shows the latter was impressed with O'Brien's savvy application of bribery and his willingness to act on his own initiative to save the government money—even if that meant manipulating a foreign ruler and technically breaking a treaty he had helped negotiate. Eaton did not extend this admiration to Cathcart, who had accomplished similar feats. At the time of Cathcart's and Eaton's arrival, O'Brien had not received correspondence or instructions from Washington for a year. On the back of his victory in persuading the dey to take the American-made ships in lieu of other tribute, O'Brien advised Eaton that "you may as well put your instructions in your pocket and concede to be governed by circumstances" and, even if the State Department broke habit and corresponded more than once a year, the distant US government could not predict the "variable winds on this treacherous coast."[49] Eaton appears to have relished O'Brien's maritime metaphors for consular autonomy, recalling that "O'Brian says giving the consuls full powers in these regencies is 'carrying out our sheet anchor' and speaking of their being confined to particular instructions he says 'Such a short scope of cable will not do in one of their sudden gales.'"[50] In short, a consul in Barbary's squally waters must act as his own captain, navigator, and crew.

A decade of captivity helped dampen O'Brien's and Cathcart's culture shock, but despite taking O'Brien's advice to heart, it was ultimately Eaton who proved the least adept at adjusting to Tunisia. He described it as a "land of rapine and sodomy," where "they are under no restraints of honor nor honesty. There is not a scoundrel among them, from the prince to the muleteer, who will not beg and steal."[51]

O'Brien and Cathcart were quickly reminded, and Eaton quickly discovered, that their diplomatic endeavors would be entirely unlike those of their esteemed colleagues in Britain, France, Holland, Spain, or Portugal. Diplomacy in Barbary was conducted without courtly decorum or even the pretense of Western notions of "honor." It was essentially a business enterprise, in which a continued "partnership" between nations depended upon the reliability of American credit and timely tribute payments, and with the terms of these partnerships constantly under review and renegotiation. Diplomacy, integrity, and business were inextricably linked in North Africa—as they were at all diplomatic posts until reforms of the diplomatic corps in 1856 granted all American consuls salaries to insulate them from conflicts of interest that accompanied private commerce. In a sign of the overlap between business and diplomacy (even for the salaried Barbary consuls), Cathcart kept a small notebook in which he wrote lists and tables that converted North African measurements of weight, distance, currency, and time. Cathcart was adhering to the advice of mercantile textbooks of the period when he created this booklet that converted measurements to assist in his private commercial enterprises with local government officials and influential merchants.[52]

Just as the consuls' public office became a means of conducting business between nations, the consuls themselves inevitably became entwined with local business communities, and the prospering or souring of these overlapping public-private relationships in turn affected diplomatic relations.[53] In North Africa the Jewish banking houses of Bacri and Busnach represented this nexus of diplomacy and commerce. A word from either family could make or break treaties or negotiations, and they held a virtual monopoly on banking and trade in each of the Barbary States. The families were informal diplomats (albeit ones with far more influence than O'Brien and Cathcart), as they were simultaneously diplomats, merchants, private bankers, managers of public treasuries, and couriers of information. Joel Barlow, when serving as O'Brien's predecessor in Algiers, called the house of Bacri "the Kings of Algiers, and that it is easier to oppose the Dey's interest than theirs."[54] O'Brien, due to proximity and necessity, had more contact with the Bacris and Busnachs than his colleagues serving in Tripoli and Tunis, and in 1802 he estimated the families' combined wealth at a staggering $5.5 million ($4.3 billion in 2018 US dollars).[55] At this time the entire US government revenue was just $15 million.[56] When they became consuls, each of the three "lighthouses" became more dependent on loans and trade with the Bacris and Busnachs to supplement their salaries. Despite their history of positive relations and continued dependence, the transition from captives to consuls made the Americans critical of the Bacris' and Busnachs' fickle and self-interested influence over public affairs.[57]

This background on the Bacris and Busnachs and their inextricable links to commerce and national affairs foreshadows the breakdown in relations between the three consuls in early 1801 and how their private trading enterprises impeded affairs between states. For his part, Cathcart began to dedicate himself to lengthy correspondence and raving against O'Brien. Each dispute might have been averted if O'Brien kept open lines of communication and if personal relations between them had not soured through earlier competitions for work and women. They also could have been defused if the US government had taken Cathcart's parting advice from captivity: "It will be absolutely necessary for a fast sailing Brig or Schooner to be employ'd as a packet [ship] from Algiers, Tunis and Tripoli."[58] It would have alleviated the misunderstandings and paranoia borne from isolation.

Eaton gave up trying to mediate a truce between the pair and conveyed the impression that Secretary of State Pickering looked upon the hostility as an embarrassed parent looks upon their squabbling children, or in his words, "as the Chancellor of Heaven does the accusing spirit informing against the elect."[59] When O'Brien took Eaton's advice and began ignoring Cathcart's correspondence, Cathcart interpreted it as a sign of professional negligence, as toxic to the national interest, and as telling of O'Brien's character that he would allow petty personal disputes to effect his professional duties. He bemoaned, "I have not received a line from Mr. O'Brien although I have wrote him six long letters. Personal pique in my opinion ought to be sacrificed when the interest of our country is at stake. I should think myself unworthy of the trust [placed] in me if I hesitated a single moment in communicating anything that involved the national interests of our citizens, even to my greatest <u>enemy</u> if I imagined he could be of any service to our common cause. I hope Mr. O'Brien may think the same, but these mushroom gentry very often forget themselves."[60]

Cathcart now shirked O'Brien, a member of the "mushroom gentry"—a common epithet for someone who had sprung up overnight into wealth and society from the dung—and he began bombarding Eaton with letters that ran as long as seven pages. Among these was a six-page report in early 1800 on the "ridiculous" superstitions of Tripoli's Muslims, the fragile status of its Jewish population, and Tripoli's greater-than-presumed independence from Algiers. Despite Cathcart's earlier admonishment of O'Brien for allegedly withholding communication due to personal disputes and to the detriment of the national interest, he now concluded that "I should inform Mr. O'Brien of this transaction but dare not as he informs the Bacri of everything I write him and they write to [Leon] Farfara [the Bacri's commercial agent in Tripoli] so that it behooves me to be very cautious in my correspondence."[61] This is Cathcart's only direct admission that he withheld diplomatic intelligence due to O'Brien's relationship with the Bacris. It is likely that over the years he withheld further intelligence without being careless enough to admit the fact.

Several months later, in a particularly caustic five-page letter, Cathcart catalogued supposed evidence that throughout 1798, while he was still in Philadelphia, O'Brien had abused his office, conspired with the Bacris and Busnachs, and repeatedly lied to the American government. Buried in this testimony is Cathcart's summary judgment that, "in short, Mr. O'Brien is a janus who keeps two journals as well as two faces. I can prove from his own handwriting that he never speaks as he thinks, and he seems to glory in the deception; his actions stink in my very nostrils, and I do not wonder that he should league with a Jew to injure his former friend; he would sacrifice, if he found it his interest to do so, Jesus Christ—but I defy him."[62] As further evidence, Cathcart discovered that tribute of jewels and watches that O'Brien sent to Tripoli in December 1800 was purchased in Algiers at twice the cost of goods available in Leghorn, Italy. Cathcart extrapolated that, since over time O'Brien had bought and distributed throughout Barbary $150,000 ($3 million in 2018 US dollars) worth of tribute, he had enriched the Bacris and Busnachs, his "masters," from whom those goods were purchased, by approximately $75,000.[63] There is no evidence, however, that O'Brien ever conspired with the Bacris or Busnachs to the detriment of the United States. It would have been impractical for O'Brien to sail to Leghorn every time he needed goods for tribute, and with the Bacris' and Busnachs' trading monopoly in Barbary, he had few alternatives for domestic trade.[64] Even if O'Brien had paid exorbitant prices to enrich the banking families, he needed the Bacris' political and financial support, if only, as Cathcart himself acknowledged, so they would not become "negative enemies." Perhaps Cathcart's relentless tirades about O'Brien won Eaton over, or perhaps it was Eaton's commercial partnership with Cathcart and his own observations of the Bacris and Busnachs. Whatever the cause, in early 1801 Eaton's initial sympathy with O'Brien and distrust of Cathcart had reversed, and he became convinced that indeed O'Brien was in league with the Bacris and Busnachs, who in turn saw it in their financial interest to be in league with France.[65]

Though they chided O'Brien without evidence, both Cathcart and Eaton happily engaged in the judicious misuse of office and even minor corruption. Such was the norm in the early consular service. According to the 1792 Consular Act, the Barbary consuls were made the only salaried consuls of the United States with the expectation that they would devote all their time to matters of state and would not be compromised by risky speculation in private trade. Nevertheless, within months of arriving in their posts, Cathcart sent Eaton a cargo of wine for sale in Tunis and in turn asked Eaton to send a load of cloth to sell in Tripoli. Although he later blasted O'Brien for allegedly keeping two sets of books to facilitate corruption, Cathcart asked Eaton to make two invoices for the price of the cloth, with one reflecting the genuine price and the other inflating the price by 25 percent, which was to be "for my government."[66] In time Cathcart and Eaton wrote of diplomacy and private trade within the same letters, in similar language, and with the same sense of urgency.[67] The State Department even tacitly sanctioned this blurring of lines, despite it contravening the spirit of the Consular Act. One department official told Eaton about the US consul at Malaga's recent profitable shipment to New York of wine, brandy, fruit, and other goods, and regretfully, informed Eaton that there were no plans for a Navy vessel to travel between the United States and Tunis for one of Eaton's private trading vessels to join in convoy. Just one month later, Eaton sent Cathcart two cargoes of wheat under the protection of the USS *Philadelphia.*[68]

In 1800 two confrontations in Tripoli highlighted the dangerous and inextricable link between private business and public diplomacy. These incidents illustrate how the tyranny of distance was not the sole source of the consuls' troubles, nor was O'Brien the only American consul whose financial dealings appeared to compromise his official duties. Whereas O'Brien's supposed indiscretions merely bruised his integrity in the eyes of his fellow "lighthouses," Cathcart's indiscretions in Tripoli created a wedge between him and the bashaw. The more minor of the two incidents involved Cathcart's short-lived attempt to buy a Tripolitan ship that was captured by the Portuguese. Although he ultimately did not buy the ship, his brief interest raised the price that the bashaw was forced to pay to reclaim it.[69] This dispute assured Cathcart made an enemy of the bashaw. It seems Cathcart failed to learn O'Brien's lesson from captivity, that "money is the God of Algiers & Mahomet their prophet."[70] Cathcart should have known the same God was worshiped in Tripoli.

The second and more damaging incident involved the cloth that Eaton sent from Tunis, which arrived in Tripoli in October 1799. Farfara, acting simultaneously as a broker for Cathcart and the local agent for the Bacris, informed Cathcart that the bashaw requested "the preference in the sale of said cloth, promising to pay for the same like any other individual."[71] Cathcart reluctantly agreed, but the bashaw, much like the American government, continually put off payment to the frustration of his creditor. Cathcart petitioned the bashaw for payment throughout 1799 and 1800. He even muddied the division between private trader and public official when he lied that the infant US Navy was sailing for Tripoli to reclaim his goods. Rather than accept that he was the victim of an understandable attempt by Farfara and the bashaw to recoup America's delinquent tribute via the private trade of its consul, Cathcart was instead convinced that "the fact is the Jews are in debt to the Bashaw for prize goods, and I imagine have paid my account to their credit."[72] Although Farfara's connection to the Bacris was through private business, and O'Brien's connection to the Bacris was predominantly through his official duties, Cathcart blurred these relations and used this incident to help convince Eaton that O'Brien was guilty of conspiracy by association with North Africa's community of Jewish merchants and bankers.

In a region where personal credibility and financial credit were a consul's two greatest assets, becoming embroiled in a personal financial dispute with any ruler in the Barbary States could lead to increased tribute demands or even declarations of war against the nation that the consul represented. Cathcart's deteriorating relationship with O'Brien and the bashaw certainly contributed to his inability to prevent the declaration of war that he had struggled to avert since his arrival. In an open letter circulated in late October 1800, Cathcart protested the bashaw's conduct toward the United States and toward the consul himself. By cannily cataloguing the bashaw's treacherous acts against the consul, side by side with those committed against the American nation, Cathcart implicitly framed himself as merely another victim of the bashaw's "arbitrary acts," who could not be held responsible for Tripoli's inevitable declaration of war six months later. Even as American colonists chastised their king for his "arbitrary" application of power, in the American imagination it was always the "Turk" who epitomized arbitrary governance. Cathcart's choice of language was almost certainly intended to arouse this association and draw a parallel between himself and earlier American patriots who endured the "arbitrary government" of King George III, which, as with Tripoli, inevitably resulted in a *just* war.

Cathcart's list of complaints in the October 1800 letter included the bashaw's refusal to accept American passports; his refusal, after Cathcart requested "above fifty times," to reimburse him 2,314 Spanish dollars for his cloth; the bashaw's attempt to rewrite Article 10 of the American-Tripolitan treaty that stipulated America would only make a one-off treaty-signing payment rather than an annual tribute; the bashaw's further rejection of Article 12 of the treaty that stipulated any dispute, such as the dispute over Article 10, may be settled by the dey of Algiers; and finally, in contravention of the treaty, Tripoli captured an American merchant ship and refused to return $217 in goods stored aboard, forcing Cathcart to pay $5.75 for the ship's anchorage before it could leave.[73]

A month before Cathcart's undiplomatic protest against the bashaw's official and personal affronts, O'Brien again stoked Cathcart's and Eaton's suspicions. On September 17 the brand new twenty-four-gun American frigate *George Washington*, the pride of the young US Navy, docked in Algiers under the city's awed gaze. In contrast to the incidents detailed above, the events surrounding the arrival of this first American-flagged frigate in Mediterranean waters did not involve the Bacris or Busnachs. The incident also earned O'Brien and William Bainbridge, the captain of the *George Washington*, the most press on American-Barbary relations since the captives were released from Algiers in 1797. All of this press was either scathing criticism or open letters by O'Brien and Bainbridge trying to explain their conduct. The incident exposes the perils of the consuls' autonomy, when their actions may be sensible "on the spot" but enraging from the distant perspective of Washington.

The *George Washington*'s mission was to deliver America's overdue tribute and impress upon the dey that the United States was equipped to protect itself from any aggression against its citizens or merchant fleet. The dey was certainly impressed by the ship, but not afraid of the nation that built it. He informed the British that he no longer needed to borrow one of their warships to transport Algerian tribute to the Ottoman sultan at Constantinople, as he now had a more impressive ship to borrow. Both O'Brien and Bainbridge insisted they lacked the authority to raise the Algerian flag and transport tribute to Constantinople on behalf of Algiers. The pair only relented after days of intense negotiations and the dey's refutation of their catalogue of excuses.[74] O'Brien justified his decision to the secretary of state as necessary "to save the peace of the United States with Algiers; to prevent captivity and detention to the ship, officers, and crew, and prevent the pretence of a sudden *war*, and pillage and slavery to the citizens of the United States."[75] Though humiliating, he calculated a five-month journey to Constantinople would cost the United States just $40,000, which he knew from painful experience was a bargain compared to the cost of mass-enslavement and ransoms. At Bainbridge's request, correspondence between himself and O'Brien and to Secretary of the Navy Ben J. Stoddert were compiled and published in American newspapers to help fortify the public impression that this national humiliation was not in vain. It was the lesser of two evils. One newspaper editor was obviously convinced, declaring, "it is evident from the whole, however that the coercion under which Capt. Bainbridge was obliged to act, was of the most imperious nature. Nor was he, or Mr. O'Brien remiss in making every prudent and practicable opposition to the degrading requisition."[76] Fulfilling the same purpose as Cathcart in his earlier framing of the bashaw's "arbitrary acts," Bainbridge wrote of "the arbitrary dey of Algiers." In this case it was not merely a number of acts by a Barbary ruler that were labeled as arbitrary and tyrannical, but the man himself.[77]

Ultimately, the Americans concluded that they could not afford to antagonize the dey by denying him use of the frigate. O'Brien knew his government and his nation's commerce could not afford a war with Algiers, and a six-ship navy was woefully insufficient to protect American interests in both the Atlantic and Mediterranean. Worse still, Bainbridge made the mistake of anchoring the *George Washington* within range of the harbor's batteries, so a refusal could also have resulted in the destruction of the glistening new frigate and the enslavement of its crew. But Eaton was not interested in explanations from Algiers. He was prone to hyperbole, but he outdid himself in his outrage that the United States had now forfeited its honor to become a "voluntary slave" to Algiers: "Genius of My Country! How art thou prostrate! Hast thou not yet one son whose soul revolts, whose nerves convulse, blood vessels burst, and heart indignant swells at thoughts of such debasement! Shade of Washington! Behold thy orphan'd sword hang on a slave—A voluntary slave, and serve a *pirate*! . . . *This is the price of peace!* But if we will have peace at such a price, recall me, and send a *slave*, accustomed to abasement, to represent the nation."[78]

When news of this latest humiliation in Barbary reached American shores, the government and public outrage equaled Eaton's—usually an impossible feat. Secretary of State James Madison warned O'Brien that the humiliation would not soon be forgotten: "The sending to Constantinople the national ship of War, the George Washington, by force, under the Algerine flag . . . has deeply affected the sensibility, not only of the President, but of the people of the United States. . . . The indignity is of so serious a nature, that it is not impossible that it may be deemed necessary, on a fit occasion, to revive the subject."[79]

On October 19, a month after the *George Washington*'s arrival in Algiers, the frigate set to sea with a cargo as bizarre as the circumstances of its mission. That afternoon, before setting sail, Bainbridge again refused to lower the American flag, so a contingent of armed Algerians boarded the frigate and raised the Algerian flag themselves. The frigate was then loaded with an Algerian ambassador and his entourage of "20 gentlemen," and a tribute to the Sultan of "100 negro Turks, 60 Turkish women, 2 lions, 2 tigers, 4 horses, 200 sheep, besides jewels and money."[80] Adding to this menagerie, the tribute may also have included twenty-five cattle, four to five antelopes, twelve to twenty parrots, and two ostriches.[81] The ship was clearly crowded, and the American crew took out their frustrations on the Muslim passengers by intentionally tacking the ship away from Mecca during the five times each day when the passengers packed the deck to pray.

When Bainbridge and his motley crew, passengers, and cargo arrived in Constantinople, it was the first time the Ottomans had heard of the new United States. They initially thought the crew must have been Native Americans and were disappointed to instead find they looked like Englishmen. This was the same response of Algerians when the crews of the *Maria* and *Dauphin* arrived as captives in 1785. Unexpectedly, and wholly unlike their experience in any of the Barbary States, the *George Washington* and its American crew were a celebrated curiosity in Constantinople and treated with greater respect than the Algerian ambassador who they accompanied.[82]

By late 1800 there was unmistakably a storm bearing down on Barbary from all directions. The relationship between the "three lighthouses" had deteriorated to the point where it affected their official duties; O'Brien's colleagues openly presumed his collusion with the Bacris and Busnachs, Cathcart's private trading and diplomatic efforts in Tripoli eroded hope in a lasting peace, and the first American warship to visit the Mediterranean had been requisitioned by Algiers, which thus relegated America to the status of a "voluntary slave" to a piratical state. Some of this disquiet stemmed from the consuls' involvement in private trade, despite their unique status as salaried consuls, and some of it came from personal baggage and personality conflicts. Some of the disquiet was also an unintended consequence of the autonomy that was required to help consuls quickly maneuver out of trouble. A significant contributing factor, however, was that each of the Barbary States was constantly on the lookout for excuses to declare war on seafaring nations, and the US government offered abundant excuses with its tardiness in delivering tribute payments.

When the storm finally hit the shores of Tripoli, it came not with a clap of thunder or the boom of a cannon, but with a casually felled flagpole. On May 14, 1801, the bashaw of Tripoli declared war with an uncharacteristically genteel tradition: his soldiers chopped down the flag outside the American consul's residence. As Cathcart succinctly put it in a three-sentence circular on the declaration of war, which was buried in the September 1801 issues of Maryland and Pennsylvania newspapers: "I am sorry to inform you that our flag staff was chopped down upon Thursday, the 14th instant, and war was declared in form by the Bashaw of Tripoli against the United States of America."[83] Three months later a lengthier account of events reached American papers, explaining that in the early evening of May 10 an Algerian known to Cathcart arrived at his residence "and told me not to be alarmed, for the Bashaw had sent him to inform me, that he declared war against the United States, and would take down the

flagstaff on Thursday the 14th." The messenger told Cathcart that if he preferred to remain in Tripoli after the formal declaration of war he "should be
treated with respect, but if I pleased I might go away." Cathcart sent his com-
pliments to the bashaw, made one last attempt to bribe him with $10,000, and
ten days later sailed for the Italian port city of Leghorn with his wife and the
first of their eleven children.[84]

This lengthier explanation, that Cathcart should "not be alarmed" at the
declaration of war, was included in compilations of news from Barbary that
spanned the past fourteen months and was collectively published as full-page
newspaper spreads. In addition to the declaration of war, one such compilation
included O'Brien's and Bainbridge's explanations for permitting the requisi-
tioning of the *George Washington* the previous year, along with Cathcart's public list of grievances against the bashaw and a description of his exchange of
metaphorical barbs with the bashaw on the streets of Tripoli.[85] In addition to
feeding the public's curiosity with the latest humiliation from Barbary, New
England readers also had more personal need to be apprised of the status of
Americans in Mediterranean waters. It was through these waters that many
of the nation's goods were taken to market, where its sons sailed, and where its
merchants invested. On a grander note, just as John Jay and David Humphreys
had advocated war with Algiers in the 1790s as a nation-building exercise that
would help transcend divisive local and partisan political differences, and create a unified national identity, now, a decade later, the war hawks turned from
pressing the need for an American national identity to the need for a firm American presence on the international stage. Cathcart, Eaton, and Jefferson argued
that a successful war with Tripoli would assure America's status as a nation to
be reckoned with, on par with Britain and France.[86]

When the bashaw declared war, Cathcart indicated he would gracefully
retreat to the company of his business partner and preferred consular "light-
house," Eaton, in Tunis. However, he decided his time would be better spent
in the comparative safety and comfort of Leghorn, where he would be positioned to coordinate lucrative business opportunities with Eaton. Cathcart kept
Eaton apprised of the Italian market value of goods, particularly wheat and oil,
which Eaton could ship from Tunis and Cathcart could sell when they arrived.[87] Like Cathcart, commercial and diplomatic interests equally motivated
Eaton, but he insisted that in the conduct of his own affairs these interests never
conflicted. In a report on suggested reforms of the consular service penned
before the outbreak of war in early 1801, Eaton advised that American consuls
should be stationed away from Barbary to avoid the clutches of the Bacris and
other corrupting influences and that their salaries should be more than doubled
to $5,000 to prevent them from dabbling in the equally corrupting influence of
private trade.[88] Yet just months into his consulship, he began engaging in trade

with Cathcart within the Mediterranean and even sent goods to the US secretary of state. In mid-1799, Eaton followed Humphreys in considering himself among the commercial avant-garde of the natural world when he dispatched new varieties of seed and livestock, namely wheat, barley and sheep, to the United States in the hope that they might flourish on New England farms. Later that same year he sent Secretary of State Pickering some fig seeds with the suggestion he plant them in Georgia, along with olives and watermelon seeds that Eaton hoped would flourish in the Southern states and along the Ohio and Mississippi Rivers.[89] At around this time, he owned at least three ships that traded between Tunis and Italy, and he confessed to Cathcart that he was "getting rich against my own inclination."[90] He wrote to his wife that he expected to soon resign and return to Brimfield, Massachusetts, with $30,000 in profits from his trading enterprises. A year earlier when he sent a cargo to New York, he included $5,000 for his wife, "to be applied in the education of your eldest children."[91] Yet while Cathcart was exiled to Leghorn, where he complained of being "as poor as Job," he encouraged Eaton's entrepreneurial vigor, advising him that "this is the critical moment which you ought to embrace with ardor as it will put you beyond the power of that capricious bitch fortune to jilt you any longer & next year you may worship your household Gods blessed with independence & free air."[92]

It was while in Leghorn discussing business that Cathcart and Eaton also refined their plan to stage a coup in Tripoli and install the bashaw's elder brother, Hamet, as an American-friendly ruler who would reign in a permanent peace with the United States and never demand tribute.[93] In a later report providing background and promising the inevitable success of this mission, Cathcart relayed to the secretary of state that he was the originator of the plan that had been fermenting in the back of his mind since his arrival in Tripoli. Eaton acknowledged that "it was suggested to me by Mr. Cathcart" in his own lengthy report to the secretary of state, sent two months before Cathcart's.[94] This plot simultaneously illustrates how much could be achieved once consuls' isolation was no longer a factor and shows the new kinds of crises that consuls could cause when given the opportunity to exercise the limits of their discretionary powers. If indeed the autonomy granted to America's consuls extended to pursuing a military campaign of foreign regime change, this prerogative would have rested with Consul General O'Brien, surely not Cathcart or Eaton. In any case, Eaton pursued the scheme with a singular vigor that reflected his manly and patriotic persona. O'Brien was kept at an informed distance, and the US government at an even greater distance.

After Cathcart notified the government of the plan, he waited over fifteen months to receive approval to go ahead. On the grounds of this delay, which Cathcart likened to a "moral impossibility," he then defended Eaton's pursuit of Hamet without government sanction. Hamet was being driven deeper into exile, thus Eaton exercised his consular autonomy to pursue him in an act "dictated by imperious necessity, and an honest zeal for the success of an enterprise which promised such vast advantages to our country."[95] Just three days before Cathcart penned this justification for embarking on a plot to pursue foreign regime change without the approval of the president, Secretary of State Madison had given his approval in a letter to Cathcart that would not arrive in Barbary for over four months. The fate of this letter is itself proof of its content: that considerable distance, local knowledge, and time delays made it difficult to micromanage diplomatic policy toward Barbary from American shores.

As a matter of precedent in American foreign relations, this letter from Madison deserves far greater attention than its two existing copies currently receive in the Huntington and New York Public Libraries. In part, the letter offers a succinct confirmation of both the extraordinary extent of a consul's prerogative and America's tepid reluctance at "intermeddl[ing] with the domestic controversies of other countries" unless the United States may turn an advantage. Madison acknowledges that "at this distance it is difficult to judge accurately of the project, or to give particular instructions for the management of it. Altho' it does not accord with the general sentiments or views of the U States to intermeddle with the domestic controversies of other countries, it cannot be unfair in the prosecution of a just war, or the accomplishment of a reasonable peace, to take advantage of the hostile cooperation of others."[96]

The plot hinged on Cathcart's questionable reading of political affairs in Tripoli, namely a recent leadership transition which he argued was "unresolved." As if plagiarized from an ancient Greek play, the present bashaw of Tripoli, Yusuf Karamanli, was the youngest son of the former ruler, but he had wrested the leadership by murdering his eldest brother and exiling his other brother, Hamet. These circumstances of Hamet's exile to the desert beyond Alexandria only helped strengthen the impression that social and political development in Barbary had indeed stalled at antiquity. Cathcart declared that from early in his consulship he had become convinced that "the inhabitants of Tripoli held the present Pacha in the greatest degree of horror imaginable & of their great desire that Hamet . . . should again assume the reigns of government, I was left no reason to doubt that should he ever be able to appear before Tripoli with any considerable force to espouse his cause, that the chief inhabitants of that Regency would declare in his favor." It was now in America's interest to raise such a force on behalf of the rightful heir. As further affirmation of Yusuf's unpopularity, Cathcart wrote that he was forced to guard constantly against the threat of coups and popular uprisings by travelling with all his treasure and jewels, his loyalists, and three to five hundred mercenaries, "who would espouse his cause no longer than until his treasure was exhausted."[97]

Cathcart was so convinced by this scheme that he even scripted Eaton's pitch to the "rightful Pasha of Tripoli" three whole years before Eaton finally lured Hamet out of the Egyptian interior. He suggested Eaton convince Hamet that his return to Tripoli had been endorsed by Allah as righteous revenge for fratricide, that his reign had been seen in premonitions by spiritual leaders who were subsequently killed by his brother Yusuf, and to "explain to him the improbability of a nation so remote from Tripoli as America is sending a Naval force to espouse his cause unless influenced by an Omnipotent decree." As Cathcart summarized: "In short, my dear sir work upon their passions, make use of their absurdities & superstitions as lawful weapons."[98]

Eaton succeeded in convincing Hamet to join him, and with seven to ten US Marines and three to five hundred Arab and Christian mercenaries, they marched almost six hundred miles in almost two months from Alexandria to Derne, now known as the Libyan town of Darnah. It is not known whether Cathcart's demeaning arguments stirred Hamet. In any case, with the assistance of US naval bombardment, Eaton's land force took Derne with one American fatality, the first on foreign soil, and raised the American flag for the first time on foreign soil after a military victory.[99] The plan was to resupply in Derne, and then, with more US Marines and naval support, to push on to Benghazi and then Tripoli to install Hamet on the seat of government.[100] At this point Hamet told Eaton that he would happily remain in Derne rather than continue to Tripoli and overthrow his brother, as planned, to which Eaton "told him very candidly that if he departed we must consider him in the light of an enemy, and that instead of my influence to assist his passage to the Kingdom of Tripoli I should give it to have him and his retinue carried prisoners of war to the United States." Rather than merely "tak[ing] advantage of the hostile cooperation of others," as Madison had reluctantly sanctioned, Eaton is clearly the instigator and unchallengeable administrator of this plan. In any case, rather than push on with, now "General," Eaton's plan, his superiors in the region reminded the industrious consul that the autonomy and initiative he exercised were on behalf of an executive that could show appreciation, or embarrassment, or find another use for those actions altogether. With Eaton's success in Derne, Tobias Lear, America's appointed negotiator to Tripoli, leveraged the victory to bring an immediate end to the unpopular war on favorable terms.[101] The US government paid Tripoli $60,000 in ransom for its captives but would never again pay annual tribute, and its commerce would henceforth be safe from Tripoli's corsairs.

When Eaton and Cathcart returned to the United States in late 1805, they were honored guests at both Federalist and Republican Fourth of July feasts in Boston. Their toasts were published and cut out of newspapers by Jefferson, who pasted them into his personal scrapbook. Eaton in particular was celebrated as

Engraving of William Eaton by Charles Balthazar Julien Fevret de Saint Memin. In Dudley W. Knox, ed., *Naval Documents Related to the United States Wars with the Barbary Powers* (Washington, DC: US Government Printing Office, 1944), V: 32.

the hero who ended the war. He was the subject of toasts, invited to dine with President Jefferson, and was happily used by Federalists to discredit Jefferson's decision-making during the war. Until his death, Eaton loudly bemoaned the government's cowardice for not pursuing total military victory in Tripoli.[102] Special rancor was saved for Lear, who was branded as directly responsible for the betrayal of Hamet and for secretly negotiating with Yusuf to invalidate Article 3 of the eventual treaty that required Yusuf to release Hamet's family who had been held hostage in Tripoli since Yusuf seized power a decade earlier.

The circumstance of the resolution to this conflict was a fitting bookend to the war, which had sidelined the consuls since Lear and other military officers arrived in the Mediterranean and began challenging the consuls' abilities. That a truce was negotiated by thwarting Eaton and Cathcart's plot of regime change is but one particularly egregious case, among dozens of others in their years of service, in which the consuls' plans and actions deviated from those preferred by the government. It is also a sign of how remarkably different American diplomacy in North Africa may have been during this period if this same speed in communications and level of political and military scrutiny had existed since the first arrival of the three American "lighthouses" in 1796.

Among the oddities surrounding the attempted coup and its fallout was the fact that Cathcart never publicly claimed credit for the plan. It is likely that Jefferson, Madison, and Cathcart kept themselves at arm's length, minimizing correspondence about and advertisement of the operation until it had run its course and made Eaton either an easy scapegoat or a national hero. Given the plan's ultimate success, at least as a public relations campaign if not as a military operation, it is unclear why Cathcart, a man of such well-documented egotism, sat silent while Eaton was crowned an honorary "General" and briefly became the toast of Washington. Perhaps Cathcart saw a failed military operation as unbeneficial to be associated with, or perhaps he thought stealing the limelight from Eaton would seem petty. Either scenario credits Cathcart with a degree of tact that he exhibited neither before nor after. Another possibility is that, during the war, Cathcart reluctantly learned that the limelight could burn as easily as illuminate.

From the beginning of the First Barbary War on May 14, 1801, the American public was firmly affixed like a barnacle upon the Barbary consuls and their misadventures. The public interest in this four-year war dwarfed all prior American discussion of Barbary, including O'Brien's and Cathcart's decade of captivity in Algiers. Newspaper mentions of *Tripoli* peaked in the year 1805 with 4,388 mentions. This even dwarfed the number of mentions of *impressment* during the War of 1812, which peaked in 1813 at just 2,322 mentions. During the years of the First Barbary War (1801–1805), *Tripoli* was mentioned no less than 12,405 times in the American press. If the period is expanded to 1794–1816, during most of which Tripoli held no American slaves and was not at war with the United States, the number balloons to 19,633, while mentions of *Barbary States, Algiers*, or *Tripoli* during the 1785–1816 period of US conflict with the region reaches 47,887 mentions.[103] Thus with the end of the First Barbary War came the end of the most active and prominent period of the consuls' lives, much to O'Brien's delight, Cathcart's grief, and Eaton's rage.[104]

After years of requests, O'Brien was finally relieved as US consul general by Lear, the recent US negotiator, in 1803. Rather than forever turning his back on Barbary as he desperately wanted, O'Brien was forced to stay until spring 1805 "on account of the situation of his lady." The birth dates for most of the

O'Briens' seven children were not accurately recorded, but "the situation of his lady" likely refers to Betsy's pregnancy with their second child. During this time Lear was grateful for the "opportunity of profiting by his knowledge and experience in affairs here, as well as in other Regencies."[105] When he and "his lady" were able, O'Brien returned to Philadelphia where he remained for five years—the longest period he had been in the United States since his capture by corsairs twenty years earlier. The remainder of O'Brien's life, split between the Pennsylvania State Legislature and the Pennsylvania town of Carlisle, is discussed in chapter six.

In contrast to O'Brien's preference for a quiet life, Cathcart's ambition and lust for the opportunities of a merchant-consul in the Mediterranean remained undiminished after he was forced from Tripoli due to war and roundly rejected by the bey as Eaton's consular replacement in Tunis and by the dey as O'Brien's replacement in Algiers. The correspondence surrounding Cathcart's rejection as consul general also serves to demonstrate the liberties taken by consuls in their communications to government, as well as their ready manipulation of communications that simply passed through them. In October 1802 the dey of Algiers wrote to President Jefferson explaining his decision to reject Cathcart as O'Brien's replacement. Without an Arabic speaker in the State Department, Jefferson had to wait seven months to receive O'Brien's translation. The editors of *The Papers of Thomas Jefferson* commissioned a retranslation of this letter and published it alongside the original. Although broadly similar, there is one notable difference between the translation sent by O'Brien and the translation by recent scholars. In both copies the dey is translated as writing that Cathcart's character is unsuitable to fill the position of consul general and "wherever he spends time he creates a great disturbance." However, O'Brien then went beyond a faithful translation to add that "he has created difficulties and brought On a war."[106] O'Brien's sly addition to the dey's letter, charging Cathcart as responsible for the outbreak of the First Barbary War, was not a necessary addition to convince the president of Cathcart's widely criticized conduct. This fraudulent addition to the letter is, however, a stark example of the powerful role of consuls in manipulating, not just forwarding, intelligence between Barbary and the United States.

From his new, and he hoped temporary, home in Georgetown (Washington, DC) in August 1805, Cathcart penned an exhausting six-page letter to Jefferson that catalogued his tragic life story in the hopes of securing employment through pity.[107] The following year, his persistence was rewarded, or perhaps punished, when he was made the State Department attaché to a visiting Tunisian delegation. The delegation, including Ambassador Sidi Soliman Mellimelli and his entourage of three bodyguards, two officials, a secretary, cook, barber, personal assistant, and four gift horses for the president, arrived in Washington on November 30, 1805.[108] The delegation was sent in response to the US Navy confiscating Tunisian merchant ships trying to run the blockade of Tripoli during the war. The bey of Tunis demanded restitution. The US Navy responded by parking its Mediterranean squadron in Tunis's harbor and demanding that the bey, under the waiting American cannons, declare his intention to declare war or remain at peace with the United States. Instead, the bey suggested he send an ambassador, Mellimelli, to smooth over the dispute. This is the same incident, detailed above, in which the commodore of the fleet was arrested by the bey and forced to pay Eaton's personal debts.[109]

President Jefferson was between meetings with congressmen when he heard the Ambassador's ship was slowly snaking its way up the Potomac. One senator recorded in his diary that the "President was in an undress[,] . . . white hose[,] ragged slippers with his toes out—clean linen—but hair dissheiveled."[110] This state of undress was in stark contrast to Ambassador Mellimelli and his entourage, who effortlessly exceeded the Orientalist expectations of Washington's curious citizens and politicians. The tall, bearded Mellimelli brought life to Washington's bitter winter by dressing in gold and red, with white silk socks and bright yellow shoes, and his head wrapped in a tall white turban. His four-foot long tobacco pipe and rose-scented snuff further incited images of Ali Baba and *One Thousand and One Nights*.[111] He became a much-sought guest of congressmen while African Americans and children pressed their noses to the windows of Stelle's Hotel, where the president had arranged for the delegation to stay. During just seven weeks this visit inspired over 650 newspaper articles.[112] Senator William Plumer's diary entries from the period reflect Washington's initial stages of curiosity in Mellimelli, followed by disinterest and then impatiently counting the days until he left with Cathcart to tour Baltimore, Philadelphia, New York, and Boston. Mellimelli and his entourage began to wear out their welcome in Washington when his personal assistant, Hadgi Mahomet, took to drink and fighting, while senators refused to allow Mellimelli the courtesy to address the Senate. They began to regret giving "this half-savage the dignified title of ambassador."[113] Adding to the mounting bills for Stelle's Hotel and the four horses, two of Mellimelli's entourage absconded to New York to rack up their own debts, which Mellimelli refused to pay on the grounds that by fleeing his service they were no longer his responsibility and he planned to leave them in America.[114]

Early in his stay, Mellimelli asked the State Department to find and pay for a prostitute. Compared to debts and drinking, students of modern diplomacy likely expect this request for a publicly financed prostitute attracted significant attention at the time, especially as it has been raised by every recent historian who has written on the Tunisian delegation.[115] It is therefore intriguing that Plumer's diary records the ambassador's devout religious faith and his request for a prostitute in successive sentences, without a hint of sarcasm: "He is a very firm believer in the Alcoran [the Quran]—he reads and expounds a lesson from it every day to his household. Our government has, on his application, provided him with one or more women, with whom he spends a portion of the night."[116] As highlighted throughout this chapter, diplomacy of the period was regularly conducted with a strong dose of eccentricity. Washington was not immune. The nonchalance displayed by Plumer and his colleagues to this publicly financed prostitute may be partially explained by the general caliber of ambassadors serving in Washington at the time, and it may be further explained by the courtesy extended to an exotic dignitary from the Orient. Between entries on Mellimelli, Plumer's diary is littered with disapproval of the new post-Revolutionary French ambassador Louis Marie Turreau: "[He] is much of a brute. He has very lately most unmercifully beat & bruised his wife" and "frequently in mid-day publicakly rode in his carriage to visit a woman of *easy virtue*. . . . This man and his wife were at the commencement of the revolution in France of the lowest grade in society."[117] As an exotic and less publicly obnoxious dignitary, at least initially, Mellimelli received kinder treatment.

Cathcart elbowed his way into the Mellimelli affair in Washington when he suggested Mellimelli be sent home with presents to prevent the bey declaring war the moment the US Navy left the Mediterranean. Secretary of State Madison agreed and Cathcart was given discretion to make the purchases as he and Mellimelli toured the nation. Under the guise of his official position, Cathcart also asked for "letters of introduction from the Department of State to some of the principle characters in the states through which we are to pass & that I may act under some sort of a commission" to prevent citizens and Mellimelli "from receiving me in the same light that they would an Indian interpreter."[118] This request is unsurprising given Cathcart's image consciousness and his strong record of private commercial networking off the back of government appointments.

Washington society and the government purse had already suffered the delegation long enough and had noticed their intention to remain in America until they were forcibly removed. The government and Washington's business community hoped a tour of the eastern seaboard would allow them to collect local goods (such as sugar and coffee) that would turn a profit in Tunis and induce their return. The tour would also bring them closer to points of departure. Unfortunately for Cathcart, he shared the same difficulty as Washington officials in prying the entourage from comfort. The first of two incidents that bookend this trying time for Cathcart began during the Philadelphia leg of the tour when Mellimelli's "superstitions" over an eclipse prevented the party's departure to Baltimore. The second incident involved the members of Mellimelli's entourage who absconded to New York and could not be induced to return, as

Cathcart sat fuming in Boston, eagerly awaiting his imminent release from minding the delegation.[119]

In Baltimore, Mellimelli hoped the US government would offer a brig as reparations to Tunis, which he could load with personal cargo that would avoid tax or freight costs and turn a handsome profit in Tunis. In a sweltering week in June, it was Cathcart's unhappy duty to scurry between Baltimore traders and compare prices for these goods. Following their stops in Philadelphia and New York, the party concluded their tour at Boston in July 1806, where Cathcart expected their immediate departure on the brig *Franklin*. Instead, they remained in Boston for two months. Mellimelli was outraged when he saw the *Franklin*, which the US government decided to give to Tunis, fully loaded with Mellimelli's cargo and awaiting the party's arrival. The brig had previously been a prize ship captured by Tunis in 1803, and thus Mellimelli feared the bey would refuse it.[120] Eventually another ship, the *Two Brothers*, was loaded with the cargo that ranged from livestock to coffee to lemons, but it only departed when Cathcart was forced to waive the export duties.[121]

Pushed far beyond his limited patience, Cathcart took a certain pleasure in transmitting news of this latest ordeal, hoping the State Department would find his suffering deserving of financial reward: "Was I disposed to foment discord the subject would give me ample means, but as that is not my aim, I will only inform you that his [Mellimelli's] phrenzy had him to every species of insolent observation. The brig Franklin finished delivering her cargo over to the ship Two Brothers yesterday afternoon & I flattered myself that in two days I would be able to deliver the United States from this political pest of society. I am disappointed. The ambassador persists in insisting that he is not subject to our revenue laws."[122] Thus Cathcart and Mellimelli parted as bitter enemies and Cathcart discovered that the treacherous waters of diplomacy and government work at "home" could be as hazardous as they were abroad. Worse still, Cathcart's hopes to raise his profile within the United States were dashed on the rocks when Federalist-aligned newspapers named him as the intermediary who was passing precious taxpayer money to the "half-savage."[123] It is difficult to argue that the delegation's visit was a success for the US government, as it cost thousands of dollars in hospitality, gifts, and a brig. However, upon Mellimelli's return to Tunis, the nation never did declare war against the United States, though in 1807 the bey demanded the modest sum of $10,000.[124]

Cathcart's frequently raised anxieties over this latest diplomatic indignity must have soon subsided, because just three months after Mellimelli's departure, he petitioned for the vacant consulship at the Portuguese archipelago of Madeira.[125] Madison gave him the post, perhaps as a reward for enduring Mellimelli or perhaps as an example of administrations using the consular service to banish the political operatives and petitioners they thought were liabilities and pests. He remained in this post from 1807 to 1815, followed by a brief stint as consul to Cadiz, Spain, from 1815 to 1816. During and between these postings, he also requested consulships in Lisbon and Liverpool and even tapped one of his in-laws who was on familiar terms with Secretary of State Madison to tout his service "in Spain, Portugal and other parts of Europe, the measures necessarily taken at home in consequence of the war, and the villainy of the belligerents [Barbary]." Not a word was mentioned of his entrepreneurial spirit that occupied much of his time as a diplomat. Rather, he was framed as a victim of "eleven years of slavery under Algerine cruelty and torture," and it was argued that he had subsequently been a selfless public servant stationed abroad for fifteen years. With a vested interest, this in-law wrote of Cathcart "having an increasing family, his great solicitude to obtain an appointment which has a prospect of affording a competent support for his family."[126]

Cathcart's decade of service in Portugal and Spain was much more typical of the early consular service than his heady four years as consul to Tripoli. His service in Tripoli produced hundreds of pages of correspondence that were printed in American newspapers and circulated throughout the Mediterranean and had great bearing on the affairs of states and the livelihood of sailors. His much longer time in the port towns of Portugal and Spain was largely spent in private trade (which did not cause diplomatic incidents, for a change) and in adherence to the intended purpose of the Consular Act of 1792 and reiterated in the supplementary Consular Act of 1803, which emphasized that a consul's primary responsibility was to aid stranded American sailors.

Even before unpacking, one of Cathcart's first acts in Madeira was to write to Eaton, his old business partner and co-conspirator: "We are now settled out of town about 20 minutes walk in the most romantic situation in the world & are busy arranging our household Gods, consequently you must only expect a short letter." Rather than spending this "short letter" on reminiscences or regrets from their time in North Africa, he outlined trading opportunities between the United States and Madeira, indicating that, despite just arriving on the island and his busy schedule "arranging our household Gods," his eyes were already open to trading opportunities. He tried to rouse Eaton's lackluster commercial spirit, writing that "I have long wished you to turn your thoughts to commercial pursuits. You have now an opportunity easy & profitable & a person [meaning himself, Cathcart] who will give you every information necessary & to whose care you have already confided property to the amount of 70,000 dollars consequently you can have no objection to recommend him to your commercial friends."[127] Despite his attempts to reaffirm the bond, Cathcart's and Eaton's connection faded. And without access to wholesale networks within Madeira and a business partner elsewhere in the Mediterranean to ship to, Cathcart was able to find and sell just one cargo of famed Madeira wine.[128]

In his first decade free from any and all Barbary affairs, Cathcart had occasion to send less than two dozen letters to the State Department, of which just six appeared as newspaper articles—and half of those six were reports on the movements of Algerian corsairs.[129] The other half dabbled in other aspects of maritime diplomacy and conflict. One explored the emotive story of Massachusetts merchant sailor John Green, "who escaped as it were miraculously from British tyranny [impressment]" by diving from a Royal Navy vessel with two others and swimming for six hours under fire. Green's two comrades drowned, but he made it ashore where an Italian actor found the exhausted sailor among the rocks and alerted Cathcart, who took pleasure in reporting the story and the small assistance he provided.[130] Other articles speak at great length about Richard W. Meade, an American merchant-turned-official at Cadiz who, in what was said to be an official act of theft, was imprisoned and had between $100,000 and $200,000 in goods confiscated and partially destroyed by the local government. The New York newspaper the *National Advocate* approvingly reprinted what they called Cathcart's "manly remonstrance. . . . As this transaction affects the honor of a national character." Since Meade had been made an American official, serving as proconsul in times of Cathcart's absence from Cadiz, "the consulate was thus violated in a manner unprecedented."[131] When Meade was released he moved to Philadelphia with his son George G. Meade, who was just a year old at the time of his father's imprisonment in Cardiz. The younger Meade grew up to graduate from West Point and lead Union troops at Gettysburg.

Cathcart's more mundane duties in Madeira included keeping a semi-annual ledger of "seamen's disbursements," which recorded payments made to American seamen who had been stranded or escaped from British impressment and were destitute, needing quick cash for food or voyage home. He noted their names, their reason for being stranded, and the amount given, which was always between $10 and $20 (equivalent to $205 and $410 in 2018 US dollars). These records were essential if consuls ever expected to be reimbursed, and they were typically forwarded to their governments every six months.[132]

Much like at other consular posts, Cathcart competed with another candidate for the consulship at Cadiz. Where in the past his poor personal recommendations failed him, now his family connections, custodianship of Mellimelli, and his relatively uneventful service in Madeira saw him best his competitor at Cadiz. His rival, a local merchant named Joseph Bloomfield, had not expected competition from an interloper like Cathcart. As was the case for consuls from most nations throughout the world, Cathcart's office granted him mercantile access and privileges beyond those of ordinary merchants, such as the "petty" and "jealous" Bloomfield with whom Cathcart clashed throughout his time at Cadiz. The conflict began when "immediately upon my arrival at Cadiz a considerable degree of enmity was manifested towards me by Mr. Joseph Bloom-field from motives of commercial jealousy, for he had entered into some arrange-ments . . . upon a supposition that he would be appointed consul at Cadiz." Shocked and disappointed at Cathcart "being appointed to supersede him in this office contrary to his expectations," Bloomfield was allegedly "determined to wreck his vengeance upon me by placing every obstacle in the way of my performing my duty."[133] For his part, Bloomfield accused Cathcart of exceed-ing his consular authority to delay and cause unspecified "difficulty" in the unloading and departure of American merchant ships, especially those that carried Bloomfield's cargoes.[134]

Finally, in April 1817 Cathcart, now with a family of seven children and more on the way, wrote to the new secretary of state, John Quincy Adams, that difficulty breaking into regulated markets (such as for tobacco) in Cadiz meant it was economically impractical to stay in the Mediterranean. He wished to relocate to the United States. After eleven years in "slavery" and "torture," an equally grueling summer touring the eastern seaboard with the Tunisian dele-gation, and a further decade in the Mediterranean, it was not fatigue or "bar-barians" that drove the Cathcart clan to American shores, but money.

Both Cathcart and O'Brien cited their diplomatic careers as selfless "public service," yet they petitioned for reimbursements until they died, at which point their families took up the cause. While serving as secretary of state, John Quincy Adams was bombarded by the pair's claims, remarking that Cathcart "besieges me with perseverance stronger than love. . . . [He] puts me out of temper with him, and out of humor with myself." He also recalled that when appointed consuls in Algiers and Tripoli, "O Brien contrived to scatter enor-mous sums of public money, and to open an inexhaustible fountain of claims for himself. Cathcart has done the same, and they will both be laying siege to Congress for more grants and allowances as long as they live."[135] Adams was also critical of their initial nomination as consuls, noting that O'Brien's "only qualification for being Consul was his having been ten years in Algiers as a slave. He took part in the negotiation of our first peace with Algiers, and claims great credit for it. Cathcart does the same, and both with little cause. There were too many makers of that treaty, and it was a very bad one."[136] If indeed there were too many makers of America's treaties with Barbary, then there were too few, too distant, too poorly paid, and too intemperate consuls assigned to keep the peace.

For O'Brien's part, between 1805 and 1808 he received $49,762, a further $10,174 in 1820, and $8,000 in 1822 (a total of $1.5 million in 2018 US dol-lars).[137] He even petitioned to be reimbursed for a failed private speculation, and he was chastised by the Senate Committee on Foreign Relations on the basis "of the danger of permitting public officers to engage in equivocal commercial speculations, in which the public agent is blended with the private adventurer in transactions which when successful turned wholly to the profit of the latter, and when disastrous to the charge of the Government."[138] In the year he died the Senate noted with palpable frustration that they "are not unmindful of the important services rendered to the Government by Captain O'Brien, in a situation of great public embarrassment and personal hazard, and were desirous that the most complete and ample justice should be done by those in whose interests he evinced so much zeal and ability; but, considering his accounts underwent a full and fair investigation, while these services were well known to the Government, and fresh in his own recollection . . . they cannot, in justice to the Government, recommend any further interposition of Government in his behalf."[139] Nevertheless, his widow and children added to his consular claims by petitioning the government for payment of his Revolutionary War pension as late as 1851. Between 1805 and 1836 Cathcart successfully petitioned the government for $10,000 as well as settlement of the debts he incurred during his consular service. In 1806 he was granted $18,417 for expenses related to Mellimelli's tour, but thirty-six years later he claimed the sum was insufficient. Congress gave him another $1,583 on the condition that it would be the last claim he would file.[140] In spite of this latest conditional payment (bringing the grand total of his reimbursements, not including forgiven debts, to approximately $835,000 in 2018 US dollars), his children continued to petition the government for four years after his death, which was almost fifty years after his first claims for reimbursement.[141] For ten years before his death in 1843, he also drew on a Revolutionary War pension for his unverifiable service on the USS *Confederacy.*

Cathcart's, O'Brien's, and Eaton's interpersonal conflicts, their business entanglements, and their readiness to rewrite diplomatic policy on the spot all reflect the haphazard and unprofessional nature of early American globalization, war making, and the ambitions of American men at the dawn of the nineteenth century. Following Cathcart's and O'Brien's release from captivity, their personal lives and career trajectories exemplify the American male's quest for "success," as defined at the turn of the nineteenth century by independence, civic accomplishment, status, and marriage. As a caricature, Eaton magnified each of these themes. Both Cathcart and O'Brien met each of criteria for "success" during their consular years to truly earn the status of self-made men. Like most men of the era, this status was not earned through dramatic upward mobility but, rather, by moving sideways. Cathcart's official diplomatic posting earned him greater status from an American perspective, but it made him far less influential within North Africa than he had been as a slave serving as chief Christian clerk to the dey of Algiers. O'Brien's position as consul general was certainly a step up from sea captain, yet it was unsolicited, did not make him fabulously wealthy, and he spent the duration as the victim of vindictive rumors circulated by his colleagues. Just as Cathcart and O'Brien were leaving the Mediterranean behind them and beginning new careers in mining the public treasury, US entanglements with the Barbary States again intensified, with the Second Barbary War against Algiers and a ballooning number of fictional and nonfictional captivity narratives. Chief among these new narrators was a Connecticut sailor, Captain James Riley, whose shipwreck on West Africa and adventure-filled march nine hundred miles across the Sahara Desert under the mastery of nomadic Berber tribes became a national bestseller and one of the most popular antebellum children's stories.

CHAPTER FIVE

Accidentally Useful and Interesting to the World

Believing that a knowledge of many of these incidents might
prove useful and interesting to the world, as well as peculiarly
instructive to my sea-faring brethren, [has] induced me to
undertake the very arduous and difficult task of preparing and
publishing a work so large and expensive.

James Riley, An Authentic Narrative, *1817*

Contact with the ocean has unquestionably exercised a beneficial
influence on the cultivation of the intellect and formation of the
character of many nations, on the multiplication of those bonds
which should unite the whole human race, on the first knowledge
of the true form of the earth, and on the pursuit of astronomy
and of all the mathematical and physical sciences.

Alexander von Humboldt, Cosmos, *1846*

In August 1815, as Richard O'Brien's and James Cathcart's diplomatic careers
drew to a close, 37-year-old Captain James Riley stood on a barren coast in West
Africa, surrounded by his drunken shipwrecked crew and fearing the cannibals
who were rumored to roam the coast. Just three months earlier his crew set sail
on the 220-ton brig *Commerce*, snaking down the Connecticut River into the
Atlantic Ocean, pausing in New Orleans and Gibraltar en route to the Cape
Verde Islands, 350 miles off the West African coast. The *Commerce* came dan-
gerously close to Africa's northwest coast after being driven off course by days
of heavy fog and Riley's rash decision to take a risky shortcut.[1] Instead of ex-
changing their cargo of wine, brandy, and 2,000 Spanish dollars for salt from
the islands, the *Commerce*'s ten-man crew and its sole passenger became stranded
when the ship struck Western Sahara's Cape Bojadore on August 18, 1815.[2]

Riley's subsequent captivity among nomadic tribes and their march across the Sahara lasted less than three months. Yet the details of his captivity floated across the Atlantic and made Riley a household name before he returned to American shores just seven months after his wreck. His thrilling and informative *Authentic Narrative of the Loss of the American Brig* Commerce went through more than 20 editions between 1817 and 1945, though it possibly sold less than 75,000 copies in total.[3] For almost 150 years, however, these editions were steady sellers, even though they never quite competed with bestsellers like Susanna Rowson's *Charlotte Temple* (1794), which went through at least 152 editions before the turn of the twentieth century, or Harriet Beecher Stowe's *Uncle Tom's Cabin* (1852), which had at least 310,000 copies printed within its first year of publication. Though not quite a member of the literary elite, Riley was a household name throughout the nineteenth century, and his *Narrative* introduced generations of Americans to North African tribal culture, political and legal structures, geography, history, fauna, and flora, as well as to a slave system where white men were slaves to African masters.

More important than the (often exaggerated) commercial success and cultural influence of Riley's *Narrative* is its broader role in the Village Enlightenment (though ironically it was not held in many village libraries) and its reflection of longer-term historical trends during the nineteenth century.[4] Contrary to claims by Riley's son, his father's *Narrative* was not read by a million people by the mid-nineteenth century, and contrary to the claims of eager scholars, it did not tangibly influence Abraham Lincoln or the antislavery movement. Instead, this chapter interprets the *Narrative* through its uncommon contribution to the Village Enlightenment. It did so chiefly through its success in embracing, and subverting, the centuries-old practice of using captivity as a vehicle for literary ethnography. Whereas authors typically used captivity as a literary device to highlight the virtues of the captive's race, religion, and nation, Riley subverts this staple of the genre by evenhandedly detailing the crew's virtues alongside their drunkenness, suicidal impulses, and attempted cannibalism of a captor's child. Similarly, rather than exclusively critiquing his captors' race, religion, and systems of governance, he occasionally celebrates their altruism, honor, and piety.

As a general rule, nonfiction narratives were more likely to detail quasi-scientific and ethnographical features—those of most value to the Village Enlightenment—while fictional accounts leaned more heavily on the virtues of religion, race, gender, and nation. As a sailor, Riley was accustomed to recording detailed observations of his surrounds and was attuned to the customs, peculiarities, and dangers of foreign ports. His *Narrative* exceeds other nonfiction Barbary captivity narratives, including Cathcart's extensive journals, for attentiveness to the flora, fauna, architecture, and peoples he encountered, and he supplements his own observations with histories of the region that he teased out of his masters and passersby. In addition to analyzing the content of Riley's original manuscript and its first published edition, this chapter traces the evolution of the *Narrative* through its various editions and the themes that each edition chose to excise or to emphasize. With no other captivity narrative continuously republished from the early-nineteenth to mid-twentieth centuries, a longitudinal analysis of how this single text was distributed, read, remembered, and recast over the course of a century serves as a mirror to the changing values and interests of editors, publishers, and readers.

Riley's captivity in North Africa was fundamentally different in law and in day-to-day experiences to Cathcart's and O'Brien's captivity in Algiers just twenty years earlier. The 1787 US-Moroccan treaty, which remains the longest-standing treaty in US history, prevented Morocco's fleet of state-sanctioned corsairs from capturing US sailors at sea or demanding tribute from the government. However, shipwrecked sailors were fair game. Since these sailors were found on shore and held by nomadic tribes, they were classed as "human salvage" rather than state-sanctioned captures.[5] Unlike their comrades captured at sea and held in Algiers, these shipwrecked sailors were not subjected to hard labor. Instead, they were typically held for only as long as it took to travel from their wreck to a city to be ransomed. Occasionally they even formed intimate relationships with their captors as they marched side by side across the desert. After all, these "captors" effectively rescued the wrecked sailors from certain death on a hostile and sparsely populated coast and merely sought a just recompense for sustaining the lives of their fragile wards. Since captors in Western Sahara were also their captives' saviors, there are no recorded cases of captives revolting against their captor-saviors, and very few tried to flee into the vast desert. Riley invoked divine intervention to justify this "voluntary slavery," arguing that "every mortal has his circle wisely marked out by heaven," and that by guiding Riley to his captors, God had given him the chance to reunite with his family.[6] Yet despite these differences between captives in Algiers and Morocco or Western Sahara, each shared the possibility that his slavery would be short-lived and enjoyed established mechanisms to facilitate ransom.[7]

In Riley's case, as soon as the *Commerce* struck the West African coast, the crew scrambled to load their longboat with provisions of food, fresh water, about 2,000 Spanish dollars in gold coins, and awkwardly, a live pig. Strangely, Riley did not order the crew to take firearms ashore for self-defense or hunting, though merchant ships typically carried a small cache of rifles and pistols and sailors had long feared cannibals and murderous savages who were rumored to prey on shipwrecked sailors along the coast. Instead, he insisted the crew salvage up to six barrels of wine, which only helped dehydrate the crew and fuel

Wreck of the brig *Commerce* on the coast of Africa—the Author's escape from the Arabs. In James Riley, *An Authentic Narrative of the Loss of the American Brig* Commerce: *Wrecked on the Western Coast of Africa, in the Month of August, 1815* (New York: T. & W. Mercein, 1817), 37.

dissent.[8] In a much-quoted initial encounter with a family of Berbers who soon plundered the sailors' belongings, Riley painted a graphic image dripping with Othering. He described the patriarch's hair as "long and bushy, resembling a pitch mop," while "his face resembled that of an ourang-outang more than a human being; his eyes were red and fiery; his mouth, which stretched nearly from ear to ear, was well lined with sound teeth. . . . I could not but imagine that those well set teeth were sharpened for the purpose of devouring human flesh!!"[9] As the family plundered, Riley repaired the longboat and his uncooperative crew got drunk.[10]

The next day a more violent group of nomads emerged from beyond the towering sand dunes that obscured the enormity of the Sahara from the coast. This new group came brandishing heavy barbaric symbolism. They immediately burned all the salvaged books, seafaring instruments, and navigational charts, representing instruments of knowledge and commerce. They trapped Riley onshore alone as his crew fled to a safe distance offshore in the repaired longboat. To spare himself, Riley called ashore Antonio Michel, a passenger from Gibraltar, whom Riley manipulated to distract the nomads as the captain fled in the longboat with the rest of his crew.[11] After the wreck, Riley's authority over the crew had slipped, as demonstrated by their getting drunk rather than assisting with vital repairs to the longboat. It was crucial for the cohesion and perhaps even the survival of the stranded sailors that Riley won back their loyalty, which would have been a doubly difficult task if he sacrificed a crewman over a passenger. The gambit of sacrificing Michel succeeded. They escaped and Riley was reunited with his crew. Michel's fate is unclear. Riley claims to see him murdered on the beach, while Archibald Robbins, an able seaman on the *Commerce*, says he was led into the desert, alive.[12]

After days in the longboat heading into the open ocean, with dwindling supplies of wine, recycled urine, and raw pig, and no sign of a friendly ship, they reluctantly returned to shore. There, they threw themselves at the mercy of a caravan of one hundred Sahrawi people native to the Western Sahara.[13] The sailors begged for sustenance and hoped to arrange ransoms from James Simpson, the US consul at Tangier. If only they had continued, starving and dehydrated, in the longboat for another two days down the West African coast, they would have reached Saint-Louis, Senegal, where the French colonial administration or the British consul could have helped the stranded crew.[14] Instead, the Sahrawis eagerly took Riley and his crew captive. The crew was repeatedly divided, resold, and fought over as they moved deeper into the Sahara, encountering diverse tribes, towns, and trials, including nearly being driven to cannibalism. Of the *Commerce*'s original crew, Riley and four others were ultimately ransomed by British consul William Willshire at Mogadore, Morocco, within eleven weeks of the wreck; two other crewmen were ransomed and returned to the United States over a year later, and the final four were never heard from again.

Captivity narratives from both the New and Old Worlds, written before and after the American Revolution, share a similar formula that is still the norm for contemporary accounts of captivity among terrorists, paramilitary guerillas, and Somali pirates, as well as from Guantanamo Bay. These contemporary narratives, like Riley's *Narrative*, typically begin with the claim that the reluctant author was strenuously encouraged by friends, family, and/or notable personalities to publish the account. This strategic positioning as a reluctant author slyly dispels readers' suspicions that an overly eager author may have embellished the account for fame or fortune. Then a brief personal biography with touching anecdotes establishes empathy. The ordeal itself is recounted in great detail and length and invariably plays on the author's isolation to explore themes of Othering, barbarism, and individual triumph over adversity. Within this time-tested formula, the particular style and content of each narrative is guided by the personal peculiarities of authors, such as their professions, religions, or social statuses. Sailors' narratives are typically a fusion of literary genres, embracing spiritual conversion tales, coming-of-age stories, and travelogues.[15] Adding to this hybrid, Cathcart's, O'Brien's, and Riley's narratives also stake out positions in public education, nation building, and policy influence.

The commercial success of Riley's *Narrative* largely owed to his enthusiastic embrace of all these genres while also feeding readers' curiosity about a little-known region and its peoples. It was a quintessential contribution to the Village Enlightenment. Although the book could not be found in many small towns, in the private collections and public libraries where it was available, it was highly sought after and passed through so many hands that it quickly wore through its binding.[16] Riley's multifaceted approach made his book a literary Rorschach test, allowing a large and diverse readership to project their preexisting interests onto the text and, in reflection, see most pronounced the content and themes that spoke most directly to them. Decades later, in the mid-nineteenth century, this approach similarly appealed to editors of anthologies and children's books, who selectively edited the *Narrative* to champion the changing interests of their generation.

Sailors, whose travel accounts were infamous for fantastic creatures and impossible survival tales, were fairly classified as unreliable sources of authentic captivity narratives or ethnoscientific data. Riley was no exception. Reviewers of the first edition of his *Narrative* noted that "some persons have considered many parts of the Narrative bordering on the marvelous," and more pointedly, that "we hope the author will reflect on the insult offered to an intelligent public in the promulgation of impossible things . . . and expunge them from the second edition."[17] Another cuttingly remarked that authors of travel narratives "are not often men whose habits of life have led them to the arduous exercise of thinking deeply, observing with accuracy, or judging with discrimination. In a word, they are not always scholars, and we should not require them to write or think as scholars." This reviewer devoted fully the first two pages of his review to a not-so-veiled attack on Riley and other inexpert travel writers for straying beyond the purview of "the humbler walks of plain narrative and simple description." Though the reviewer believed Riley's account was generally truthful, he suspected "a very high colouring to his descriptions" of some specific events.[18] This skeptical reception led New York governor Clinton DeWitt to encourage Riley to personally publish the captivity narrative of another American sailor, Judah Paddock, who also shipwrecked on Africa's northwest coast and shared similar experiences in captivity. Clinton's endorsement of both narratives, and his rationale for the latter's publication, was even printed on the first page of Paddock's narrative in 1818, just one year after Riley's.[19] The idea was that this new narrative, in addition to that of Archibald Robbins published in late 1817, would verify Riley's account as authentic.[20]

In spite of Riley, Robbins, Paddock, Cathcart, O'Brien, and other captives lacking scholarly qualifications, and the likelihood that their accounts were rife with embellishment and misinterpretation, captives' credentials often exceeded those of the travel writers who dominated the literary-ethnography market. Travel writers were temporary spectators who locals served and showed their censored selves. Captives made for far better ethnographers. They served their local masters, lived with them, and became intimately familiar with every aspect of their lives and relationships with each other, their animals, and the environment. Mary Louise Pratt sees many parallels between captivity and ethnographic fieldwork, including "the sense of dependency, lack of control, the vulnerability to being isolated completely or never left alone."[21] Pauline Turner Strong could have also been talking about late eighteenth-century American captives in Barbary, especially the shipwrecked captives like Riley, when she wrote that, for seventeenth-century colonists held captive by Native Americans, their Anglo-American identity grew through constant struggle against "a threatening but enticing wilderness," in which captives sought to "domesticate this wilderness as well as the savagery within [themselves]." All the while captives stood in opposition to the native Others who were typically portrayed as "savage, bestial, demonic, and seductive."[22]

Strong argues that within this general framework, captivity narratives of different eras served different sets of cultural and political functions. The prominence of particular functions ebbed and flowed every few generations to reflect changing political climates and readers' interests. Religious confessions were particularly popular from 1682 to the early eighteenth century, but they were supplanted by political propaganda, which remained the most popular until the mid-eighteenth century. Sensationalism and sensibility then held prominence until the early nineteenth century, when historically and ethnologically rich captivity narratives became the preference.[23] Riley's *Narrative* shows that there was also significant overlap of these periods and functions. He seamlessly incorporates extensive and recurring passages of religious confession, political propaganda, sensationalism, and ethnography. Riley's traditional narrative structure allowed him to probe the unique themes these genres lend themselves to with greater depth and frequency than the prescriptive diaries of O'Brien and Cathcart, and it ultimately allowed him to publish a more authentic, compelling, and successful work of literary ethnography than other captive or noncaptive competitors.

From beginning to end, the first edition of Riley's *Narrative* explicitly tied itself to the goals of the Village Enlightenment, boasting its contributions to the knowledge base of man and its practical applications for future sailors in the region. Riley framed the narrative on its very first page by advising that "these incidents might prove useful and interesting to the world, as well as peculiarly instructive to my sea-faring brethren."[24] He later paused to note the dangers of navigating off the Florida Keys, "as so many vessels of all nations who navigate this stream have perished with their cargoes, and oftentimes their crews, I mention this incident to warn the navigator of the dangers he is in when his vessel is acted upon by these currents."[25] The book closed with lengthy appendices of advice for future sailors navigating off the Moroccan coast, and in case those sailors were ever shipwrecked, Riley included a twenty-six-page Arabic alphabet and vocabulary to help negotiate with and understand their captors. Between these overtly self-conscious bookends, Riley crafts an account that is equally a narrative of captivity and of discovery. This fixation on accidental scientific discovery was echoed in the subsequent narrative of Archibald Robbins, who reflected that "the crew of the Commerce seem to have been designed to suffer themselves, that the world, through them, might learn."[26]

The types of knowledge that Riley catalogued across a weighty 580 pages fit into three broad categories: (1) graphic information designed to shock and appall readers; (2) information with direct value to social scientists, physical scientists, or traders; and (3) information purely of interest in itself. The first type includes Riley's unnecessarily explicit detail and recurring mentions of the taste of his own urine and that of camels. For the benefit of readers, he advised that camel urine "was bitter, but not salt[y] . . . which we preferred to our own."[27] Even when Riley stole and drank the urine of the ship's African American cook, Richard Delisle, to avert dehydration, he did so unapologetically and without feeling the need to justify his theft, noting simply that "the only taste it had for me, was a salt[y] one, and it seemed (if possible) to increase my burning thirst."[28] These separate, and shocking, incidents arise at least six times during the weeks of marching across the Sahara. That is a similar frequency to his graphic descriptions of camel milk and honeycomb causing "violent diarrhea" and "continual dysentery" where "our bowels seemed to ferment like beer."[29] The most gratuitously gruesome incident is a series of state-sanctioned executions and amputations of criminals' limbs in a town the captives were passing through. This dispassionate two-page account toward the end of Riley's captivity graphically catalogues how the inexperienced executioner "began cutting very leisurely with his knife round the neck (which was a very thick one) and kept cutting to the bones until the flesh was separated . . . and [he] threw it on a mat that was spread to receive the mutilated limbs of the others. There were eight more who were sentenced to lose a leg and an arm each, and nine to lose only one arm," which were all dispatched "in the same leisurely and clumsy manner."[30]

This appalling type of information bridges the first and second types of knowledge found in Riley's *Narrative* by cataloguing the process by which local professional butchers were invited to bid for the job of amputating and executing state prisoners, and how once the commission was completed, they were forced to flee the jurisdiction under fear of reprisals from the victims' friends and family. The butcher-cum-executioner who Riley witnessed left behind a wife and seven children when he fled with the proceeds of his butchery. Unlike authors of earlier captivity narratives and diaries, including Cathcart, Riley

Destructive locust of Africa. In James Riley, *An Authentic Narrative of the Loss of the American Brig* Commerce: *Wrecked on the Western Coast of Africa, in the Month of August, 1815* (New York: T. & W. Mercein, 1817), 473.

rarely seized upon these distressing encounters to portray his captors, their culture, or their governance through an Orientalist or Othered lens. The regions of Morocco that Riley passed through were governed by far more brutal and arbitrary rulers and customs than those in Algiers, yet he remained the steely-eyed ethnographer. These graphic incidents are instead used as evidence in the *Narrative*'s concluding chapter to bolster Riley's claim of the inherent injustice of slavery, including as practiced in the United States.

The second type of information—original scientific, commercial, and anthropological data—is also presented dispassionately. Because of Riley's conscious desire to make his captivity an educational experience for others, the sophisticated discussion of these fields is given greater weight than in other prominent captivity narratives, such as Mary Rowlandson's *Sovereignty and Goodness of God* or Cotton Mather's *Captivity of Hannah Dustan*, and is more factual than in Robert Adams's *Narrative of Robert Adams, a Sailor, Who Was Wrecked on the Western Coast of Africa, in the Year 1810*. While traversing the desert and observing rock formations and cliffs, Riley (drawing on his familiarity with the sea) became convinced that "the sea had gradually retired from this continent," though he acknowledged his limited scientific training, confessing, "I must leave it to philosophers to account for the cause."[31] At other times he lacked the self-awareness to see that his scholarly shortcomings led to absurd scientific conclusions. He fervently believed that "hundreds and thousands of Arabs on this vast expanse of desart actually live to the age of two hundred years of our calendar." Riley explained that they achieved this extraordinary feat through daily routines, nutritious food and aversion to alcohol, a dry climate, and a physically active lifestyle.[32] Despite advancing the occasional scientific impossibility, Riley was generally a fount of new data on a little-known region, ranging from extremely detailed descriptions of plants (even recording their odor when burning), to a description of the ceremony of business transactions in the desert (which always involved threats of violence), to a five-page account of Moroccan snake charmers.[33] He also made a point of highlighting how his newly acquired local intelligence about plentiful fish stocks with a high profit margin could enrich adventurous American merchants. He similarly reiterates, over ten painfully detailed pages, how his observations of North African locusts could help avert disaster if a locust plague infested America's agricultural regions.[34]

In its initial reviews and for decades after publication, Riley's *Narrative* received its greatest praise for these and innumerable other contributions to scientific and cultural knowledge of Morocco and Western Sahara. One otherwise skeptical early reviewer cited its geographic contributions as "although uncertain . . . the most valuable part of the book."[35] As late as 1875, newspapers from Missouri and Texas were still using Riley's topographical observations of the Sahara's underwater past to contextualize for readers the emerging evidence that "the earth's surface of sea and land has been for unknown ages constantly changing."[36] Contributions such as these drove initial sales and clearly made a deep cultural impression, continuing to serve as go-to frames of reference in science communication for up to sixty years after the *Narrative*'s initial publication.

The third and final type of information spanning Riley's *Narrative*, information that is of interest in itself but of no discernible value beyond that, is the most common. This is where Riley finds his unique voice. Like many more purely academic scientists and ethnographers, Riley acknowledged that the information he provides is sometimes not obviously valuable or applicable at the moment, though it may become an invaluable benchmark for future scholars and curious readers seeking to verify and build on others' accounts of the sparsely documented Sahara. His devotion to this type of highly personalized knowledge, primarily commentary and analysis of interactions with his masters and passing communities, is the hallmark of the captivity narrative genre. What distinguishes Riley's inclusion of this type of information from the accounts of countless other white slave predecessors is both the range of his experiences and the publication of subsequent narratives that largely verified his account. This verification was essential for the *Narrative* to serve, as Riley hoped, as a reliable scholarly benchmark and practical guide.

The author and his men's first interview with Mr. Willshire, with a distant view of Mogadore. In James Riley, *An Authentic Narrative of the Loss of the American Brig* Commerce: *Wrecked on the Western Coast of Africa, in the Month of August, 1815* (New York: T. & W. Mercein, 1817), 296.

Unlike most other captives, especially Americans, who were confined to North African port cities like Algiers and Tripoli, Riley traversed the vast and surprisingly diverse Sahara. While Cathcart's and O'Brien's daily routines revolved around the same people, places, and menial tasks, Riley's experience of captivity changed each day, exposing him to myriad communities, ethnicities, and towns. His encounters extended far beyond the predominant master-slave relationship in North African port cities. Riley described Sidi Hamet, his final and longest-term master, as "a very intelligent and feeling man," "generous and humane," and "most courageous." His account includes frequent examples of Sidi putting himself at risk or sacrificing precious resources for Riley's comfort.[37] This glowing review of Sidi's character inspired one South Carolina father to name his son Sidi Hamet, surely making him the only American child to be named after a desert-dwelling, nomadic, Muslim, slave master. The honor also indicates the potential influence of the inclusion of this type of information, which helped deconstruct monolithic stereotypes about Muslims, the people of North Africa, and the agricultural potential of the region. Devoted readers of Riley's *Narrative* also named a slew of other people and places after those they found in the *Narrative*, including the nineteenth-century, New York–born historian Consul Willshire Butterield; the town of Willshire, Ohio; and the town of Mogadore, Ohio, alongside Mogadore Reservoir near Akron.[38]

In spite of Riley's success in deconstructing American stereotypes of North

Africans and Muslims, he had much less success in combating Americans' stereotypes of Jews. Mordecai Manuel Noah, a prominent Jewish writer and diplomat in the early American republic, even chastised Riley for including passages that can be interpreted as critical of North African Jewish communities, despite these two passages being amongst dozens of others that were neutral or positive. Noah argues that Riley was guilty of two specific counts of "gross libels on the general chastity of [Jewish] females": first, for writing that Jewish women "are considered by the men as having no souls, nor are they allowed to enter the Synagogues, but once a year"; and second, for alleging that, near the end of his captivity while in the Moroccan city of Safi, two "handsome and stylishly dressed" Jewish teenagers drew him into their home and tried to seduce him.[39] North Americans had little direct contact with Jews within their own national borders, so Americans' cultural impressions of Judaism were formed through reading the accounts of captives, consuls, and travelers in North Africa.[40] Given the role of this literature in creating an American perception of Judaism, and the popularity of Riley's *Narrative*, Noah's emphasis on these few unflattering reflections is understandable. Especially given his personal experience of anti-Semitism in the United States and the practice of Judaism in North Africa, having been US consul to Tunis soon before Riley's captivity—a position from which he had been controversially fired by Secretary of State James Monroe for the offence of practicing diplomacy while Jewish.[41]

Whereas foreigners' typical passing references to Jewish communities in North Africa were of encounters with individual merchants in capital cities, Riley's complementary observations are of whole communities in smaller towns and cities. These include an entire chapter devoted to comparing "present Arabs and ancient Jews" and scattered passages, ranging from five to seventeen pages, that detail circumcisions in Mogadore, the process of global collections to support rabbis in Jerusalem, and the institutionalized sexual abuse suffered by Jewish women in Morocco.[42] Riley equated the lack of legal recourse available to the fathers or husbands of the abused women with the legal standing of slaves in the United States and West Indies, remarking, "should a Jew attempt to resist a Moor on any occasion, he [or she] is sure of getting a sound drubbing, and his [or her] testimony cannot be taken against a Moor, any more than that of a negro slave in the West Indies and the Southern States of America, can be given against a white man."[43] Nevertheless, a small number of readers in the United States almost immediately cited Riley's observations as reinforcing their own anti-Semitic prejudices, tragically validating Noah's critique of the *Narrative*. One Pennsylvanian journalist in 1818, just a year after the publication of Riley's *Narrative*, was astonished that a Jewish judge ("one of the *circumcision*") was appointed in Pennsylvania "to sit in judgement over *Christians*." When associate judges in neighboring counties resigned in protest, the newspaper ironically opined, "what a pity that [Pennsylvania governor William Findlay] did not send to Mogadore for a couple of associates, as Captain Riley's *Narrative* informs us that there are some of the circumcision to be found at that place."[44]

Dispersing these three types of knowledge throughout Riley's *Narrative* — knowledge that is either shocking and appalling, directly applicable, or with no immediate value—culminated in an uncommonly entertaining, intellectually stimulating, and commercially successful product. Spinning this adversity into an opportunity for fame and fortune was still far from assured. British, European, and North American captives had already pursued this publishing path and received only modest short-term public interest.[45] In part, Riley's success is attributable to the unique circumstances of the initial newspaper syndication of his captivity and the regular reinterpretation of his *Narrative*, as detailed below.

In the *Sequel to Riley's Narrative*, Riley's son claimed that by 1851 his father's ordeal "has been read by more than a million now living in these United States."[46] That estimate is a gross exaggeration. More important than its ultimate sales figure, however, is that in three respects—its distribution, evolution, and legacy—Riley's *Narrative* serves as a singularly reflective mirror to the changing infrastructure and interests of the nation across the nineteenth century.

Riley began drafting his manuscript in North Africa in the midst of post-traumatic stress that struck soon after being ransomed. He described his condition as "the tempest that was gathering in my brain." The tempest left him "delirious" and "bereft of my senses—and for the space of three days knew not where I was."[47] Later, William Willshire told Riley how he had looked: "continually bathed in tears, and shuddering at the sight of every human being, fearing [he] should again be carried into slavery."[48] Even when stabilized, his dreams were filled with visions of captivity that lasted until "I would hit my head against something, which would startle and awaken me."[49] An author in this volatile mental state is clearly unable to reliably recount in excruciating detail a nine-week ordeal across a manuscript of over six hundred handwritten pages. Yet surprisingly, the details of Riley's account are almost entirely supported by the narrative of his crewman Archibald Robbins, published just months later. The only notable difference is the ultimate fate of Antonio Michel, the elderly passenger who Riley claimed to sacrifice to nomadic scavengers at the site of their wreck. Robbins assured Riley that he was not responsible for Michel's death, as he and other crewmen "saw the Arabs load his back with plunder, and force him to carry it over the sand hill." Robbins had clearly read Riley's *Narrative* before publishing his own, and it's possible he amended other recollections to conform to the captain's already published account. As a junior member of New England's tight-knit merchant sailor community, Robbins may also have been inclined to smooth over Riley's sacrifice of Michel and reluctant to jeopardize his own prospect of future employment.[50]

Biographers and friends of the *Narrative*'s editor, Anthony Bleecker Jr., repeatedly claimed that, "from the crude notes, journals, and log-books which Capt. James Riley furnished, [Bleecker] drew up that gratuitously popular 'Narrative of the Brig Commerce,' which obtained so wide a circulation both in this country and abroad."[51] Yet there is no actual evidence that Riley's manuscript received more than occasional tweaks. It is hard to argue that Bleecker pieced together the *Narrative* from logbooks and scattered notes, since the *Commerce*'s logbook was never recovered from the wreck, and there is no evidence that Riley gave Bleecker any document other than his completed manuscript. Furthermore, the original handwritten manuscript of Riley's *Narrative* was barely altered for either style or content before publication.

The matter of authorship is somewhat complicated, however, by the fact that the original manuscript is not penned in Riley's or Bleecker's handwriting.[52] It is possible that Riley provided crude notes and journals, which Bleecker drew on when compiling the original manuscript, with a polished draft (the earliest surviving copy of which is held by the New-York Historical Society) then produced by a professional scribe.[53] In this case, the minor edits on that manuscript, which are all in Bleecker's handwriting, simply reflect modest changes to his own draft. Alternatively, Riley could have drafted the manuscript and hired the scribe long before contacting Bleecker. In any case, Riley's articulate and prodigious correspondence in the years after his captivity, and the style of that correspondence, is ample evidence that he could have drafted the manuscript himself.

Within the handwritten manuscript, the overwhelming majority of Bleecker's edits were spelling corrections and the addition or deletion of one or two words in a sentence. In fact, his few substantive revisions reinforce rather than alter Riley's established course. For example, one small revision made Sidi appear more cunning in his protection of Riley from a caravan of less honorable nomads. Another made Riley's observations of North African fish stock seem more commercially useful.[54] Both points were already amply made elsewhere. Even in removing passages and entire pages, Bleecker confined himself to excising material about old battles and older towns, which was made redundant by dozens of similar entries throughout the manuscript. He also purged several passages that could be perceived as anti-Semitic, while at the same time leaving dozens more pages on the lives, laws, and governance of North African Jewish communities.[55]

The Bleecker family's interest in and tradition of shaping North American captivity narratives further complicates Anthony Bleecker's contested role in Riley's *Narrative*. Long before Bleecker edited America's bestselling nonfiction

Barbary captivity narrative, his aunt, Ann Eliza Schuyler-Bleecker, penned the nation's first fully fictional captivity narrative. No previous scholar has unearthed this familial connection and asked if it inspired Bleecker's role in Riley's *Narrative* and his approach to editing the manuscript. Set during the French and Indian War, and written in the form of a letter to a fellow rural New Yorker, *The History of Maria Kittle* (published posthumously in 1793 but likely written decades earlier) adheres to the established norms of the captivity narrative genre. It quickly establishes its protagonist as an intellectually curious, empathetic, and popular everywoman.[56] Though set on a vastly different continent in a different century, and populated with culturally different captors and a captive of a different gender, this first fictional narrative parallels Riley's account. Both narratives play on tropes of discovery-by-disaster, of captivity as a path to realizing divine Providence, and of a hostile wilderness with still more hostile inhabitants.[57]

Though connected by blood, a shared passion for literature, and an eerie coincidence in captivity narratives, and separated by just a few years and a few miles, there is no surviving evidence that Anthony and Ann Eliza corresponded on this topic or any other. Nor is there any surviving evidence that Anthony was raised on the stories of his prolific aunt. It is hard to believe that such kindred spirits in such close proximity missed each other entirely, but when Ann Eliza's severe depression drove her to burn most of her writing and correspondence, it became impossible to uncover the truth.[58] Solving the mystery of Ann Eliza's influence on young Anthony would be significant in understanding the development of American captivity narratives in the history of American literature. Alas, the destruction of Ann Eliza's work and the absence of Anthony's correspondence or journals means this mystery might forever remain unsolved.

Although it's uncertain how many copies of the first edition of Riley's *Narrative* were printed and sold, Donald Ratcliffe convincingly argues that it's unlikely to be greater than four thousand, which was "not out of scale with other books of the period."[59] Far from a bestseller, it was initially a barely modest seller. Ratcliffe traces the true scope of Riley's "readership" (or the amount of people who read his account in some form) to three periods: beginning before the *Narrative*'s publication, then receiving a second wind in the 1830s, and then being recently revived in the early twenty-first century when Dean King penned a bestselling amalgamation of Riley's and Robbins's accounts.[60] Between the *Commerce* striking ground in 1815 and the final republication of Riley's *Narrative* in 1965, news of his captivity was widely circulated, first through newspaper articles while he was still in North Africa and then in the form of a book that went through, by Paul Baepler's count, at least twenty-five editions, not including King's 2005 amalgamation.[61] Each of the estimated forty-four thousand copies of the *Narrative* printed between the years 1817 and 1859 would have needed to be read by over twenty-two people each to reach the one million readers Riley's son claimed.[62]

The speed and geographic distribution of Riley's *Narrative* in the nineteenth century is largely thanks to near-simultaneous transformations in US infrastructure and communication technologies that neatly coincided with Riley's publication. The network of local newspapers throughout the United States that circulated news from Cathcart and O'Brien decades earlier was radically changing by the time of Riley's captivity. During Cathcart's and O'Brien's time, the soon-to-be-united United States had less than 75 post offices and fewer than 1,875 miles of post roads. By the time of Riley's captivity, those numbers exploded to over 2,610 post offices and 39,378 miles of post roads, facilitating far speedier and more comprehensive distribution of news to an increasingly information-hungry citizenry.[63] Over the same period the number of public libraries in New England grew at a similar rate. And readers were clear in their particular interest in the most up-to-date histories, biographies, political science books, and travel narratives.[64] Precisely the sort of fresh and unfiltered knowledge that Riley and the Village Enlightenment offered.

The same year Riley first published his *Narrative* (1817) was also a watershed moment in how information, goods, and people were transported across the United States.[65] In that year, construction began on the Erie Canal, making the steamboat a viable means of transport on the Ohio and Mississippi Rivers and increasing the speed and frequency of transportation. A year later, the National Road, the nation's first major highway, was opened. The brief initial reports that "Captain Riley and his crew were made slaves by the Moors" were printed in January 1816 before the completion of these major transport-infrastructure programs and received only modest syndication in newspapers in Connecticut, New York, Virginia, Massachusetts, and Washington, DC.[66] Despite being unable to benefit from these imminent internal "improvements," as infrastructure projects were called, the fate of the *Commerce*'s crew soon spread thanks to the tradition of free postage for newspapers and the fact that more than half of newspaper editors in the nation's interior received the East Coast papers directly from the publisher. Each edition mainly consisted of nonlocal news, so editors, such as one from the *Mobile Advertiser*, "must plead our excuse for the barrenness of our columns today," when the post from New York and abroad arrived too late to print.[67] The thirst for and coverage of foreign news was so insatiable that Riley's story became widely known from towns to homesteads thanks to its newspaper coverage in 1816 and 1817, rather than through the repeatedly published book.[68] Within a month, a wider circle of at least seventeen newspapers, from Salem to Richmond to Albany, syndicated the first account penned by Riley of his capture and release, but with no details of the captivity in between.[69] In spite of the scant details of his ordeal, these articles were enough to whet the public's appetite for Riley's first edition, sold by subscription.[70]

Just as the *Narrative*'s distribution tracks a course of changing communication technology and infrastructure through the nineteenth century, so too do shifts in the emphasis that readers attach to various themes within the *Narrative* make it an ideal case study of the nation's shifting interests. Over the nineteenth and twentieth centuries, the published editions of Riley's *Narrative* were abbreviated and adapted to highlight different themes and lessons from his captivity. Each substantive revision was a unique product of its time, published and remembered by readers for filling a perceived information gap in one subject or another. Reviewers of the first edition could not have been more explicit in identifying scientific observation as the true value of Riley's *Narrative*, writing, "the personal narrative, affecting as it is, is but secondary in value to the information—the vast body of facts given by Capt. Riley."[71] Of secondary interest were the thrilling survival story, the lessons in manly fortitude, and the notable faith in divine Providence. All of these were recurring themes in Riley's *Narrative*, but readers now considered them far less significant than in previous American-Barbary captivity narratives. Presidents Abraham Lincoln, John Adams, and Thomas Jefferson all owned and read Riley's *Narrative* during the time this hierarchy of interests drove sales.[72]

By the 1830s, the once-struggling early republic had become a more assertive Jacksonian democracy, and Riley's original 580-page book shed more than half its pages. The same highly detailed scientific content for which it had originally been praised was the first to be cut. The harrowing survival story, with its moral and religious lessons, now became the driving focus for a new generation of young readers, and those were also the lessons deployed in newspapers by evangelists and antislavery advocates. From around 1833, moral and religious themes were carefully forged as the new anchors of the *Narrative* as it was heavily edited for anthologies.[73] Still, the *Narrative* continued to serve as a Rorschach test, with readers interpreting it as espousing whatever cause was dear to them, irrespective of whether their interpretation was broadly shared by other readers of their time.

As early as 1817, long before the *Narrative*'s inclusion in anthologies, one newspaper published an entire editorial on the theme that Riley's recovery from slavery served as a reminder that "God is our refuge and strength."[74] By 1824, antislavery newspaper columnists were using Riley's *Narrative* to take sly jabs at Southern slavery: "We have a large number of such adventurers [slaves] in our southern states who we sincerely wish would be as fortunate as the renowned Captain has been, and be allowed to return to their own country and publish, if they please, a narrative of *their adventures* in this land of liberty."[75] The peak of this religious and moral reinterpretation came in the early 1830s when the *Narrative* was adapted as a pair of children's books by Samuel Goodrich in his popular Peter Parley series. In one of these books, *The Story of Captain Riley, and His Adventures in Africa*, Goodrich merely edited Riley's *Narrative*, leaving much of the text intact. There were, however, notable omissions. Some of those omissions, which conflicted with Goodrich's idea of popular moral education, included the abandonment (and perhaps death) of Antonio Michel, the crew getting drunk after the wreck, frequent mentions of diarrhea and drinking urine, and most importantly, Riley's closing commitment to advocate for antislavery policies in the United States. As a substitute for these telling omissions, Goodrich indulged in his own conclusion that "Captain Riley had made one Friend who, amid all his trials, never forsook him. . . . This Friend was the Christian's God."[76]

The same decade the children's books were published, the abolitionist newspaper *The Emancipator* "ask[ed] all slaveholders to read the two journals" of Riley and Judah Paddock, whose narrative Riley had personally published to prove the veracity of his own.[77] The reporter saw the narratives as such explicit texts of comparative slavery that he recited a line that never appeared in any edition of either narrative: "You *Christian* dog—how dare you complain when you fare so much better than you treat black men which your nation *steals* from our coast and enslaves forever."[78] The next year the same newspaper again invoked Riley's *Narrative* as justification for helping runaway slaves, writing, "we have no doubt that Capt. Riley, shipwrecked on the coast of Africa and made a slave by the natives, had a right to escape if he could; and if in our power, we should think it our duty to assist him. Another class of cases is equally clear."[79]

Lincoln mentioned Riley's *Narrative* far more subtly in his authorized 1860 campaign biography.[80] We will never know if Lincoln mentioned reading the book, the young emancipator's first nonfiction narrative, because a new edition had just been published and it was on the public's mind. Or, whether it was a dog whistle: perhaps Lincoln hoped proslavery readers would simply hear it as a common childhood appreciation for Riley's adventure yarn, while antislavery advocates would hear it as an acknowledgement that Riley helped young Lincoln develop his opposition to slavery. That level of subtlety was certainly unnecessary given the biography's frequent and explicit discussions of Lincoln's long-held moral and policy positions on slavery. But the mere two-word mention of *Riley's Narrative* in the eighty-six-page campaign diary has not stopped scholars from making unfounded and hyperbolic claims about Riley's influence on the young emancipator.[81]

Though Riley's *Narrative* was widely read in newspapers, published editions, and children's books, in gauging its impact on Lincoln and the nation, scholars have habitually erred in taking the size of Riley's readership as a measure of its actual influence. In reality, Riley had no discernible influence on the messaging, organization, or membership of the colonization or abolition movements. Nor is there any evidence he changed the minds of any policymakers or members of the general public on matters of slavery. Contemporaries occasionally cited his *Narrative* as proof of the immorality of slavery, but Riley himself was never cited as tangibly changing the debate. Nevertheless, historian Robert J. Allison argues that Riley's explicit engagement with questions of morality and politics, namely the slavery debate, is what made his *Narrative* more popular and enduring than other captivity narratives.[82] Others argue instead that the unrivaled success of Riley's *Narrative* derived from his simple, approachable writing style or his self-awareness of his limited qualifications and preference to dwell only on subjects he was most qualified to speak to.[83]

Ultimately, it is impossible to isolate a single, dominant cause of the *Narrative*'s success above others in the genre. What kept people reading, generation after generation, was that it lent itself to uncommonly many different readings. To readers with little knowledge of Islam, Judaism, and North Africa, it was an educational and thrilling read, whereas to antislavery advocates it was a rousing affirmation of their cause. To contemporary popular history authors in the early twenty-first century, "when one of the great challenges we face is to find common ground for Muslims, Christians, and Jews, the plight of the crew of the Commerce achieves a new relevance."[84] And to contemporary scholars it is "a commentary on American character and a sermon on American sinfulness."[85]

The exaggerated commercial and cultural impact of Riley's *Narrative* has persisted in popular and scholarly literature since the nineteenth century. In its many revised forms the *Narrative* did not make a verifiable contribution to the antislavery movement or to Lincoln's opinion of slavery, and it almost certainly did not enjoy a million-person readership. Moderating these excessive claims, however, does not negate Riley's very real contributions to the Village Enlightenment, to the captivity narrative genre, and to Americans' understanding of a little-known region and its peoples.

True, by the time of Riley's captivity in 1815, American Orientalism and basic knowledge of the Muslim world was already well-established in the American public sphere. Thanks to rapidly increasing US-Mediterranean contact, North African and Ottoman Orientalism was well on its way to being tamed and commodified in the United States through fads in fashion, portraiture, architecture, domestic furniture, and ornate smoking rituals.[86] But beyond its value in original scientific observations and putting a piercing spotlight on American hypocrisies, an oft-overlooked contribution that sets Riley's *Narrative* apart from preceding and subsequent American-Barbary captivity narratives is that he consciously challenged the established dichotomy of American Orientalism that contrasted American virtue with North African barbarism. Riley held himself and his crew accountable for their sins, such as drunkenness and attempted cannibalism, and commended supposedly "barbarian" North Africans for their virtues, including donations of food to the captives by impoverished locals, charismatic leadership qualities, and frequent praise of his "generous and humane" master, Sidi Hamet.

Alas, even the *Commerce*'s crew who safely returned to American shores lived up to the stereotype of sailors' melancholy and intertwined fates. Many were stalked by misfortune. Among the least fortunate was James Clark, who was almost immediately diagnosed with tuberculosis and suffered chronic pain and depression before dying at the age of just twenty-nine. Worse still was the fate of Thomas Burns, whom the *Connecticut Courant* reported, "having been annoyed, as he says, by a *white Cat*, loaded his gun, and went out in the evening for the purpose of shooting it." Instead of shooting the cat he shot a "young man dead on the spot," claiming the man's white vest and cravat had made him a cat-like target. Burns was never prosecuted for the shooting, though he, his wife, and his daughter all soon fell ill and died. In the *Courant*, Burns was merely remembered as "one of the unfortunate sufferers with Capt. Riley, on the great desart of Sahara."[87] So contagious was this curse of the *Commerce* that it even extended to their former captor Sidi, who was reportedly murdered while endeavoring to fulfill his pledge to track down and ransom William Porter, an able seaman on the *Commerce* who was eventually ransomed.[88] Other crewmen offer more encouraging signs that the physical trauma of marching across the Sahara did not adversely impact their long-term health. Nor did it impact their capacity to live, raise families, and contribute to American commercial and infrastructure projects for many decades afterward.[89] In tribute to the US consul in Gibraltar and the British consul in Morocco who paid Riley's ransom, Riley renamed his two youngest sons Horatio Sprague Riley and William Willshire Riley. And evincing the tight-knit communities of sailors and their families, the daughter of Aaron Savage, the *Commerce*'s second mate, married one of Riley's sons, and they gave their first child the middle name of Willshire, to honor the man who had freed their fathers. Archibald Robbins, who married the niece of George Williams, the *Commerce*'s first mate, in turn gave their first child the middle name of Riley.[90]

In addition to incorporating the Riley family name within the Robbins lineage, Robbins also paralleled Riley's post-captivity life. Both contributed to significant internal national improvements such as the Erie Canal, and both pushed the boundaries of US settlement by colonizing the Ohio frontier. As will be shown in the following chapter, the same is broadly true of Richard O'Brien and James Cathcart. O'Brien settled in Carlisle, Pennsylvania, which became a conduit for supplying the expanding interior with necessary goods and would-be frontiersmen from the East Coast. Meanwhile, Cathcart similarly sent forth his children to Indiana, with explicit instructions to build a family political and commercial dynasty in the new territories. He instilled in his children the hard lessons of upward mobility learned in Algiers, supplemented with insider knowledge of federal land sales and cynical interpretations of Jacksonian democracy. This shift in the former sailors' focus to the US interior is hardly atypical. It merely reflects the land-based lives of sailors before taking to sea, after they retired from sea, and during the years spent on farms and in port towns in between voyages.

CHAPTER SIX

Sailing the Inland Sea

I shall not rest contented 'til I have explored the Western
Country, & traversed those lines . . . which have given bounds to
a New Empire.

George Washington, October 12, 1783

Richard O'Brien, James Cathcart, and James Riley established themselves on
America's terrestrial frontier decades before Horace Greeley's famous recommendation to "Go West, young man, and grow up with the country," away
from toxic cities and port towns.[1] Rather than growing from boys to men in the
West and redefining American identity as inseparable from the rugged country,
the trio performed their rites of passage on the maritime frontier, expanding
American commercial, diplomatic, and military presence into the Mediterranean and defining American identity against what they found in captivity.
Now, for the final voyage of their lives, they moored their ships and turned
to the landed frontier in the wake of the Louisiana Purchase. These were not
gaudy men, interested in charting a grand destiny in the West; neither were they
vocal champions of manifest destiny. Nevertheless, they inadvertently served as
trailing members of its advance team.

The pattern of tragedy and bad luck that haunted the trio in North Africa followed them ashore as the sailors pivoted west. O'Brien died in relative ano-nymity a decade after moving to a small town between Philadelphia and Pitts-burgh. Cathcart went as far as to design his own palatial homestead, to be built where his children settled in Indiana—but only after the federal government reimbursed decades-old expenses, which it never did. Instead, he died bitter and despondent in Washington, DC. At the same time, Riley, having settled his family on the Ohio frontier, returned to sea, only to die on the Caribbean before fulfilling his pledge to bring William Willshire, his now destitute former redeemer, to a new life in the United States.

The three redeemed captives never "settled." Instead, in the spirit of Alexis de Tocqueville's observation of Americans as "restless in the midst of abun-dance," they continued to contribute to the Village Enlightenment and exper-iment in self-making.[2] Rather than resting on their laurels of successful careers in diplomacy and publishing, the trio repeatedly forged entirely new careers in unfamiliar parts of the country. While their experiences upon returning to American shores were not identical, the differences were ones of degree, not of kind.

In an era of relatively small government, it is striking that during these later years back in the United States each of these men held state or federal govern-ment appointments, and in Riley's case, both. Just as when they served on the maritime frontier, their connection to, and reliance upon, government on the terrestrial frontier belies the stereotype of the rugged individualist—no matter how much Cathcart, O'Brien, and especially Riley tried to cultivate this image of themselves. After all, western settlement was supported through infrastruc-ture projects that were largely financed by government, and security was pro-vided by military outposts. Early settlers were often former government sur-veyors of the region (like Riley) who hoped to subsidize their settler aspirations through further government employment, such as becoming operators of post offices or liaisons between government and local Native American tribes through the Office of Indian Trade.[3] In subsidizing frontiersmen and serving as a crucial safety net for these "rugged individualists," governments accepted these finan-cial burdens of settlement at their own peril. Twice, during the so-called panics (more accurately, the "crippling recessions") of 1819 and 1837, the precarious financial positions that governments put themselves in to build internal im-provements felt like ropes they had tied around their own necks.[4]

Even on the micro level of the settler community, frontiersmen were rarely truly alone. From the late eighteenth century onward, these communities pooled their resources to survive and exchanged their labor, in a system they termed *changing works*, to improve their standard of living.[5] Despite this necessity in sharing resources and labor, Riley never explicitly acknowledged the role of changing works and mutual assistance in raising his town in western Ohio, nor did O'Brien mention reciprocal working relationships or shared resources on his farm in Pennsylvania, or the Cathcart family on their estate in Indiana. But it is safe to assume that the systems of cooperation that were already firmly established by the late eighteenth century were still fully functioning during the Jacksonian era and had taken much of the wind out of claims to rugged individualism on the frontier.

It is unsurprising that scholarship on Cathcart, O'Brien, and Riley almost ceases as they transition away from international affairs and into other subfields of historical inquiry.[6] Non-elites who somehow leave a mark on the popular imagination invariably leave behind few sources. They typically find their whole lives being consigned to just one small role or event in historical memory. Even if they largely fell off the historian's radar, however, O'Brien, Cathcart, and Riley hardly fell off the map. Their later years on the home front are powerful evidence that non-elite individuals restlessly pursued lives as professional amateurs, endeavoring to leave their marks in ever-more domains.

Once they returned from Algiers, Richard and Elizabeth O'Brien, along with their two young children, briefly settled in Philadelphia. Richard was elected to the state legislature as a Democratic-Republican Party representative, serving just one term from December 1808 to April 1809. Perhaps O'Brien was elected on the basis of his modest fame from over a decade of captivity in Algiers and his service as consul general; or perhaps it was simply that he was a professional sailor in a port city. Pennsylvania politics was a short-term and classically democratic hobby, rather than an elitist occupation. Whereas colonial-era politicians enjoyed reelection after reelection, in post-Revolutionary Pennsylvania legislators experienced a constant turnover, serving an average of just one or two terms each between 1775 and 1821. This turnover was not due to political volatility or increased voter participation. Instead, it was the consequence of county political leaders' efforts to pass around the job to as many leading local men as possible.[7] Since O'Brien was included, it seems likely the rotation was not limited to political leaders. O'Brien had never held elected office or befriended any party patrons.

As a legislator, O'Brien was one of the quietest Democratic-Republican representatives to ever grace the Pennsylvania House of Representatives.[8] As a fitting start, his first act was to ask for a few days' leave.[9] His name appears only two dozen times in the House Journal. Most of his thoughts are on the construction of roads, speaking on behalf of the US Marines, and anxiety over the state's eroding shore defenses.[10] His most notable contribution was the introduction of a bill for the welfare of Philadelphia sailors. The act stipulated that if a local sailor died at sea and no relative was found to claim his estate then it would be put in a fund "for the benefit of poor and disabled sailors belonging to the port of Philadelphia, their widows and children."[11] His only political wave to breach state boundaries was a speech reported in the Massachusetts *Salem Gazette*, and even then, the interest was in O'Brien's amusing maritime metaphors rather than his policy position.[12] The *Salem Gazette* did not even bother providing any context for the legislation that O'Brien was railing against—its details remain a mystery—but instead the paper relished in reprinting almost eight hundred words of warning that the commerce bill, if passed, "will get your state chart[ed] into the squally latitudes," imploring the legislature "not to steer after the top light of this rear admiral [the bill's champion], for, so certain as you do, he will dash you on the shoals. I therefore request this house heave all aback, and save the ship from this dangerous lee-shore." He graphically brought readers to shore in the same fashion: "What is proposed in this bill, is to destroy your light-houses—to destroy the light and usages of nations, and leave us jumping in the dark."[13]

In the decades preceding O'Brien's election, the number of petitions to the legislature had ballooned and become the point of origin for the overwhelming majority of state statutes successfully passed into law.[14] In an earlier period (in 1790), just half of Pennsylvania legislators submitted even one lone petition to the legislature. That figure steadily climbed, rising to 86 percent of legislators by the time O'Brien was elected.[15] Thus the bulk of O'Brien's work was to serve as a medium for his constituents' petitions. In fact, the only mention of O'Brien in the only scholarly book devoted to the Pennsylvania legislature in the early republic is to commend his staggering fifteen petitions, in contrast to the mere one or two typically tabled by his colleagues.[16]

O'Brien's first petition was from the German Jewish community asking to hold a lottery to raise funds to build a synagogue.[17] O'Brien's committee approved the lottery, though suggesting "that all places of worship should be built at the expence of a more moral system than that proposed by lotteries, or from any other gambling system or institution."[18] Several other petitions that O'Brien dutifully tabled conflicted with his own policy positions, such as two from communities of sailors that warned the continued embargo was driving the nation's maritime workforce abroad, and more graphically stated, "should they from sad necessity, abandon our ports and forsake their native land, it would lop off the right arm of commerce, and deaden the vital spirit of agriculture."[19]

Although a former merchant sailor, O'Brien curiously ran as a candidate (and then spoke as a representative) in favor of the 1809 Non-Intercourse Act, which was signed by President Thomas Jefferson just days before leaving the Oval Office and was essentially a continuation of his Embargo Act of 1807.[20] By forbidding American maritime trade with Britain and France, the Non-

Intercourse Act aimed to force the navies and privateers of both nations to reconsider their custom of ignoring American neutrality and preying upon its commerce and impressing its sailors. Instead, the acts crippled American shipping. They were also deeply unpopular and commonly violated by smugglers, who thrived during these years.

O'Brien's support for measures that impeded US trade and put thousands of sailors out of work is surprising given his own background in maritime trade, his continued support for seamen, and his public disregard for the acts' architects, President Jefferson and James Madison.[21] In light of this unlikely support for the embargo, one newspaper editor asked during the campaign whether O'Brien was personally benefiting from the embargo by owning merchant ships that were registered in foreign ports and enjoying a brisk trade while his neighbors' ships languished in dry dock.[22] Nevertheless, O'Brien gave voice to dissenting positions, and he dutifully read to the chamber the petitions from sailors who reported that the acts had left them to "the aid of the public, or abandoning their country and engaging in a foreign service."[23] Having dutifully read his constituents' petition, O'Brien insistently added that "the ocean being of equal property of all nations and states, that the state of Pennsylvania as one of the United States, will never abandon or surrender its rights to navigate the same: and our present temporary embargo shall never be considered by this state as an abandonment of any of our maritime rights."[24]

Following his turn in the legislature, O'Brien retired with his family to Carlisle, Pennsylvania, where he made even less of a public mark than in his legislative career. The written record contains only two subsequent references to him. One was in 1812 when he was made chairman of the Cumberland County Democratic-Republican Party.[25] O'Brien's name does not appear again in the *Carlisle Gazette* until twelve years later, upon his death on February 14, 1824, aged 66. Even then, he was granted just a single line: "DIED - At Washington City, on Sunday morning last, Commodore Richard O'Brien, of this place, and late Consul to the Barbary Powers."[26] It does not even mention why he was in the capital.

When they acquired about seven hundred acres of farmland on the periphery of Carlisle, the O'Briens joined a community that historian Judith Ridner aptly describes as "a town in-between."[27] The town, thriving and economically diverse in the early nineteenth century, "occupied a contested space between east and west, north and south, Europe and America, and Euro-American and Native American."[28] A visitor found Carlisle in 1812 to be "a flourishing town in the midst of, and mingling in undistinguishable association, with fields and forests of extended fertility and luxuriant foliage. The town presented a diversified picture of houses and trees," with "the farmer and the merchant in unison."[29] In contrast to this glowing review, another visitor over thirty years after the O'Briens settled in Carlisle found the town "very pretty," but added that its "Society does not take rank with the enlightened and intelligent of other country towns," locating it among merely the "third and fourth rank in the state."[30] The small town's middling society and lack of opportunity for making overnight fortunes would have appalled Cathcart; but for the same reasons, Carlisle was an ideal retirement site for O'Brien, finally far removed from the opportunistic Cathcarts of the world.

When the O'Briens arrived in 1809 or 1810, the town's population had grown to twenty-six thousand, and it had grown divided.[31] The violent political divisions that erupted in the town's public squares following the ratification of the Constitution and the Whiskey Rebellion had died down by the turn of the century, but divisions in wealth steadily widened.[32] Whereas in 1795 the bottom 50 percent of taxable households held 13 percent of the town's wealth, their holdings plummeted to just 3 percent by 1808, with an additional 18 percent of the otherwise taxable townspeople having no taxable property at all.[33] At the time of his death, O'Brien's will lists assets that placed him squarely in between the wealthier and poorer classes of Carlisle, which was itself "in between" regions, demographics, and nationwide financial extremes.[34]

Given O'Brien's quiet life and the scarcity of sources detailing his postconsular years, it is unsurprising that this period remains fallow ground for historians. Yet when viewed in the context of his Revolutionary War years, Algerian captivity, and leadership of America's first consuls to North Africa, these twilight years in the Pennsylvania countryside take on the light of a typical cosmopolitan American life that had come full circle. O'Brien's birth to Irish parents in the northernmost reaches of the Massachusetts colony, early introduction into Atlantic seafaring, English wife, and considerable experience abroad made him appealing as a political candidate. His persisting use of maritime metaphors on the floor of the Pennsylvania assembly and in everyday conversation reveals an enduring connection to the sea. Yet he evidently found solace in a quiet country life, away from the risks and isolation of the sea. He never shared in Cathcart's bitterness or Riley's impulse to reinsert himself into political advocacy. He did, however, share their interest, at a comfortable distance, in nation building on the western frontier.

As a more ambitious self-maker and more reliable correspondent, Cathcart's post-consular careers and contributions are both more significant and better documented than O'Brien's. Whether surveying the Louisiana Territories, toiling in the US Treasury Department, or instilling his children with the knowledge and ambition to build a political dynasty on the Indiana frontier, all Cathcart's subsequent pursuits mark his further (sometimes inadvertent) contributions to the Village Enlightenment and the creation of an American empire in the

West. This phase of Cathcart's life was meant to be his final trick, the pinnacle of his upward thrust into high public office and/or great wealth. Instead, his flood of ambition ran up against an even stronger tide of disinterest and party machinery, which left him relegated to the role of family consigliere to a generation that ultimately realized his ambitions in high politics, influence, and manifest destiny.

Within a year of returning to American shores from his final consulship in Cadiz, Spain, Cathcart successfully petitioned the federal government to become a naval agent, leading a three-man party to survey live oak and red cedar stocks in the Louisiana Territories, with the aim to help rebuild the US Navy after its decimation in the War of 1812.[35] The surveying party began in New Orleans in January 1819, snaking up the Mississippi River to Bayou Plaquemine, alternating between inland routes and a small single-masted sailboat as they hopped from one bayou to the next.[36] While assessing flora that hugged the Mississippi, Cathcart prophetically found that "the mind naturally expands in contemplation of the destiny which awaits it [the Mississippi]; the only grand outlet to the increasing commerce of an Empire, equal now to many, and in no distant period will be superior in wealth, population and resources to any in Europe."[37] After surveying the bayous west of New Orleans, the party made their way to Mobile, Alabama, where they travelled over a hundred miles by steamboat up the Tombigbee River to the town of St. Stephens, then overland west about fifty miles to Claibourne on the Alabama River. Having endured plagues of giant mosquitoes and Spanish "land pirates," witnessing the arbitrary murder of slaves, being trapped on an island which the group accidentally set fully ablaze, and sharing a small boat with an unruly monkey, Cathcart finally returned to Washington in May of 1819 to write his report.[38]

The protagonists of the Village Enlightenment were sometimes underappreciated, before their time, and often themselves unaware of the scope of their own contributions. Cathcart's final report for the Navy Department totaled almost one hundred handwritten pages with an additional twenty-two-page index. Yet the Navy Department sat on it for eight years before even mentioning the expensive exercise to Congress, neglecting to forward the report until 1832, fully thirteen years after its completion. Even then, the report merely accompanied a statement of expenses paid to government surveyors of the region.[39]

As with his earlier semipublic writings for government, Cathcart was certain his report would filter through the corridors of power, land on the desks of influence, secure him future employment, and perhaps even be quoted in newspapers. Instead, it was roundly ignored. This is despite sharing the same style, scope, and fields of interest as John C. Frémont's famous surveyor journals of his US Army–sponsored 1842 and 1843 travels through the South-Pass and Oregon Trail.[40] More than the quarter century between their surveys, the chief difference between Frémont's and Cathcart's expeditions was their prescribed goals. Cathcart's government brief was to traverse unsurveyed lands and simply count trees. Frémont, in contrast, was tasked with popularizing already-established travel routes, and—with eager government endorsement—his accounts were circulated widely in newspapers. As American public imagination turned west, Frémont became a household name in the same way and for the same reasons that Riley had a generation earlier.

Officially, Cathcart was only meant to document tree stock and justifications for expenses. Yet his ambitious journal, which aimed for but never achieved the stature Frémont later enjoyed, provides invaluable contributions to the environmental, social, and economic history of the Louisiana Territories. Importantly, Cathcart made these contributions during a tipping point when the purchase of the territories brought changes in approaches to land management and the movements of people.[41] Throughout his travels, Cathcart relished the opportunity to continue the style of his Barbary captivity journals and proffer his informed opinions on myriad fields of science and policy. Subjects that caught his attention ranged from the New Orleans system of funding welfare, through taxation on gambling, to observations of slavery that triggered lengthy explanations of his support for the colonization movement (transporting American slaves to Africa rather than allowing them to remain free in the United States).[42] The brief company of a pet monkey on his boat even provided an opportunity to correct the scientific record, noting that the monkey's spontaneous leap into the Mississippi River "proves that the Ape species have not so great an antipathy to the water as is generally imagined."[43]

The environmental and social histories of the Mississippi Valley ebbed and flowed according to the currents of the empire that controlled the region at a given moment. In the decades before the Louisiana Purchase, different parts of the region passed between the control of Native Americans and British, Spanish, and French governments. The Louisiana Purchase in 1803 brought the whole region, for the first time, under the power of a single, expanding North American empire.

By the time of the Louisiana Purchase, the population of the area was only starting to rebound, having halved during the eighteenth century to a low of just fifty thousand after waves of disease, war, and malnutrition.[44] The relatively modest land management strategies of the French colonial era helped to slowly transition the once variable and lush flood plains into dry farmland. King Cotton now thrived under American care on the same lands where rice once thrived for the French.[45] This transition brought a cycle of constructing more levees, which enabled more plantations tended by ever-more slaves who supplied the labor for more levees and caused ever-more destructive floods, forever transforming the region's ecology and demographics.[46]

Cathcart and his surveying party repeatedly stumbled into cross-cultural disputes that inevitably accompany such transitions. Chief among them was the customary belief in the region that timber belonged not to individuals or governments but to whoever harvested it.[47] Louisiana towns were literally built on this tradition of logging. After the Louisiana Purchase, a toxic distrust of the federal government sprouted among the illegal loggers as the US government began to exert control over the region and sought to use these natural resources as a source of revenue. The same loggers who had lived off ill-gotten cedar, oak, and cypress for generations were now threatened with $1,000 fines and a year in jail for logging government land.[48] They defended this tradition with violence and intimidation and were only discouraged once General Andrew Jackson and the US Army were called in.[49] Cathcart waded uneasily into this muggy climate of illegal logging and enduring tensions about whether squatters' land claims would be maintained under the Louisiana Purchase. After finding a prize ridge of live oak on private property, Cathcart was convinced that the landowners would freely give the trees to anyone willing to clear the land—but that if the US government were to benefit, the price would suddenly become exorbitant, "for patriotism is a plant which does not grow in this climate & Uncle Sam is consider'd fair game."[50]

Rather than feeling frustrated, Cathcart should have felt at home amid this environment of contested loyalties and identities. Now, however, his familiar roles were reversed. No longer a petitioner, Cathcart now served as an agent of government, and he railed against those who feigned multiple allegiances in the service of self-interest—just as he had done throughout his life. As an agent of the federal government, Cathcart found that his party was "view'd by every class of people [as spies] with a very jealous eye, upon a supposition that we have been sent here on purpose to collect information for the government."[51] Rather than simply shunning the presumed spies in his surveying party, the locals launched an active campaign of disinformation and cunningly conspired to "place every obstacle in the way of our procuring land carriages, provisions & every other [necessity], & their information is so contradictory, & in almost every instance palpably false, that it needs but little penetration to perceive, that it is studied on purpose to deceive."[52] In the only study to explore this later period of Cathcart's life, literature scholar Jacob Rama Berman argues that to Cathcart this environment "look[ed] a lot like Barbary," with its "impenetrability, chaos, disorder, and heterogeneity."[53] Cathcart himself never drew the parallel between Louisiana and Barbary that Berman stresses. Nevertheless, there is certainly a parallel between the negotiable allegiances of Cathcart and Louisiana's inhabitants. As late as the 1820s in the unpoliced Louisiana Territories, Cathcart found "bands of Pirates" who roamed the bayous and thwarted Louisiana's assimilation into the greater commercial and political nation.[54] Without a hint of irony, Cathcart was particularly offended that these pirates "wear any flag that suits them, but denominate themselves Patriots."[55] This accusation of the fair-weather patriot describes no one better than Cathcart, who draped himself in both the colonial and British flags during the Revolution, and then again during captivity.

Added to the region's motley crew of land pirates and pliable identities were the "medly of foreigners." Cathcart found riverside villages of "mongrel Indian, French, and Negro," and aboard his steamship up the Mississippi River were "hybrids with their gibberish—French Spanish Italian Congo & English mixed."[56] The recent immigrants included a French and an Irish family. Cathcart characterized the French family as possessing "true French levity . . . & endeavour'd to be, or at least to seem happy," and he said the "melancholy" Irish family "seem'd to expect to find an asylum in these wilds . . . & look'd as if they had seen better days."[57] Rather than migrating to America for unique commercial opportunities or to take advantage of religious or political liberties, Cathcart thought "the whole tenor of their conduct, seem'd to say . . . I must work for my living, & whether I work in France, Brabant, or Louisiana, provided I get enough to eat & drink, it is very immaterial!"[58] According to Berman, the multicultural and multilinguistic Louisiana Territories were an assault on Cathcart's image of a culturally homogenous America.[59] True, Cathcart was quick to indict the few multicultural and multilingual thieves and squatters who impeded his work. Yet he expressed (admittedly, restrained) affection for the law-abiding immigrants who simply aspired to begin anew in the Louisiana Territories and had more immediate concerns than displaying their embrace of US identity as soon as they touched dry land, or in this case, muddy bayous.

Hoping to quickly transform his consular career into wealth and influence within the United States, Cathcart soon grew despondent when his ill-informed contribution to domestic viniculture was embarrassingly syndicated by newspapers throughout the nation, but his otherwise excellent survey report was buried.[60] Doubling down on his perceived failures since returning to the United States, Cathcart spent six years unsuccessfully petitioning America's leading political figures for a job that suited his experience and sacrifices. Yet he was forced to settle for a position as a bureaucrat in the Treasury Department until his death in 1843.[61] He did not quietly suffer the indignity of failing to secure more lucrative or glamorous employment to support his ten children, "notwithstanding that I am master of the French, Spanish, Portuguese, & Italian languages," or of having likewise failed to extract decades-old reimbursements from the federal government, which he planned to use to build a palatial homestead in Indiana and birth a political dynasty.[62] Fuming to his chosen heir, Charles Cathcart, from his twilight years in "the city of deception," Washington, DC, the elder Cathcart lamented that his final decades in the Treasury Department merely served "to promote the interests of the mushrooms of the present day, men without talent, without honor, without patriotism, without honesty or any of the virtues that dignifies the human heart & who like incubi hang on the body politic, slaves, vile slaves, ready to make a tyrant for unholy curse, saddled & bridled waiting at the stable door of the treasury for a Dictator to mount them & spur them on to any thing however base that would promote their own interest."[63]

During the Jacksonian era, Cathcart felt patriotism had become dramatically diluted and manipulated since the supposed purity of the Revolutionary era. By 1833, he wrote that "it has degenerated to mere pretext to promote personal interest, it is merely a war of the In's and Out's."[64] His decades of service beyond American shores immediately after the Revolution made for quite a shock when Cathcart returned to find a radically different America with a whole class of newly rich domestic industries nurtured through high tariffs and a national bank to build and bind the nation through finance.[65] And none of these developments worked to benefit Cathcart or his family. They were now squarely amongst the "Out's."

Redirecting his bitterness, Cathcart nurtured in his children the same Machiavellianism that he saw in contemporary politics and which he had excelled at during his station-climbing captivity in Algiers. Beyond surveying the Louisiana Territories, Cathcart's contributions to settling the West extended, by proxy, through his children. Cathcart forcefully urged his four eldest sons, Charles, James, Henry, and John, to all move to the Indiana frontier. Once settled on a farm on the outskirts of the small town of La Porte, about seventy miles from Chicago, Cathcart senior sent them correspondence with such frequency and tenor as to verge on harassment.[66] He implored Charles to seek election as a congressman in the growing state, noting that "you no doubt would gain honor but lose money by being elected," and advised that to mitigate financial losses he should "in the mean time acquire property which is power!"[67]

From his vantage point in the Treasury Department, Cathcart senior funneled information to Charles about likely policy developments "on nullification, tariff, land arrangements & [the national] bank" that would form the agenda in the next sessions of Congress. The foreknowledge, he told his son, will "enable you to steer your political course accordingly."[68] Within a year of arriving in La Porte, Charles's forays into local land speculation made him one of the wealthiest men of the county and secured him the resources to realize his father's dreams of building a family compound dubbed "Cathcart's retreat."[69]

Beyond passing along publicly available information, supplemented with his own insider Washington knowledge, Cathcart also directly speculated on land. He supplied Charles with a semisecret map from the Treasury Department in early 1836 that outlined a proposed railroad line from Michigan City, Indiana, near La Porte, to Maumee Bay on Lake Erie. Cathcart advised Charles to buy land along the route to sell later at an exorbitant profit.[70] Months later his keen eye on fiscal policy and a looming government surplus, which was distributed among the states according to population, and likely to be spent on infrastructure, led Cathcart to send Charles $6,000 to buy more land along the Michigan City to Maumme Bay route.[71]

Since the 1770s, land speculators and squatters had been pandemic on the frontier, guided only by individual initiative and largely ignoring central governments' attempts to restrain their activities.[72] These settlers clashed with Native Americans for land and with their own imperial governments over land policies, ultimately influencing settlement policy among Revolutionary leaders who shared those two common enemies and were eager to secure support on the untamed frontier.[73] Just one year after the Revolution, when the "rage for privateering" subsided, George Washington found a new "rage for speculating" in the Ohio Valley, where, in his words, "men in these times, talk with as much facility of fifty, a hundred, and even 500,000 acres as a Gentleman formerly would do of 1000 acres."[74]

Rather than greedy villains and counter-revolutionaries, American land speculators during the earliest years of the republic were invaluable in funding critical infrastructure that ultimately helped settle the frontier.[75] Little had changed by the time the Cathcarts sank their financial teeth into Indiana. Land purchases on the frontier certainly had a role in funding new infrastructure, but describing the relationship between speculators and the government as a "public-private partnership," as historian Michael Blaakman does, inaccurately implies a modest level of benevolence and shared interest in the successful outcome of a given infrastructure project. Instead, the speculator's sole interest was to find a greater fool (whether the government or a private citizen) to buy their land at the greatest possible profit in the shortest possible time. Whereas the government's interest was building roads, canals, and rail for the long-term welfare of the region. These goals are not mutually exclusive. Neither, however, are they entirely collaborative or aligned.

The Jacksonian era was awash with and depended upon speculators for the same reasons as the early republic.[76] In the later period, as in the earlier one, settlers and squatters on the frontier speculated in small neighboring parcels while large outfits traded in thousands of acres at a time. The only difference was one of scale. In 1835, however, these two competing David and Goliath types of speculators came to a head in Cathcart's Indiana when Native Americans in reservations around La Porte sold large swathes of their land for a pittance to unscrupulous large-scale speculators from outside the region.[77] More than merely missing out on a good deal, pioneers who squatted on these lands were convinced they had legitimate claims and hoped to one day sell their stakes during a land boom. Sensing a political opportunity to ingratiate himself with the community, Charles Cathcart threw his support behind the squatters and ventured to Washington to meet President Jackson, who immediately agreed to nullify sales of lands on which settlers had made internal improvements.[78] Riding on this victory, Charles was elected to the Indiana state senate, then the US House of Representatives and the Senate, achieving heights, peddling influence, and shaping national discourse in ways that his father often dreamed of for himself.[79] Cathcart senior's final letter to his son was typical, fuming at unrealized potential and hinting at the overdue compensation which he felt entitled to after finally setting allegiances on American shores: "I am verging on 77 years of age, have spent a very eventful life, brought up & educated as well as I was able eleven children, born in three quarters of the globe whilst I was faithfully serving an ungrateful country."[80]

Just as earlier generations took to sea to see the world and prove their worth, they were soon compelled to go west, where the absence of luxury cultivated masculine resilience. Riley was part of the advance party for that coming influx. This was still a good many years from Horace Greely's suggestion that America's young men move west. And many more years before the terrestrial frontier became home to tired tributes to masculinity by younger, coddled, and untested men from the cities who had something to prove.[81] Like O'Brien and Cathcart, Riley leveraged his somewhat greater fame from captivity into a brief career in local politics and then to exploit the emerging opportunities on the western frontier. His post-captivity years intersected with the territorial, commercial and sensitive political issues of the time far more dramatically than they did for Cathcart or O'Brien. Riley's post-captivity career wedded the waters of the Erie Canal, global maritime commerce, western settlement, the Village Enlightenment, and slavery. Yet the old salt could not shake the pull of the sea. Returning to maritime trade at the ancient seafaring age of 51, he negotiated the tides of good and bad fortune until dying at sea twelve years later.

Capitalizing on his triumphant return from captivity and the recent publication of his *Narrative*, Riley was the toast of Washington, DC, welcomed into the homes of socialites and employed for three congressional sessions by James Simpson, the US consul at Tangier, to lobby for reimbursements and a substantial salary increase.[82] Hoping to restore his health after the physical trials of captivity, Riley then embarked on a four-thousand-mile tour of the western states, venturing down the Ohio River from Pittsburgh to Kentucky, where he was impressed with the speed with which settlers had tamed the land "into fruitful fields; and, as if by magic, had raised up towns and cities."[83] On horseback he trekked through Ohio, Indiana, Illinois, and New York, describing the Great Lakes as the "Mediterranean of the interior of America."[84] Surprisingly,

Riley claims that this unconventional and arduous approach to physical therapy considerably improved his health. Based on this taste of the frontier he successfully lobbied the federal government to make him surveyor of far northwest Ohio lands acquired through treaty just a year earlier.[85]

Riley put down roots on the Ohio frontier in mid-1819, soon buying land in the same northwestern part of the state he surveyed. He promptly moved his family into a rustic log cabin and plotted the town of Willshire, named for the British consul who ransomed him from captivity just four years earlier.[86] In this town, Riley, echoing Cathcart, sought to "establish my children in a new country where with proper industry and energy and good conduct they might rise with the country."[87] This "rise" in what Riley saw as a "new country" in the West was facilitated by a growing population, agricultural development, and navigable rivers, which, after continued investment in canal infrastructure, Riley anticipated soon becoming arteries connecting the fertile interior to the cities of the Atlantic coast.[88]

It was only after Riley retreated from the West that this vision, typified by the Erie Canal, transformed frontier towns into cities and farms into agricultural powerhouses. Opened in 1825, the canal saw so much traffic that its entire debt for construction was repaid in just twelve years, and as late as the 1850s, up to thirteen times as much freight was transported along the canal as all the railways in New York. The canal contributed to a trebling of US economic output and to the trebling of Ohio's population in the first twenty-five years of its operation.[89] Riley's vision for Ohio was soon realized, but the footloose sailor did not stay put long enough to fully benefit from the transformation.

Despite already proving his mettle through trials in Morocco, Riley's accounts of his years settling the Ohio frontier are littered with similar fantastical "miracles" that critics found in his *Narrative*. Less than a decade after bounding to prominence through newspaper accounts of captivity and his published *Narrative*, the public now eagerly followed his move westward. Newspapers editorialized that Riley was "still struggling with difficulties, and laboring to establish his future comfort," and through syndicated columns they traced everything from his roadside robbery at the hands of Irish-born "land pirates" to his "bountiful contribution to the fund of marvelous" by allegedly trekking the frontier with about one hundred pounds of live rattlesnakes clenching to his boots.[90]

Though Riley achieved his lofty goals of building a town and taming the wild "forests [which] bow before the axe of the redeemed Captive," his frontier experience was far more rugged, financially ruinous, and debilitating to his health than the moderate experiences of O'Brien and Cathcart.[91] During the Riley family's first winter on the frontier, wolves and other dangers "frightened sleep from my wife and children for a season."[92] In their first summer, the whole family was struck with "bilious and remittent fevers," and each summer the fevers returned, lasting until October, at which point "dysenteries, cramps, and chronic pains would taper off the fevers, so that I was not able to attend much to my business until in February or March, and then not with my usual vigor."[93] The whole family shared in these recurring illnesses that kept them grounded for the entirety of every summer, autumn, and winter they spent on the frontier. In spite of this ordeal, Riley still confessed, "the settlers were generally more miserable, if possible, than ourselves; sick, and destitute, not only of the comforts, but even of the necessaries of life."[94] The situation for settlers did not improve over the decades, with forty of Willshire's seventy-five residents dying of cholera in 1854.[95]

Like the Cathcarts in Indiana, though without a hint of their self-interest, Riley parlayed his landed influence into a brief political career, taking a seat in the Ohio state legislature in late 1823. For just one term he represented a community that is now made up of fourteen counties in northern Ohio. Rather than advancing the causes of education and internal improvements that he campaigned on, his failings in political communication inadvertently sank a special appropriation for Ohio University. Likewise, canal construction bills that Riley favored were shelved after the figures he promoted were shown to be so wildly inaccurate that one legislator accused Riley of "an intention to mislead, or mental derangement."[96]

For all his failings as a policy wonk and political campaigner, it was an impassioned commitment to antislavery advocacy that drew him to politics, drove him in the legislature, and inspired him to continue work for the American Colonization Society until his death. As early as 1819, Riley began living up to the concluding pledge of his *Narrative*—to invigorate popular antislavery sentiment and legislate for an end to US slavery at a politically achievable pace.[97] Though most Ohioans at the time were not interested in the slavery debate, communities of Quakers in the east of the state and Presbyterians to the south made Riley's voice one in a small chorus.[98] While still surveying the frontier, and caught up in the national whirlwind surrounding whether to admit Missouri as a slave state, Riley found time to write a passionate letter to Governor Ethan Allen Brown pleading with him to use his influence over the state legislature and Ohio's congressional delegation to reject the admission of another slave state.[99] Drawing on his own captivity and conversations with settlers in Ohio, Riley chastised Americans and Christians for their hypocrisy, detailing the "demon like butchery" that slaves in the United States endured. He sketched a chilling image for Governor Brown of how, "When the subject of slavery is brought forward—every nerve & sinew about my frame is strangely affected, the blood thrills quickly through my heart to the extremities, my former sufferings among barbarians, rushes across my mind like a torrent." He went on to say,

"I thank my God I am in a Christian Land—where all enjoy freedom & religious toleration. In the midst of these gratifying reflections I am suddenly transported to the Banks of the Mississippi where I behold hundreds of Black Slaves—who have been snatched & torn from their native country by CHRISTIAN CUPIDITY & where they are doomed with their posterity to perpetual slavery."[100]

Riley's single term in the legislature also coincided with struggles for independence in Greece and throughout South America, struggles which US citizens viewed through myriad lenses, much as they viewed Riley's *Narrative* through the lens of their own interests. Antislavery advocates perceived the string of successive revolutions as South Americans overthrowing the Spanish colonial slave system. Most ordinary citizens saw the revolutions as the world beginning to follow the lead of the United States. Meanwhile, senior politicians like President James Monroe and Secretary of State John Quincy Adams saw the revolutions as an opportunity to capitalize on the recent US acquisition of the Louisiana Territories and the Floridas and to push towards a hemisphere-wide removal of European colonies.[101] In perhaps Riley's only savvy maneuver during his short political career, he combined these sentiments and held up the revolutions as a mirror for the United States, which had failed to live up to its own revolutionary ideals and was now being surpassed by the neighboring independence movements that it had inspired.[102] In 1825, at the first Fourth of July celebration held in Willshire, Riley spoke of the South American revolutions as representing the "steady march [of] the principles contained in our Declaration of Independence in the New World." He regretted that the United States could not "lead the van in the cause of freedom and equality until our glorious Declaration shall be fulfilled, and we can with truth proclaim liberty throughout all the land to all the inhabitants thereof."[103]

Behind the unwavering rhetoric was Riley's equally unflappable commitment to the African colonization movement, the same policy solution that he championed in his *Narrative* and until his death over two decades later. Almost all of Riley's writings on slavery were intended for public consumption, so it is unclear whether his sustained support for the American Colonization Society really was (as he initially claimed in his *Narrative*) underpinned by a sincere belief that freed slaves allowed to remain in the United States would be unable to fend for themselves and inevitably trigger civil strife.[104] As a preferable alternative, Riley and the colonization movement argued that slaves should be purchased at market value and transported to Africa, where they would help "civilize" the local population and not threaten domestic US stability.[105]

In time, these pro-colonization arguments eroded as the movement lost ground to the abolitionists, who critiqued the colonization movement as a veiled continuation of the same prejudices and colonialism that were responsible for slavery in the first place. These abolitionists pointed to the movement's policy of mass deportation as evidence of its disinterest in the welfare of former slaves.[106] Now, sixteen years after first throwing his support behind the colonization movement in his *Narrative*, Riley stopped alluding to the inability of freed slaves to sustain themselves and ceased holding them responsible for potential ensuing unrest. He seems to acknowledge the critiques of the movement, and with tragic prescience, he pivoted the likely blame for post-abolition unrest towards "the lack of education of the white population," who would bring on "a servile war; which, if not prevented by this, [colonization,] or some other means, must at some future time deluge our country in blood—must end in a strife which cannot cease but by the total extermination of one or the other party."[107]

In search of better health and a new purpose in life, Riley pulled up stumps in 1826 for the alleged medicinal benefits of New York's sea air, soon convincing himself and his physician that a return to seafaring could only improve his health.[108] Following increasingly dangerous and disease-prone professions was a pattern for Riley, who treated his ailments from captivity with a grueling six years of touring and settling the West, and then treated his new frontier ailments by returning to one of the most dangerous professions of the era. About one-third of all sailors ended their sailing careers by dying at sea, and most of those deaths were by disease. So taking to sea as a cure for existing ailments was like dropping anchor in hope of picking up speed. Riley returned to sea at the age of 51. A sailor of that age was such a rarity that the seminal quantitative study of the preceding generation of American sailors does not even count those over the age of 49.[109]

With this unlikely return to sea, Riley, the Jack Tar ethnographer, again immersed himself in amateur study and commentary on fields already explored in his *Narrative*—notably, diplomacy, commerce, geography, governance in North Africa, and avoidable dangers in seafaring. He now built on these fields with further contributions to the Village Enlightenment, but they were published piecemeal rather than in a single popular narrative.[110] These new contributions included recommendations to government on restructuring the consular system, the commercial benefits of increased American naval presence in the Mediterranean, commentaries on medicine and the maladministration of healthcare, comparative lessons in the development of national infrastructure, and untapped commercial opportunities in North Africa.[111] Buying and captaining two ships of his own, Riley quickly progressed from short hops between New York and Norfolk to more extended trips to the Caribbean and New Orleans. Eventually his voyages stretched to Gibraltar, to rekindle a personal and trade relationship first sparked in his captivity, and even back to Mogadore, where an untapped market for oriental goods lay in wait for an adventurous merchant sailor and where Riley's friend and patron Consul Willshire served as a practiced local agent. Together they established this trade with North Africa in the 1830s, almost a decade before the first Ottoman merchant ship docked in New York and two decades before a fascination with consuming Ottoman culture gripped the United States, when gentlemen wore fezzes and installed oriental smoking rooms in their homes.[112]

Almost as soon as he returned to the sea, Riley again wrecked the ship he captained, this time off Florida en route to New Orleans. As before, he took the opportunity to document for public interest the dangers in navigating this passage and to write at great length about the parasitic local salvage operators who mercilessly charged for their services fully half the value of wrecked ships and their cargo. Upon refusing these "extortionate demands of the civilized inhabitants on the coast of Florida," Riley was unsuccessfully sued by those "ugly customers."[113] Later, based on his observations in Gibraltar, Riley felt qualified and compelled to write to the secretary of the navy that the United States has a commercial interest in a greater naval presence in the Mediterranean to secure access to trade.[114] Simply legislating policies that gave American merchants free access to the oceans were insufficient. Riley now expected the federal government to instruct its military to play an active role in facilitating private commerce. In a lengthy letter to the secretary of state that dripped with frustration, Riley advised reforms to the consular system to limit consulships to US citizens, who must remain stationed at their post and be given sufficient salaries to prevent them charging exorbitant fees on American merchant ships that pass through their port.[115]

Riley finally returned to Mogadore in 1832 at the staggering seafaring age of 55—this time escaping quietly after a tidy trade in local goods and a long-awaited reunion with Willshire.[116] Having established his reputation as an exotic trader, Riley was welcomed back to North African shores not as a destitute captive but as an influential foreign dignitary to be courted and shown the lands in style. Initial contacts at the ports of Algiers and Tangier blossomed from tentative trading prospects into a tour of over one thousand miles from Mogadore to Tangier to Algiers at the behest of local rulers. No longer running across the Sahara behind camel caravans and surviving on meals that often caused severe diarrhea, Riley was now the guest of local royalty and introduced to the most prominent political and trading houses across North Africa. As when a captive, Riley took this opportunity to thoroughly document the diverse architecture, governance, and ethnography along the one-thousand-mile trail, far surpassing his *Narrative* and the accounts of fellow American captives in sheer range of geography and comparative analysis.[117] In the words of his son, this knowledge was imparted "without pretensions to scholarship. . . . It is COMMON SENSE inditing its own ideas and impressions."[118] Riley's embrace of his scholarly limitations underpins his unique brand of "common sense" contributions to the Village Enlightenment which so effectively embedded in the popular imagination. Likewise, his embrace of life as a perennial frontiersmen, whether at sea, in North Africa, or in the American West, moderated his aspirations in upward mobility so that he could enjoy greater successes than O'Brien without Cathcart's bitterness of unfulfilled dreams.

When Riley died at sea at the age of 62, his memorials far exceeded both the number and detail of those for O'Brien and Cathcart.[119] Still, Riley's memorials paid little tribute to his role as a case study in successful American self-making and agile reinvention—as a man who found in disaster and poor health new opportunities for pivoting careers and contributing to the body of human knowledge in an array of fields. Instead, the obituaries framed his life through the narrow lens of his popular *Narrative* and as an ongoing romantic tragedy. Even his holding of "nearly the entire monopoly" of the US–North African trade was implied as a shackle that bound him to his former captivity. Rather than being remembered for successfully raising a family, passionately campaigning against slavery, and building frontier communities under unremitting hardship, Riley was portrayed by newspaper editors as a figure of tragedy whose "robust frame seemed to have given away to disease, and he finally sank under it, removed from his family and friends."[120] In contrast, Riley's son only mentioned North Africa in passing when remembering his father's "strange and eventful" career. Instead, and more faithfully, his son chose to remember that "he had mingled in every grade of human society: from the most exalted ranks in Christendom to the extreme limits of barbarism. He had mingled and conversed, in their native tongue, with the Red Men of an American wilderness; and had been kindly greeted by Presidents of the United States and heads of the Executive Departments."[121]

From O'Brien's, Cathcart's, and Riley's prominent earlier years, when their exploits were widely syndicated in US newspapers, the trio faded into near-anonymity once they returned to the United States. The source of their brief brush with fame, falling victim to Barbary captors, was not of their making. What the public, diplomats, and politicians saw as the trio's invaluable commentaries from captivity were, in fact, self-interested responses to circumstances forced upon them. Once free and at "home" in the United States, where two of the trio had actually spent a minority of their lives, they hoped to build on their unsought notoriety, this time on their own terms. Though free, they nevertheless lacked the self-determination and clout to attain their chosen professions. Again, they turned to the federal and state governments for assistance. Out of necessity they each became amateur Renaissance men, with varying degrees of success and ambition, always responding to circumstances rather than entirely charting the course of their own lives.

O'Brien took to this perpetual adaptation with resigned acceptance and little ambition, and consequently seemed entirely satisfied with his lot in life. Riley was more ambitious and self-promoting, though also accepting of his own limitations and job rejections. He never mentioned grudges over lost job opportunities, nor complained at repeatedly losing fortunes through global financial crises or ruinous government policies. He even miraculously spun his international tour for healthcare into commercial opportunities for himself and (unsolicited) educational opportunities for others. Perhaps because his exploits were so well known, Riley was the only one of the trio not to cite his experience in North Africa as a qualification for future employment.

Cathcart, however, was all too happy to blame others for his perceived professional failings. Clouded by his spectacular ambitions, Cathcart failed to see how his unique ability to make enemies at first contact contributed to his fate. It is ironic that Cathcart's surname means "a river running through a narrow channel," stubbornly finding a route through seemingly immovable obstacles.[122] In his own way, he lived up to this surname, navigating political and economic obstacles to move upwards, not merely sideways. Yet of the trio, Cathcart was the least content with his circumstances, fuming about his alleged persecution until the last time his pen touched paper. Though none of these sailor-frontiersmen achieved the typical hallmarks of the self-made man, boasting great wealth and infamy that outlived them, each was consoled that their children built upon their fathers' accomplishments to achieve greater security and opportunity as wealthy politicians, surveyors, and wives to community leaders.

Opportunities of Empire

I was buoyant and, like a tennis ball, the harder I fell the higher I bounced.

James Cathcart, June 17, 1833

In celebration of the Louisiana Purchase, an Anti-Federalist amateur poet penned, in just seven rousing stanzas, a sweeping tribute to America's unique global advantages spanning the nation's past, present, and future. At the time of writing, decades since the Revolution and in the thick of America's 1801–1805 war with distant Tripoli, the author nevertheless saw "the harsh menace of war us no longer assailing . . . exempted from terror, and alarms of invasion."[1] He gazed toward new frontiers ripe for exploitation. In the United States, no game laws "deprive us the produce of our woods or of streams," the Louisiana Territories were "a new link of the Union," and American spirit would "erect in her wild woods a temple." Looking east to the high seas "our highest ambition is freedom and trade / On the ocean's highway we'll ne'er yield to monopoly." The jubilant author bounces through these varied arenas of nation building as if he were James Cathcart's metaphorical tennis ball. Like most patriotic prose, this poem—titled "National Prosperity"—ignores the hardships and hard-learned lessons from when the ball drops. Cathcart, Richard O'Brien, and James Riley remade themselves and the nation in each arena the poet canvasses. But it is their celebrated hardships en route, as much as their triumphs, that facilitated self-making and opportunities for advancement.

More than merely embodying the convergence of world events, passively bobbing in a sea of tidal forces, O'Brien, Cathcart, and Riley each navigated new opportunities as the United States grew from a collection of colonies into a global power. Their lives chart the opportunities of a growing empire, from its birth in the Revolution, through its adolescence during the early republic and its self-discovery through global trade and westward expansion, to the eve of the Civil War, the nation's rite of passage into adulthood. Through these opportunities the trio of sailors became active agents in shaping how America perceived the world, how the world perceived America, and also, how Americans perceived themselves.

As the American colonies transitioned into a republic, her sailors built on their experiences of carrying multiple logbooks and the flags of various nations to facilitate deceit and improve their odds of safely traversing the seas. So too, when imprisoned, they raised the flag of greatest convenience. During the Revolution, Cathcart tacked from serving in the Continental Navy to the Royal Navy, and, like most sailors of the era, both he and O'Brien likely took to sea for fortune rather than patriotism. As a captive, Cathcart repeatedly drifted between allegiances to Britain, Algiers, and the United States, and both his and O'Brien's diaries and correspondence catalogue shrewd interventions into emerging American nationalism, winning the favor of diplomats and inspiring charity drives throughout the United States. Far from these pliable loyalties and financial priorities being unique to sailors, recent scholarship stresses these traits were equally prevalent among land-bound citizens of the Revolutionary era.[2]

From their captivities, O'Brien, Cathcart, and Riley each made unique lay contributions to the fields of ethnography, geography, and comparative politics. In doing so, they joined a so-called Village Enlightenment of non-elite citizens whose personal experiences complemented and contested the claims of professional researchers and cultural elites. For the trio, as captives or as consuls, this meant nudging the course of US government policy toward, and public awareness of, the Orient. Back on the terrestrial frontier, the sailors, who in fact spent very little of their lives at sea, exploited their past ordeals to pursue available opportunities that were increasingly on the western frontier.

During the trio's final years on the terrestrial frontier, Alexis de Tocqueville toured the same lands, where he found American sailors a fitting metaphor for broader national character traits and approaches to commerce. Tocqueville saw sailors as exemplars of Americans', even landlubbers', instinctive embrace of high-risk, high-reward commercial ventures. His assessment reads as if it's the résumé of O'Brien, Cathcart, or Riley:

> An American will build a house in which to pass his old age and sell it before the roof is on; he will plant a garden and rent it just as the trees are coming into bearing; he will clear a field and leave others to reap the harvest; he will take up a profession and leave it, settle in one place and soon go off elsewhere with his changing desires. If his private business allows him a moment's relaxation, he will plunge at once into the whirlpool of politics. Then, if at the end of a year crammed with work he has a little spare leisure, his restless curiosity goes with him traveling up and down the vast territories of the United States. Thus he will travel five hundred miles in a few days as a distraction from his happiness.[3]

Despite his observations of Americans' perennial restlessness both on land and on sea, Tocqueville's actual discussion of American sailors and maritime commerce in *Democracy in America* is fleeting. The book is appropriately lauded for its breadth and insights, but it is surprising that this seminal text fell victim to the ongoing problem in scholarship that sailors are treated as independent of the land.[4]

The collective biographical approach of this book hopefully goes some way in addressing this historiographical lacuna and revealing connections that have been missed due to scholarly silos isolating specific regions, themes, and periods from one another. Previous scholarship that touched on O'Brien, Cathcart, or Riley, and the various macro developments that intersected with their lives, has done so in isolation of what came before and after. Much is lost, both on a micro and macro scale, in this unnatural fragmentation of individuals' lives. For individual biographical subjects, this means we are denied an accurate sense of the deep-rooted motives, concerns, and skills that inspire their actions. And on a grander scale, it means we are less informed of the factors truly inspiring social, political, and commercial movements. For example, if O'Brien's, Cathcart's, and Riley's lives were examined piecemeal, with an eye to either their maritime service, consular years, or lives on the frontier, they would merely appear as down-on-their-luck patriots who held a few very different careers over the course of their lives. Yet by examining their *whole* lives, it's possible to see that each man clearly adapted his narrow skill set to a wide array of spheres and employment sectors: maritime networks were adapted into advocacy networks, the skills of a sailor were adapted into skills as a surveyor, and so on.

This approach also reveals an underappreciated lifelong capacity of ordinary individuals to maneuver through and contribute to American development while simultaneously advancing their own interests. Even the most astute maritime scholars can underestimate the true agency of these individuals by focusing on their time at sea.[5] Although American sailors were often victims of forces beyond their control, they were far from powerless. They were so practiced in managing the perception of powerlessness that each, in his own way, turned it into an asset.

Epilogue

One important field that even this wide-ranging book could not accommodate is the centuries-long evolving role of Barbary captivity narratives in American political and cultural discourse. By the time the first US citizen was captured in North Africa, the fictional and nonfictional narratives of white captives in Barbary and the Ottoman Empire were already a centuries-old literary genre that had personally touched early American colonists. As early as 1575, Miguel de Cervantes, author of *Don Quixote*, and his brother Rodrigo were held captive in Algiers. Rodrigo was ransomed by the Cervantes family but Miguel remained a captive for five years, attempting escape four times. His captivity in Algiers inspired poems, two plays, and a lengthy story of captivity in *Don Quixote*.[1] Before the colonial Virginian leader John Smith's much-mythologized travels with Pocahontas, he was a veteran of battles against the Ottoman Empire and was held captive in Tartary (contemporary North Asia) before he killed his captor and escaped.[2] Smith's coat of arms includes three Turks' heads as a tribute to his years battling the Ottomans. When he reached Massachusetts in 1614, he named the colony's northern peninsula Tragabigzanda (since renamed Cape Ann) in honor of his initial captor in Constantinople, whom he respected, and he also named a trio of islands off the same peninsula the Three Turks' Heads (since renamed the Straitsmouth, Thacher, and Milk Islands).[3] In Daniel Defoe's 1719 novel, Robinson Crusoe was captured by a "Turkish rover of

Sallee" while sailing between the Canary Islands and the African coast. Defoe depicted Crusoe as being instantly reduced "from a merchant into a miserable slave" until his escape two years later.[4]

Regrettably, the first nonfiction Barbary captivity narratives penned by colonial Americans (by Abraham Browne in 1655 and Joshua Gee in 1687) collected dust for centuries before they were eventually published. Thankfully, other North Americans held in Barbary soon had better luck in regularly publishing their nonfictional accounts, accompanied by novels, plays, and poetry. Most of these were republished over decades and syndicated throughout the country.[5] It was these fictional novels and plays, more so than the nonfiction narratives, that explicitly engaged with the politics of the moment, using American captivity in North Africa as a mirror to more palatably make forceful and controversial commentaries on American masculinity, identity, slavery, and religion. Susannah Rowson's 1794 play, *Slaves in Algiers*, for example, centered on stoic female captives and, in doing so, advocated for women's rights within the United States. Just a few years later, Royall Tyler's 1797 novel, *The Algerine Captive*, used a captive and captor's amicable debates on comparative religion to comprehensively deconstruct Americans' blind faith in monotheistic Christianity.[6]

The inverse experience of slavery—white slaves to African masters—made Barbary captives into powerful and unobjectionable instruments for authors, playwrights, and politicians attempting to foster antislavery sentiment in the public sphere.[7] Benjamin Franklin's last published work during his lifetime was a 1790 newspaper article that exploited the nation's fixation on Barbary captives to expertly satirize the proslavery arguments of Georgia's congressman James Jackson. Under the penname Historicus, Franklin feigned approval of Jackson's arguments for the continuation of African American slavery and noted that his logic was identical to that used by a fictional ruler of Algiers to justify the enslavement of white American Christians.[8]

Fictional and nonfictional Barbary narratives therefore served as important mediums for gestation of the slave narrative literary genre, which grew into the antebellum African American slave narrative. American captives provided an opportunity for preachers to frame slavery as an important moral issue, which helped lay the ideological groundwork for the popular antislavery movement that led to the Civil War.[9] Between 1784 and 1815, newspapers, novelists, and captives were the primary sources of information about the morally repugnant condition of white slavery. Those narratives were then picked up by churches and theatres, which provided ordinary citizens with the opportunity to financially assist in the redemption effort.[10] The concepts, strategies, and audiences that championed this early antislavery discourse continued to expand and evolve from the late eighteenth century to the mid-nineteenth century. Over time, the comparative slavery subtext and attacks on the "peculiar institution" became more explicit and grew into full-frontal attacks with the onset of the Civil War.

In Boston almost 60 years after Franklin's final piece of scorching satire, the antislavery firebrand Charles Sumner picked up the torch and labeled the American antebellum slave states the "Barbary States of America." Sumner issued a terrifying warning: "Hitherto we have been oppressors; nay, murderers! for many a negro has died by the whip of his master, and many have lived when death would have been preferable. Surely, the curse of God and the reproach of man is against us. Worse than the seven plagues of Egypt will befall us. If Algiers shall be punished sevenfold, truly America seventy and sevenfold."[11] Then, worse than a warning, Sumner accused enlightened Americans of falling behind the abolitionist trend of barbaric North Africa, where "the Barbary States of Africa are changed to Abolitionists; from the untutored ruler of Morocco comes the declaration of his desire, stamped in the formal terms of a treaty, that the very name of Slavery may perish from the minds of men; and only recently from the Bey of Tunis has proceeded that noble act by which, 'for the glory of God, and to distinguish man from the brute creation,'—I quote his own words—he decreed its total abolition throughout his dominions. Let Christian America be taught by these despised Mahometans."[12] The antislavery movement did well in co-opting American-Barbary captivity, but the captives themselves deserve little credit. As a group, they were not especially prone to antislavery activism during their captivity or after they were freed. The credit belongs to antislavery activists, who were much like the captive sailors they drew on—each group unapologetically manipulated circumstances or material at hand to advance their cause.

Introduction · Victims of American Independence?

1. *Newburyport Herald* (Newburyport, MA), December 21, 1824, vol. 28, no. 76, p. 1; *Salem Gazette* (Salem, MA), December 24, 1824, vol. 2, no. 102, p. 2.

2. Robert C. Davis, *Christian Slaves, Muslim Masters: White Slavery in the Mediterranean, the Barbary Coast, and Italy, 1500–1800* (New York: Palgrave Macmillan, 2003), 31.

3. Lotfi Ben Rejeb, "'The general belief of the world': Barbary as Genre and Discourse in Mediterranean History," *European Review of History* 19, no. 1 (February 2012): 17; Fatima Maameri, "Ottoman Algeria in Western Diplomatic History with Particular Emphasis on Relations with the United States of America, 1776–1816" (PhD diss., University Mentouri, Constantine, 2008), ch. 1; Frank Lambert, *The Barbary Wars: American Independence in the Atlantic World* (New York: Hill and Wang, 2005), 31–34.

4. Lambert, *Barbary Wars*, 7–10.

5. Richard O'Brien to Thomas Jefferson, June 8, 1786, in Dudley W. Knox, ed., *Naval Documents Related to the United States Wars with the Barbary Powers* (Washington, DC: US Government Printing Office, 1939), I: 3.

6. John Adams and Thomas Jefferson to John Jay, March 28, 1786, in *The Diplomatic Correspondence of the United States of America* (Washington, DC: Blair & Roves, 1837), II: 341–343; Walter Lowrie and Matthew St. Clair Clarke, eds., *American State Papers: Documents, Legislative and Executive, of the Congress of the United States* (Washington, DC: Gales and Seaton, 1833), II: 18; Milton Cantor, "Joel Barlow's Mission to Algiers," *Historian* 25, no. 2 (February 1963): 191.

7. Davis, *Christian Slaves, Muslim Masters*, ch. 1; Robert C. Davis, "Counting European Slaves on the Barbary Coast," *Past and Present* 172 (August 2001): 118.

8. Christine E. Sears, *American Slaves and African Masters: Algiers and the Western Sahara, 1776–1820* (New York: Palgrave Macmillan, 2012); Christine E. Sears, "Slavery as Social Mobility? Western Slaves in Late-Eighteenth Century Algiers," in *Rough Waters: American Involvement with the Mediterranean in the Eighteenth and Nineteenth Centuries,* Research in Maritime History 44, ed. Silvia Marzagalli, James R. Sofka, and John McCusker (Liverpool, UK: Liverpool University Press, 2010); Lawrence A. Peskin, "The Lessons of Independence: How the Algerian Crisis Shaped Early-American History," *Diplomatic History* 28, no. 3 (June 2004); Lambert, *Barbary Wars*; James R. Sofka, "The Jeffersonian Idea of National Security: Commerce, the Atlantic Balance of Power, and the Barbary War, 1786–1805," *Diplomatic History* 21, no. 4 (Fall 1997); Martha Elena

Rojas, "'Insults Unpunished': Barbary Captives, American Slaves, and the Negotiation of Liberty," *Early American Studies* 1, no. 2 (Fall 2003); Paul Baepler, ed., *White Slaves, African Masters: An Anthology of American Barbary Captivity Narratives* (Chicago: University of Chicago Press, 1999); Hannah Farber, "Millions for Credit: Peace with Algiers and the Establishment of America's Commercial Reputation Overseas, 1795–96," *Journal of the Early Republic* 34, no. 2 (Summer 2014); William Ray, *Horrors of Slavery; or, The American Tars in Tripoli*, ed. Hester Blum (New Brunswick, NJ: Rutgers University Press, 2008); Richard B. Parker, *Uncle Sam in Barbary: A Diplomatic History* (Gainesville: University of Florida Press, 2004); Robert J. Allison, *The Crescent Obscured: The United States and the Muslim World, 1776–1815* (New York: Oxford University Press, 1995).

9. This approach draws on a growing body of scholarly biographical (and collective biographical) microhistories, including Gary Nash and Graham Russell Gao Hodges, *Friends of Liberty: A Tale of Three Patriots, Two Revolutions, and the Betrayal That Divided a Nation; Thomas Jefferson, Thaddeus Kosciuszko, and Agrippa Hull* (New York: Basic Books, 2008); Alfred F. Young, *The Shoemaker and the Tea Party: Memory and the American Revolution* (Boston: Beacon Press, 1999); Linda Colley, *The Ordeal of Elizabeth Marsh: A Woman in World History* (New York: Pantheon Books, 2007); Emma Rothschild, *The Inner Lives of Empires: An Eighteenth-Century History* (Princeton, NJ: Princeton University Press, 2011).

10. Myra Glenn, "Forging Manhood and Nationhood Together: American Sailors' Accounts of Their Exploits, Sufferings, and Resistance in the Antebellum United States," *American Nineteenth Century History* 8, no. 1 (2007): 28; Thomas Philbrick, *James Fenimore Cooper and the Development of American Sea Fiction* (Cambridge, MA: Harvard University Press, 1961), 49, 66.

11. Adam Smith, *An Inquiry into the Nature and Causes of the Wealth of Nations* (London: Alex, Murray & Co., 1872), 332.

12. Colley, *Ordeal of Elizabeth Marsh*, xix.

13. Colley, *Ordeal of Elizabeth Marsh*, 300.

14. Baepler, *White Slaves, African Masters*, 307.

15. James Riley to unknown, July 3, 1824, in "Founding of Willshire," *Northwest Ohio Quarterly* 16 (1944): 43.

16. David Jaffee, "The Village Enlightenment in New England, 1760–1820," *William and Mary Quarterly* 47, no. 3 (July 1990): 328.

17. Nathan Hatch quoted in Jaffee, "Village Enlightenment," 339.

18. Nathan Hatch quoted in Jaffee, "Village Enlightenment," 327.

19. Nathan Hatch quoted in Jaffee, "Village Enlightenment," 342.

20. Nathan O. Hatch, *The Democratization of American Christianity* (New Haven, CT: Yale University Press, 1989), 10–11, 27–30, 46.

Chapter 1 · Farmers, Privateers, and Prisoners of the Revolution

Epigraph. Peter E. Jones, "Grant Us Commission to Make Reprisals upon Any Enemies Shipping," *Rhode Island History* 34, no. 4 (November 1975): 106.

1. Barnabas Downs, *A Brief and Remarkable Narrative of the Life and Extreme Sufferings of Barnabas Downs, Junior* (Boston: E. Russell, 1786), 6.

2. Downs, *Brief and Remarkable Narrative*, 7.

3. Downs, *Brief and Remarkable Narrative*, 9.

4. Downs, *Brief and Remarkable Narrative*, 12.

5. Barnabas Downs quoted in Samuel J. Hough, ed., *Barnabas Downs: Shipwreck in Plymouth Harbour, December 1778* (Yarmouthport, MA: Parnassus Imprints, 1972), intro.

6. On the fraternal relationship between sailors on shore and community support for former sailors, see Margaret S. Creighton, "Fraternity in the American Forecastle, 1830–1870," *New England Quarterly* 63, no. 4 (December 1990).

7. Michael A. McDonnell, "War and Nationhood: Founding Myths and Historical Realities," in *Remembering the Revolution: Memory, History, and Nation Making from Independence to the Civil War*, ed. Michael A. McDonnell et al. (Amherst: University of Massachusetts Press, 2013), 24; John. A. Ruddiman, *Becoming Men of Some Consequence: Youth and Military Service in the Revolutionary War* (Charlottesville: University of Virginia Press, 2014), ch. 1 and 2.

8. Jesse Lemisch, "Listening to the 'Inarticulate': William Widger's Dream and the Loyalties of American Revolutionary Seamen in British Prisons," *Journal of Social History* 3, no. 1 (Autumn 1969): 14–16; Peter Linebaugh and Marcus Rediker, *The Many-Headed Hydra: Sailors, Slaves, Commoners, and the Hidden History of the Revolutionary Atlantic* (Boston: Beacon Press, 2000), 221–224, 229, 234–235.

9. Jesse Lemisch, *Jack Tar vs. John Bull: The Role of New York's Seamen in Precipitating the Revolution* (New York: Garland Publishing, 1997), 4.

10. Daniel Vickers and Vince Walsh, "Young Men and the Sea: The Sociology of Seafaring in Eighteenth-Century Salem, Massachusetts," *Social History* 24, no. 1 (January 1999): 26–28.

11. Richard O'Brien to James Cathcart, November 12, 1794, in James Cathcart, *Tripoli: First War with the United States, Inner History, and Letter Book* (LaPorte, IN: Herald Print, 1901), 141.

12. Case Files of Pension and Bounty-Land Warrant Applications Based on Revolutionary War Service, compiled ca. 1800–ca. 1912, documenting the period ca. 1775–ca. 1900, record group 15, pension number R7751, publication number M804, National Archives, Washington, DC, hereinafter cited as NADC; Mathew Irwin to George Washington, July 9, 1789, "Founders Online," accessed January 8, 2015, http://founders .archives.gov/documents/Washington/05-03-02-0079-0001.

13. Gardner Weld Allen, *Massachusetts Privateers of the Revolution* (Boston: Massachusetts Historical Society, 1927), 123, 133, 296.

14. James Cathcart to his sons, April 16, 1833, Papers of Charles William Cathcart, box 1, folder 1, p. 3, Michigan State University Archives, hereinafter cited as MSUA; James Cathcart, pension number: S 12413, Case Files of Pension and Bounty-Land Warrant Applications Based on Revolutionary War Service, compiled ca. 1800–ca. 1912, documenting the period ca. 1775–ca. 1900, M804, roll 0499, record group 15, NADC.

15. Vickers and Walsh, "Young Men and the Sea," 20–21.

16. Vickers and Walsh, "Young Men and the Sea," 19.

17. Jesse Lemisch, "Jack Tar in the Streets: Merchant Seamen in the Politics of Revolutionary America," *William and Mary Quarterly* 25, no. 3 (July 1968): 373.

18. Lemisch, "Jack Tar in the Streets," 373–374; Lemisch, *Jack Tar vs. John Bull*.

19. At this time about one third of the foreign-born sailors in New York were Irish. Lemisch, *Jack Tar vs. John Bull*, 5.

20. Vickers and Walsh, "Young Men and the Sea," 23.

21. Vickers and Walsh, "Young Men and the Sea," 24, 33; Daniel Vickers, *Farmers and Fishermen: Two Centuries of Work in Essex County, Massachusetts, 1630–1850* (Chapel Hill: University of North Carolina Press, 1994), 251–252.

22. James Riley, *An Authentic Narrative of the Loss of the American Brig* Commerce: *Wrecked on the Western Coast of Africa, in the Month of August, 1815* (New York: T. & W. Mercein, 1817), 3; Vickers, *Farmers and Fishermen*, 206.

23. Vickers, *Farmers and Fishermen*, 251–252; Riley, *Narrative*, 4.

24. Riley, *Narrative*, 5.

25. Andrew Sherburne, *Memoirs of Andrew Sherburne: A Pensioner of the Navy of the Revolution* (New York: Books for Libraries Press, 1970), 18.

26. Sherburne, *Memoirs*, 23.

27. Sherburne, *Memoirs*, 33.

28. US Continental Congress, "Extracts from the Journals of Congress Relative to the Capture and Condemnation of Prizes" (Philadelphia: John Dunlap, 1776), 44.

29. Benjamin Rush to Richard Henry Lee, December 21, 1776, in Peter Force, ed., *American Archives: A Documentary History of the United States of America* (Washington, DC: Government Printing Office, 1853), series 5, III: 1511–1512.

30. Abigail Adams to John Adams, September 29, 1776, Massachusetts Historical Society, accessed December 19, 2017, www.masshist.org/digitaladams/archive/doc?id =L17760929aa.

31. Francis D. Cogliano, " 'We All Hoisted the American Flag': National Identity among American Prisoners in Britain during the American Revolution," *Journal of American Studies* 32, no. 1 (April 1998): 20.

32. Michael J. Crawford, "The Privateering Debate in Revolutionary America," *Northern Mariner/le marin du nord* 21, no. 3 (July 2011): 221.

33. John A. McManemin, *Captains of the State Navies during the Revolution* (Ho-Ho-Kus, NJ: Ho-Ho-Kus Publishing Company, 1984), 70.

34. Congress, "Extracts from the Journals of Congress."

35. Case Files of Pension and Bounty-Land Warrant Applications Based on Revolutionary War Service, compiled ca. 1800–ca. 1912, documenting the period ca. 1775–ca. 1900, record group 15, pension number R7751, publication number M804, NADC; "Pension application of Richard O'Brien," R7751, f8 VA, accessed December 19, 2017, http://revwarapps.org/r7751.pdf.

36. Mathew Irwin to George Washington, July 9, 1789, "Founders Online," accessed December 19, 2017, http://founders.archives.gov/documents/Washington/05-03-02-0079 -0001.

37. Charles Henry Lincoln, *Naval Records of the American Revolution, 1775–1788* (Washington, DC: Government Printing Office, 1906), 258.

38. Willis John Abbot, *Naval History of the United States*, 2 vols. (New York: Peter Fenelon Collier, 1886), I: 153–154.

39. Dumas Malone, ed., *Dictionary of American Biography* (New York: Charles Scribners' Sons, 1934), XIII: 611–612.

40. Case Files of Pension and Bounty-Land Warrant Applications Based on Revolutionary War Service, compiled ca. 1800–ca. 1912, documenting the period ca. 1775–ca. 1900, record group 15, pension number R7751, publication number M804, NADC.

41. Cathcart to his sons, April 16, 1833, Papers of Charles William Cathcart, Box 1, Folder 1, p. 3, MSUA.

42. John A. McManemin, *Captains of the Continental Navy* (Ho-Ho-Kus, NJ: Ho-Ho-Kus Publishing Company, 1981), 122–123; McManemin, *Captains of the State Navies*, 71, 87.

43. McManemin, *Captains of the State Navies*, 87.

44. Emily Blanck, *Tyrannicide: Forging an American Law of Slavery in Revolutionary South Carolina and Massachusetts* (Athens: University of Georgia Press, 2014), 6.

45. Blanck, *Tyrannicide*, 96.

46. Blanck, *Tyrannicide*, 97–98.

47. Blanck, *Tyrannicide*, 103.

48. Benjamin Guerard to John Hancock, October 6, 1783, in Terry W. Lipscomb, ed., *The Letters of Pierce Butler, 1790–1794: Nation Building and Enterprise in the New American Republic* (Columbia: University of South Carolina Press, 2007), xxvii.

49. Blanck, *Tyrannicide*, 137.

50. Blanck, *Tyrannicide*, 144.

51. Cathcart to his sons, April 16, 1833, Papers of Charles William Cathcart, box 1, folder 1, p. 3, MSUA; Cathcart, pension number: S 12413, NADC M804, Revolutionary War Pension and Bounty-Land Warrant Application Files.

52. James L. Howard, *Seth Harding, Mariner: A Naval Picture of the Revolution* (New Haven, CT: Yale University Press, 1930), 100–103.

53. Nathan Perl-Rosenthal, *Citizen Sailors: Becoming American in the Age of Revolution* (Cambridge, MA: Harvard University Press, 2015), 70.

54. The Frigate *Confederacy* Papers, 1776–1786, collection 222, Historical Society of Pennsylvania, hereinafter cited as HSP.

55. Cathcart to his sons, April 16, 1833, Papers of Charles William Cathcart, box 1, folder 1, p. 3, MSUA; James Cathcart, *The Captives: Eleven Years a Prisoner in Algiers* (La Porte, IN: Herald Print, 1899), 28, 106.

56. William Hooper, Revolutionary War Pension and Bounty-Land Warrant Application Files, pension number: S. 18452, M804, NADC; Mary Allen, widow of Ambrose Allen, Revolutionary War Pension and Bounty-Land Warrant Application Files, pension number: W. 20577, M804, NADC; War Department Record of Cathcart's Revolutionary War Claim, approved March 13, 1833, Cathcart Family Papers, 1785–1962, box 3, New York Public Library, hereinafter cited as NYPL.

57. John A. McManemin, *Captains of the Privateers during the Revolutionary War* (Spring Lake, NJ: Ho-Ho-Kus Publishing Company, 1985), 252.

58. McManemin, *Captains of the State Navies*, 88.

59. Vickers and Walsh, "Young Men and the Sea," 27.

60. McManemin, *Captains of the State Navies*, 90.

61. McManemin, *Captains of the State Navies*, 90. The Preliminary Articles of Peace, signed on November 30, 1782, halted warfare within North America, but battles still raged at sea until the Treaty of Paris, signed on September 3, 1783. Thus, Cathcart's final imprisonment lasted less than a year.

62. Captain Harding to Governor Trumbull, June 8, 1782, in Louis F. Middlebrook, *History of Maritime Connecticut During the American Revolution, 1775–1783* (Salem, MA: Essex Institute, 1925), 51; Howard, *Seth Harding, Mariner*, 147–148.

63. Navy Board, Navy Pay Office, Ships' Pay Books (Series II), *Enterprize*, August 15, 1781–May 26, 1784, ADM 34/298, United Kingdom National Archives, hereinafter cited as UKNA; Navy Board, Navy Pay Office, Ships' Pay Books (Series II), *Leander*, January 1, 1781–April 30, 1784, ADM 34/449, UKNA.

64. *Rivington's Royal Gazette* (New York, NY), April 21, 1781, and "Private Journal of Capt. Joseph Hardy," in Howard, *Seth Harding, Mariner*, 146, 258.

65. Lemisch, "Listening to the 'Inarticulate,'" 7–9.

66. Paul A. Gilje, "Loyalty and Liberty: The Ambiguous Patriotism of Jack Tar in the American Revolution," *Pennsylvania History* 67, no. 2 (Spring 2000): 178.

67. Within that 12 percent of American-born defectors there is an underrepresentation of Americans born in New England, indicating a greater sense of patriotism and loyalty of sailors from this region. Cogliano, "'We All Hoisted the American Flag,'" 33–34. This flexible notion of loyalty was equally prevalent among civilians in colonial port towns, where ambiguous allegiances were essential to survival as towns drifted between colonial and British occupation. Donald F. Johnson, "Ambiguous Allegiances: Questioning Loyalties in Revolutionary Cities under British Military Rule," McNeil Center for Early American Studies Seminar Series, January 23, 2015, p. 2.

68. Lemisch, "Listening to the 'Inarticulate,'" 17–18; Gilje, "Loyalty and Liberty," 174.

69. Charles Herbert quoted in Cogliano, "'We All Hoisted the American Flag,'" 35–36.

70. John Green to Thomas Powell, September 15, 1781, and Green to J. Nesbitt & Co, September 13, 1781, "John Green Letter Book, 1781–1783," Captain John Green Papers, *1781–1801*, J. Welles Henderson Archives and Library of Independence Seaport Museum, hereinafter cited as ISM.

71. Cathcart claims to have been held on each ship, but does not specify which he escaped from.

72. Christopher Hawkins, *The Adventures of Christopher Hawkins*, ed. Charles Ira Bushnell (New York: Privately Printed, 1864), 32–33, 42, 47–48, 73–89, 287, 289; Thomas Andros, *The Old Jersey Captive: or a Narrative of the Captivity of Thomas Andros* (Boston: William Peirce, 1833), 25–35, 61; Lemisch, "Listening to the 'Inarticulate,'" 18n59.

73. Andrew Sherburne, *Memoirs of Andrew Sherburne: A Pensioner of the Navy of the Revolution*, 2nd ed. (Providence, RI: H. H. Brown, 1831), 110, 118; Albert G. Greene, ed., *Recollections of the Jersey Prison-Ship; Taken and prepared for publication from the original manuscript of the late Captain Thomas Dring, of Providence, R.I., one of the prisoners* (Providence, RI: H. H. Brown, 1829), 50–56.

74. Greene, *Recollections of the Jersey Prison-Ship*, 84.

75. Douglas Bradburn, *The Citizenship Revolution: Politics and the Creation of the American Union, 1774–1804* (Charlottesville: University of Virginia Press, 2009), 7–8.

76. Lemisch, "Listening to the 'Inarticulate,'" 15n45; John K. Alexander, "Jonathan Carpenter and the American Revolution: The Journal of an American Naval Prisoner of War and Vermont Indian Fighter," *Vermont History* 36 (1968): 75.

77. Alexander, "Jonathan Carpenter," 77.

78. Francis D. Cogliano, "'Relics of the Past Generation': Maritime Prisoners of War and the Memory of the American Revolution," in *Pirates, Jack Tar, and Memory: New Directions in American Maritime History*, ed. Paul A. Gilje and William Pencak (Mystic, CT: Mystic Seaport, 2007), 96–97.

79. Cogliano, "'Relics of the Past Generation,," 105.

80. Robert Forbes, *Personal Reminiscences* (Boston: John Wilson & Son, 1876).

81. Paul A. Gilje, *Liberty on the Waterfront: American Maritime Culture in the Age of Revolution* (Philadelphia: University of Pennsylvania Press, 2004), 70–71.

82. Marcus Rediker, *Villains of All Nations: Atlantic Pirates in the Golden Age* (Boston: Beacon Press, 2004), 23.

83. Leon Fink, *Sweatshops at Sea: Merchant Seamen in the World's First Globalized Industry, from 1812 to the Present* (Chapel Hill: University of North Carolina Press, 2011), 12.

84. Perl-Rosenthal, *Citizen Sailors*, 32, 133–134.

85. Gregory E. Fehlings, "America's First Limited War," *Naval War College Review* 53, no. 3 (Summer 2000): 108.

86. Captain John Green Papers, 1781–1801, box 27, 81, 38. 31–32d, ISM.

87. Brown & Ives Records, box 534, folder 4, John Carter Brown Library, Providence, RI; James B. Hedges and Jeannette D. Black, "Disaster in the South Seas: The Wreck of the Brigantine Eliza and the Subsequent Adventures of Captain Corey," *American Neptune* 23, no. 4 (October 1963), 233–254.

88. I. C. Campbell, "The Historiography of Charles Savage," *Journal of the Polynesian Society* 89, no. 2 (1980), 143–166, accessed September 30, 2019, http://www.jps.auckland.ac.nz/document/?wid=3954.

89. Riley, *Narrative*, 6.

90. W. Willshire Riley, ed., *Sequel to Riley's Narrative: Being a Sketch of Interesting Incidents in the Life, Voyages and Travels of Capt. James Riley* (Springfield, OH: George Brewster, 1851), 389.

91. Riley, *Sequel to Riley's Narrative*, 390.

92. William Radcliff to James Riley, February 27, 1836, in Riley, *Sequel to Riley's Narrative*, 394.

93. Perl-Rosenthal, *Citizen Sailors*, 252.

94. Perl-Rosenthal, *Citizen Sailors*, 254–255.

95. Riley, *Sequel to Riley's Narrative*, 392.

96. "The Embargo," in *Scrapbooks of Clippings Compiled by Thomas Jefferson's Family, 1800–1808*, Jefferson Library, Charlottesville, Virginia, microfilm.

97. Riley, *Narrative*, 20–22.

98. Christopher Magra, *The Fisherman's Cause: Atlantic Commerce and Maritime Dimensions of the American Revolution* (Cambridge: Cambridge University Press, 2009), 170–173, 188.

99. In the colonial, Revolutionary, and post-Revolutionary eras, it was standard practice for merchant ships, privateers, and slave ships to carry the flags of multiple warring and neutral nations. *United States v. La Jeune Eugenie*, 26 F. Cas. (C.C.D. Mass. 1822) (No. 15,551); Samuel J. Bayard, *A Sketch of the Life of Com. Robert F. Stockton* (New York: Derby & Jackson, 1856), 51; Perl-Rosenthal, *Citizen Sailors*, 55–56.

Chapter 2 · *Diaries of Barbary Orientalism and American Masculinity in Algiers*

Epigraphs. Richard O'Brien, May 17, 1790, *Remarks and Observations in Algiers*, Historical Society of Pennsylvania; James Cathcart, "Account of Captivity," James L. Cathcart Papers, 1785–1817, Library of Congress, 68–69.

1. Martha Elena Rojas, "'Insults Unpunished': Barbary Captives, American Slaves, and the Negotiation of Liberty," *Early American Studies* 1, no. 2 (Fall 2003): 163, 181.

2. Edward W. Said, *Orientalism* (London: Routledge & Kegan Paul, 1978), 290–291.

3. Robert Battistini, "Glimpses of the Other before Orientalism: The Muslim World in Early American Periodicals, 1785–1800," *Early American Studies* 8, no. 2 (Spring 2010).

4. It is important to note that Americans' manufacturing of Barbary Orientalism was not a strictly linear process and included outliers such as William Shaler (consul general to Algiers, 1815–1828) who refuted the typical claims that North Africans exhibited "extraordinary bigotry, fanaticism, or hatred of those who profess a different religion." Instead, Shaler "found them civil, courteous, and humane." William Shaler, *Sketches of Algiers, Political, Historical, and Civil* (Boston: Cummings, Hillard and Company, 1826); William Shaler, *Communication on the Language, Manners, and Customs of the Berbers or Brebers of Africa* (Philadelphia: Abraham Small, 1824); Lotfi Ben Rejeb, "'The general belief of the world': Barbary as Genre and Discourse in Mediterranean History," *European Review of History* 19, no. 1 (February 2012): 15, 23.

5. Toby L. Ditz, "Afterward: Contending Masculinities in Early America," in *New Men: Manliness in Early America*, ed. Thomas A. Foster (New York: New York University Press, 2011), 256.

6. Mark E. Kann, *A Republic of Men: The American Founders, Gendered Language, and Patriarchal Politics* (New York: New York University Press, 1998); Mark E. Kann, *On the Man Question: Gender and Civic Virtue in America* (Philadelphia: Temple University Press, 1991); E. Anthony Rotundo, "Body and Soul: Changing Ideals of American Middle-Class Manhood, 1770–1920," *Journal of Social History* 16, no. 4 (Summer 1983); E. Anthony Rotundo, *American Manhood: Transformations in Masculinity from the Revolution to the Modern Era* (New York: Basic Books, 1993); Michael Kimmel, *Manhood in America: A Cultural History* (New York: Free Press, 1996); Dana D. Nelson, *National Manhood: Capitalist Citizenship and the Imagined Fraternity of White Men* (Durham, NC: Duke University Press, 1998).

7. Declaration of Independence, July 4, 1776, National Archives, accessed December 19, 2017, https://www.archives.gov/founding-docs/declaration-transcript [italics mine].

8. Gillian Weiss, "Barbary Captivity and the French Idea of Freedom," *French Historical Studies* 28, no. 2 (Spring 2005): 257–258.

9. Toby L. Ditz, "Shipwrecked; or, Masculinity Imperiled: Mercantile Representations of Failure and the Gendered Self in Eighteenth-Century Philadelphia," *Journal of American History* 81, no. 1 (June 1994): 53.

10. Ditz, "Shipwrecked," 22; Christine E. Sears, *American Slaves and African Masters: Algiers and the Western Sahara, 1776–1820* (New York: Palgrave Macmillan, 2012), 29.

11. John J. McCusker, "Worth a War? The Importance of the Trade between British America and the Mediterranean," in *Rough Waters: American Involvement with the Mediterranean in the Eighteenth and Nineteenth Centuries,* Research in Maritime History 44, ed. Silvia Marzagalli, James R. Sofka, and John McCusker (Liverpool, UK: Liverpool University Press, 2010): 16–17.

12. Silvia Marzagalli, "American Shipping into the Mediterranean during the French Wars: A First Approach," in *Rough Waters: American Involvement with the Mediterranean in the Eighteenth and Nineteenth Centuries,* Research in Maritime History 44, ed. Silvia

Marzagalli, James R. Sofka, and John McCusker (Liverpool, UK: Liverpool University Press, 2010): 49–50.

13. Mathew Carey, *A Short Account of Algiers, and of Their Several Wars Against Spain, France, England, Holland, Venice, and Other Powers of Europe* (Philadelphia: J. Parker, 1794), 9–10. Also see Charles Albert Keene, "American Shipping and Trade, 1798–1820: The Evidence from Leghorn," *Journal of Economic History* 38, no. 3 (1978); Charles Albert Keene, "The American Commitment to the Mediterranean Marketplace, 1776–1801" (PhD diss., University of California, Santa Barbara, 1979).

14. Thomas Jefferson, "Report of the Secretary of State relative to the Mediterranean Trade," in Walter Lowrie and Matthew St. Clair Clarke, eds., *American State Papers: Documents, Legislative and Executive, of the Congress of the United States* (Washington, DC: Gales and Seaton, 1833), I: 104–105.

15. Marzagalli, "American Shipping," 58.

16. John Lloyd Stephens, *Incidents of Travel in Greece, Turkey, Russia, and Poland* (New York: Harper & Brothers, 1838), I: 175.

17. Stephen T. Riley, "Abraham Browne's Captivity by the Barbary Pirates, 1655," in *Seafaring in Colonial Massachusetts*, Publications of the Colonial Society of Massachusetts 52 (Boston, 1980), 41–42.

18. For a discussion of the contrasts between the circumstances of captivity in North Africa and slavery in North America, and the relationship between Native American captivity narratives and Barbary narratives, see Robert J. Allison, *The Crescent Obscured: The United States and the Muslim World, 1776–1815* (New York: Oxford University Press, 1995), 107–118.

19. James Cathcart, *The Captives: Eleven Years a Prisoner in Algiers* (La Porte, IN: Herald Print, 1899), 17.

20. In addition to these three officers, up to one-third of American common sailors held in Algiers between the years 1785 and 1796 paid the fee for papaluna status or had the fee paid for them by the US government. Sears, *American Slaves and African Masters*, 67.

21. Cathcart, *Captives*, 56–57; Sears, *American Slaves and African Masters*, 77–79.

22. Cathcart, *Captives*, 109–110.

23. Cathcart, *Captives*, 117.

24. Cathcart, *Captives*, 122–123.

25. Cathcart, *Captives*, 157.

26. Cathcart, *Captives*, 156, 177.

27. Captain Timothy Newman to Cathcart, unknown date, Cathcart Family Papers, box 1, New York Public Library, hereinafter cited as NYPL.

28. Cathcart, *Captives*, 87.

29. Paul Baepler, "White Slaves, African Masters," *ANNALS of the American Academy of Political and Social Science* 588, no. 90 (July 2003): 91.

30. Ann Thomson, *Barbary and Enlightenment: European Attitudes towards the Maghreb in the 18th Century* (Leiden: E. J. Brill, 1987), 13–14; Filippo Pananti, *Narrative of a Residence in Algiers: Comprising a Geographical and Historical Account of the Regency [. . .]* (London: Henry Colburn, 1818), 101–102; Rejeb, "'The general belief of the world,'" 17–18.

31. Timothy Marr, *The Cultural Roots of American Islamicism* (Cambridge: Cambridge University Press, 2006), 28; Fatima Maameri, "Ottoman Algeria in Western

Diplomatic History with Particular Emphasis on Relations with the United States of America, 1776–1816" (PhD diss., University Mentouri, Constantine, 2008), 64–65.

32. Said, *Orientalism*, 290.

33. Said, *Orientalism*, 293–294.

34. Said, *Orientalism*, 290.

35. Battistini, "Glimpses of the Other," 470.

36. O'Brien, December 28, 1789–January 7, 1790, *Remarks and Observations*.

37. O'Brien, January 10, 1790, *Remarks and Observations*.

38. O'Brien, October 22, 1790, *Remarks and Observations*.

39. Cathcart, "Account of Captivity," 1–6.

40. Cathcart, "Account of Captivity," 5.

41. Cathcart, "Account of Captivity," 11.

42. Cathcart, "Account of Captivity," 14–15.

43. Cathcart, "Account of Captivity," 12.

44. Cathcart, "Account of Captivity," 28, 91, 106.

45. For example, in 1802 Jefferson joined Joel Barlow, an American negotiator to Algiers during the final year of Cathcart's and O'Brien's captivity, in translating and publishing *The Ruins, or A Survey of the Revolution of Empires* by the Abbe Constantin de Chassebouef Volney. Combined with Volney's other book on the Orient, *Travels through Egypt and Syria*, which Jefferson had also read, these texts served as warnings that even enlightened societies will inevitably regress to barbarism and fade to ruins if they fail to keep in check the tyrannies of religion and the state. Glenn James Voelz, "Images of Enemy and Self in the Age of Jefferson: The Barbary Conflict in Popular Literary Depiction," *War and Society* 28, no. 2 (October 2009), 25–26; Allison, *Crescent Obscured*, 50.

46. Cathcart, *Captives*, 86, 89.

47. Allison, *Crescent Obscured*, 52–53; Nabil Matar, "John Locke and the 'Turbanned Nations,'" *Journal of Islamic Studies* 2, no. 1 (1991): 72–73.

48. While Glenn focuses on antebellum sailors, the same principle applies to other periods. Myra C. Glenn, "Troubled Manhood in the Early Republic: The Life and Autobiography of Sailor Horace Lane," *Journal of the Early Republic* 26, no. 1 (Spring 2006): 62.

49. Again, see Kann, *Republic of Men*; Kann, *On the Man Question*; Rotundo, "Body and Soul"; Kimmel, *Manhood in America*; Nelson, *National Manhood*; Kathleen Wilson, *The Sense of the People: Politics, Culture, and Imperialism in England, 1715–1785* (Cambridge: Cambridge University Press, 1998), 185–205, 219.

50. Glenn, "Troubled Manhood," 70.

51. Rotundo, "Body and Soul," 25, 27.

52. O'Brien, August 10 and November 4–6, 1790, *Remarks and Observations*.

53. O'Brien, December 8 and 16, 1790, *Remarks and Observations*. Similar passing references to employment are made in January 2–3, 17, and 19 of 1791. When a new Algerian corsair, which presumably the American captives worked on, was launched in February 1791, O'Brien recorded that it was "launched under the Algerine banners with the American stripes." It is unclear if this was to honor or mock the American workers. In either case, O'Brien was impressed by the four thousand locals who came out to celebrate the launch, "which was done in a very capital manner." O'Brien, February 16, 1791, *Remarks and Observations*.

54. O'Brien, August 17, 1790, *Remarks and Observations.*

55. Cathcart, *Captives*, 24.

56. Cathcart, *Captives*, 137–138. Cathcart's well-recorded acts of charity were not confined to O'Brien, and they included providing meals for American captives who were assigned to hard labor; supplying food and clothes for a former shipmate, James Harnet, during his four years in the local insane asylum; and paying for Harnet's burial upon his death. Though Cathcart mentions O'Brien at least forty-nine times in his journals, O'Brien only once mentions Cathcart in his diary, and rather than affirming Cathcart's self-described benevolence and sacrifice, this single entry notes Cathcart's financial and political troubles when serving as the clerk of the Bagnio Gallera in early 1791. Sears, *American Slaves and African Masters*, 82, 100–101; O'Brien, February 10, 1791, *Remarks and Observations.*

57. O'Brien, April 25, 1790, *Remarks and Observations.*

58. Myra Glenn, "Forging Manhood and Nationhood Together: American Sailors' Accounts of Their Exploits, Sufferings, and Resistance in the Antebellum United States," *American Nineteenth Century History* 8, no. 1 (2007): 36.

59. Sears, *American Slaves and African Masters*, 55.

60. Cathcart, *Captives*, 12.

61. Cathcart, *Captives*, 25.

62. Cathcart to O'Brien, March 2, 1793, in "The Diplomatic Journal and Letter Book of James Leander Cathcart, 1788–1796," *Proceedings of the American Antiquarian Society* 64, pt. 2 (Worcester, MA, 1955): 320, hereinafter cited as "Diplomatic Journal."

63. Cathcart to O'Brien, unknown date, in "Diplomatic Journal," 325.

64. O'Brien, November 13, 1790, *Remarks and Observations.*

65. O'Brien, February 20, 1791, *Remarks and Observations.*

66. O'Brien, November 16 and December 5, 1790, *Remarks and Observations.*

67. O'Brien, January 9, 1791, *Remarks and Observations.*

68. Cathcart, *Captives*, 26. The common usage of *arbitrary* was synonymous with *tyrannical* during the Revolution. Thomas Paine employed this usage in *Common Sense*, and among the list of charges in the Declaration of Independence that claimed to prove King George III's "absolute Tyranny over these States," one charge read, "For abolishing the free System of English Laws in a neighbouring Province, establishing therein an *Arbitrary government.*" Yet in the popular imagination of North Americans and Europeans, it was the "Turk," not the Christian monarch, who epitomized arbitrary governance. Marr, *Cultural Roots of American Islamicism*, 25–26; Allison, *Crescent Obscured*, 35–48.

69. Cathcart, *Captives*, 168, 176, 178, 183, 246, 261–263.

70. Cathcart, *Captives*, 168.

71. Greta LaFleur, *The Natural History of Sexuality in Early America* (Baltimore: Johns Hopkins University Press, 2018), 84.

72. "Report of the Secretary of State, in relation to American prisoners at Algiers," December 30, 1790, Lowrie and Clarke,, *American State Papers*, I: 101.

73. Paul A. Gilje, "Loyalty and Liberty: The Ambiguous Patriotism of Jack Tar in the American Revolution," *Pennsylvania History* 67 (Spring 2000): 182.

74. Cathcart, *Captives*, 21.

75. O'Brien, November 30, 1790, *Remarks and Observations.* The pair happily exploited both the more nuanced and more straightforward concepts of American liberty

and slavery. Rhetorically, their frequent references to themselves and their comrades as "miserable slaves" starkly highlight the dichotomy between their current state and the lot of their countrymen.

76. François Furstenberg, "Beyond Freedom and Slavery: Autonomy, Virtue, and Resistance in Early American Political Discourse," *Journal of American History* 89, no. 4 (March 2003): 1300, 1302–1303. While it does not explicitly discuss the role of captives or sailors, for an astute analysis of how non-elite citizens shaped and reflected the cultural notion of liberty, see Michal Jan Rozbicki, *Culture and Liberty in the Age of the American Revolution* (Charlottesville: University of Virginia Press, 2011), 164–180. According to Furstenberg, during the colonial era agency meant "God's agency, once the mover of all worldly deeds," which, during and after the Revolution, "was increasingly supplanted by human agency." This shift also reflects a change in fictional and nonfictional Barbary captivity narratives in the pre- and post-Revolutionary eras, whereby captives looked to God for their freedom in the earlier period and looked to their nation and themselves in the later period. Furstenberg, "Beyond Freedom and Slavery," 1305–1306.

77. Nicholas Wood, "Barbary Slavery, American Freedom: Race, National Power, and National Rights in the New Nation," McNeil Center for Early American Studies Seminar Series, Rutgers University, March 23, 2012, pp. 25–26.

78. O'Brien to Humphreys, November 12, 1793, Despatches from US Ministers to Portugal, M43, roll 3, National Archives at College Park, hereinafter cited as NACP, published verbatim in Lowrie and Clark, *American State Papers*, I: 417.

79. O'Brien to Humphreys, Carmichael, and Short, January 6, 1794, Despatches From US Ministers to Portugal, M43, roll 3, NACP.

80. Cathcart, "Account of Captivity," 144–149.

81. Cathcart, "Account of Captivity," 147.

82. Cathcart, "Account of Captivity," 147.

83. Cathcart to unknown, unknown date, Cathcart Family Papers, box 1, NYPL. Robert Allison speculates that this incident "touched a nerve in Cathcart" because he too was Irish and wonders if Cathcart played a role in the arrests because he operated a competing tavern. Reflecting on this incident and Cathcart's moral outrage, historian H. G. Barnby also speculates that "James Cathcart, for all his pious protests at the behaviour of his fellow Irish-born seamen, must surely have found some entertainment during the course of his eleven years' captivity. . . . It is difficult to imagine a man like Cathcart," a wealthy slave, "who later fathered a very large family, remaining celibate between the ages of 18 and 28." Allison, *Crescent Obscured*, 118–119; H. G. Barnby, *The Prisoners of Algiers: An Account of the Forgotten American-Algerian War, 1785–1797* (London: Oxford University Press, 1966), 145–146.

84. O'Brien, April 25, 1790, *Remarks and Observations*; Cathcart to Philip Werner, May 20, 1791, in Cathcart, *Captives*, 153.

85. LaFleur, *Natural History of Sexuality*, 92.

Chapter 3 · Captivity by Correspondence
Epigraph. Richard O'Brien, on behalf of American captives, to John Adams, Minister Plenipotentiary to the Court of St. James, February 13, 1787, "The Correspondence, Journals, Committee Reports, and Records of the Continental Congress (1774–1789)," M247, item 104, vol. 6, National Archives, Washington, DC.

1. Nathan Perl-Rosenthal, "Private Letters and Public Diplomacy: The Adams Network and the Quasi-War, 1797–1798," *Journal of the Early Republic* 31, no. 2 (Summer 2011): 284, 308–309.

2. Martha Elena Rojas, "'Insults Unpunished': Barbary Captives, American Slaves, and the Negotiation of Liberty," *Early American Studies* 1, no. 2 (Fall 2003): 162.

3. Anne Goldgar, *Impolite Learning: Conduct and Community in the Republic of Letters, 1680–1750* (New Haven, CT: Yale University Press, 1995), 2–3.

4. Lawrence A. Peskin, *Captives and Countrymen: Barbary Slaves and the American Public, 1785–1816* (Baltimore: Johns Hopkins University Press, 2009), 23.

5. Jesse Lemisch, *Jack Tar vs. John Bull: The Role of New York's Seamen in Precipitating the Revolution* (New York: Garland Publishing, 1997); Peter Linebaugh and Marcus Rediker, *The Many-Headed Hydra: Sailors, Slaves, Commoners, and the Hidden History of the Revolutionary Atlantic* (Boston: Beacon Press, 2000); Paul A. Gilje, *Liberty on the Waterfront: American Maritime Culture in the Age of Revolution* (Philadelphia: University of Pennsylvania Press, 2004).

6. James Cathcart, "The Diplomatic Journal and Letter Book of James Leander Cathcart, 1788–1796," *Proceedings of the American Antiquarian Society* 64, pt. 2 (Worcester, MA, 1955): 323–324, hereinafter cited as "Diplomatic Journal."

7. O'Brien to Humphreys, November 12, 1793, in Walter Lowrie and Matthew St. Clarke, eds., *American State Papers: Documents, Legislative and Executive, of the Congress of the United States* (Washington, DC: Gales and Seaton, 1833), I: 417.

8. Richard D. Brown, *Knowledge is Power: The Diffusion of Information in Early America, 1700–1865* (New York: Oxford University Press, 1989), 112.

9. Konstantin Dierks, *In My Power: Letter Writing and Communications in Early America* (Philadelphia: University of Pennsylvania Press, 2009), especially ch. 2.

10. James Cathcart, *Note Book Giving Weights and Measurements of Algiers and Time, Also*, January 14, 1798, La Porte County Historical Society, Indiana. This notebook was compiled after Cathcart's captivity when he returned to Barbary as consul to Tripoli, where he complemented his government salary with private commercial enterprise.

11. February 23–March 22, 1795, expenditures of the Skjoldebrand brothers, and "Imports made by his excellency the Dey of Algiers which he desires Consul Logie to forward to the Court of Portugal as his terms for concluding a Permanent & Lasting Peace," Cathcart Family Papers, box 1, Manuscripts and Archives Division, New York Public Library, hereinafter cited as NYPL.

12. O'Brien to unknown, December 29, 1792, in *Providence Gazette and Country Journal* (Providence, RI), August 3, 1793, vol. 30, no. 31; "Remarked from the Journals of Slavery of O'Brien," in *The Medley or New bedford Marine Journal* (New Bedford, MA), November 21, 1794, vol. 3, no. 3; O'Brien to "a friend in Baltimore," November 9, 1795, in *Claypoole's American Daily Advertiser* (Philadelphia, PA), January 27, 1796, no. 5241; O'Brien to Lisbon merchants, August 26, 1785, in *Charleston Evening Gazette* (Charleston, SC), February 17, 1786; O'Brien, "General Warning," August 27, 1785, in *Salem Gazette* (Salem, MA), November 28, 1786; O'Brien to Dohrman, January 16, 1786, in *Charleston Evening Gazette* (Charleston, SC), June 16, 1786; O'Brien to Dohrman, January 26, 1786, in *Maryland Gazette* (Annapolis, MD), June 8, 1786; O'Brien to John Adams, October 12, 1795, in *Maryland Gazette* (Annapolis, MD), January 14, 1796.

13. Peskin, *Captives and Countrymen*, 23.

14. Cathcart, "Diplomatic Journal," 436; James Cathcart, *The Captives: Eleven Years a Prisoner in Algiers* (La Porte, IN: Herald Print, 1899), 171.

15. Christine E. Sears, "Slavery as Social Mobility? Western Slaves in Late-Eighteenth Century Algiers," in *Rough Waters: American Involvement with the Mediterranean in the Eighteenth and Nineteenth Centuries,* Research in Maritime History 44, ed. Silvia Marzagalli, James R. Sofka, and John McCusker (Liverpool, UK: Liverpool University Press, 2010); Christine E. Sears, *American Slaves and African Masters: Algiers and the West Sahara, 1776–1820* (New York: Palgrave Macmillan, 2012), 87.

16. O'Brien to unknown, December 29, 1792, in *Providence Gazette and Country Journal* (Providence, RI), August 3, 1793, vol. 30, no. 31; "Remarked from the Journals of Slavery of O'Brien," in *The Medley or Newbedford Marine Journal* (New Bedford, MA), November 21, 1794, vol. 3, no. 3; O'Brien to "a friend in Baltimore," November 9, 1795, in *Claypoole's American Daily Advertiser* (Philadelphia, PA), January 27, 1796, no. 5241; O'Brien to Lisbon merchants, August 26, 1785, in *Charleston Evening Gazette* (Charleston SC), February 17, 1786; O'Brien, "General Warning," August 27, 1785, in *Salem Gazette* (Salem, MA), November 28, 1786; O'Brien to Dohrman, January 16, 1786, in *Charleston Evening Gazette* (Charleston, SC), June 16, 1786; O'Brien to Dohrman, January 26, 1786, in *Maryland Gazette* (Annapolis, MD), June 8, 1786; O'Brien to John Adams, October 12, 1795, in *Maryland Gazette* (Annapolis, MD), January 14, 1796.

17. O'Brien to Jefferson, June 8, 1786, in Dudley W. Knox, ed., *Naval Documents Related to the United States Wars with the Barbary Powers* (Washington, DC: US Government Printing Office, 1939), I: 1–6.

18. O'Brien to Jefferson, June 8, 1786, in Knox, *Naval Documents,* I: 1–6.

19. Hannah Farber, "Millions for Credit: Peace with Algiers and the Establishment of America's Commercial Reputations Overseas, 1795–96," *Journal of the Early Republic* 34, no. 2 (Summer 2014).

20. In one of the few signs that Jefferson placed responsibility in the captives, he wrote that "Mr. Lambe is instructed to make no bargain without your [O'Brien's] approvation, and that of the other prisoners, each for himself." Jefferson to O'Bryan [*sic*], November 4, 1785, in Thomas Jefferson Randolph, ed., *Memoir, Correspondence, and Miscellanies, From the Papers of Thomas Jefferson* (Boston: Gray and Bowen, 1830), I: 353–354; also see Jefferson to William Carmichael, November 4, 1785, I: 350; James L. Cathcart Papers, container I: 36–37, microfilm, Library of Congress, hereinafter cited as LOC.

21. O'Brien to William Carmichael, July 11, 1786, Dispatches from US Consuls in Algiers, M23, roll 1, National Archives at College Park, hereinafter cited as NACP; O'Brien to Jefferson, June 8, 1786, in Knox, *Naval Documents,* I: 1–6; James L. Cathcart Papers, container I: 48–52, microfilm, LOC.

22. Nathaniel Cutting to Secretary of State Edmund Randolph, February 10, 1794; Michael Murphy to Secretary of State, November 17, 1794; Joel Barlow to Secretary of State Timothy Pickering, March 18, 1796, all in Knox, *Naval Documents,* I: 63–68, 86–87, 140–142.

23. Thomas Jefferson, "Report of the Secretary of State relative to the Mediterranean Trade," in Lowrie and Clarke, *American State Papers,* I: 105.

24. Jefferson to Humphreys, July 13, 1791, in Lowrie and Clarke, *American State Papers,* I: 290.

25. Jefferson to Admiral John Paul Jones, June 1, 1792, in Lowrie and Clarke, *American State Papers*, I: 290–292.

26. "Extract of a letter from the Secretary of State to Colonel David Humphreys," in Lowrie and Clarke, *American State Papers*, I: 528; Humphreys to Washington, February 8, 1793, in Frank Landon Humphreys, *Life and Times of David Humphreys*, 2 vols. (New York: G. P. Putnam's Sons, 1917), II: 159–160.

27. Cathcart's and O'Brien's exploitation of Revolutionary vocabulary mirrors Michal Rozbicki's description of participants in Shays' Rebellion. Michal Jan Rozbicki, *Culture and Liberty in the Age of the American Revolution* (Charlottesville: University of Virginia Press, 2011), especially ch. 6. Throughout their captivity, Cathcart and O'Brien experimented with similar catchphrases, referring to themselves as "Victims to Slavery," "American Livestock," and "Liberty in Bondage." O'Brien to William Carmichael, February 19, 1790, *Remarks and Observations in Algiers*, Historical Society of Pennsylvania; Cathcart, "A List of Beyliques American Livestock, Now Slaves in Algiers," July 1, 1794, box 1, folder Correspondence 1785–1794, Cathcart Family Papers, NYPL.

28. Ernest Renan, "What is a Nation?," in *Nation and Narration*, ed. Homi K. Bhabha (London: Routledge, 1990), 19.

29. O'Brien, "Extract of a Letter from Capt. Richard O'Brien, a Prisoner at Algiers, Dated December 29, 1792, and Eighth Year of His Captivity," *Providence Gazette and Country Journal* (Providence, RI), August 3, 1793, vol. 30, no. 31, p. 3.

30. O'Brien to Humphreys, March 26, 1793, quoted in Peskin, *Captives and Countrymen*, 37.

31. James L. Cathcart Papers, container I: 142–143, LOC, also printed verbatim in Cathcart, *Captives*, 143–145.

32. Cathcart to Humphreys, unknown date, 1794, in "Diplomatic Journal," 327.

33. "An Address: Delivered by Mr. Hallam, at the Theatre in Philadelphia, previous to an entertainment performed for the benefit of the American captives in Algiers," in *Scrapbooks of Clippings Compiled by Thomas Jefferson's Family, 1800–1808*, Jefferson Library, Charlottesville, Virginia, microfilm. Other clippings in the scrapbook reference later American captives during the First Barbary War and include Fourth of July toasts by Cathcart and William Eaton and poetry by American captive William Ray.

34. Paul A. Gilje, "Loyalty and Liberty: The Ambiguous Patriotism of Jack Tar in the American Revolution," *Pennsylvania History* 67, no. 2 (Spring 2000): 165.

35. Nathan Perl-Rosenthal, *Citizen Sailors: Becoming American in the Age of Revolution* (Cambridge, MA: Harvard University Press), 32, 68–70, 76, 187; Sears, *American Slaves and African Masters*, 55.

36. Charles Logie to Lord Sydney, December 20, 1785, FO 3/6, United Kingdom National Archives, Kew, hereinafter cited as UKNA; Richard B. Parker, *Uncle Sam in Barbary: A Diplomatic History* (Gainesville: University Press of Florida, 2008), 220–222.

37. For the French experience with Barbary, see Gillian Weiss, *Captives and Corsairs: France and Slavery in the Early Modern Mediterranean* (Stanford, CA: Stanford University Press, 2011), 27; Gillian Weiss, "Barbary Captivity and the French Idea of Freedom," *French Historical Studies* 28, no. 2 (Spring 2005).

38. Cathcart to Philip Werner, May 20, 1791, in "Diplomatic Journal," 319.

39. Cathcart to Philip Werner, May 20, 1791, in "Diplomatic Journal," 319; Cathcart, *Captives*, 152–153.

40. Cathcart to William Wilberforce, January 12, 1794, FO 95/1/3, UKNA. Cathcart's latest approach may have been encouraged by the successful ransom in 1790 of Charles Colvill, a Scottish-born sailor captured on O'Brien's ship *Dauphin*. After unsuccessful attempts at soliciting private ransom from friends in America, Colvill turned to old friends in Scotland, who subsequently had a British member of parliament persuade Charles Logie to facilitate the 825 sequins, or US$1,485, ransom in an unofficial capacity, as it was contrary to official British policy to aid in the ransom of crew on American-flagged vessels. O'Brien, February 24 and May 27, 1790, *Remarks and Observations*.

41. Edward Church, American consul at Lisbon, to Secretary of State Jefferson, October 12, 1793; O'Brien to President Washington, November 5, 1793; and Pierre Eric Skjoldebrand to Humphreys, November 13, 1793, all in Lowrie and Clarke, *American State Papers*, I: 296, 415, 417–418; O'Brien to Humphreys, November 12, 1793, and O'Brien to Humphreys, January 6, 1794, Despatches from US Ministers to Portugal, M43, roll 3, NACP; Peskin, *Captives and Countrymen*, 103–104, 116; Sears, *American Slaves and African Masters*, 73; O'Brien to Humphreys, August 21, 1794, Despatches From US Ministers to Portugal, M43, roll 3, NACP.

42. Cathcart, February 25, 1796, in "Diplomatic Journal," 371.

43. Robert Montgomery to Cathcart, August 22, 1795, in Cathcart Family Papers, box 1, NYPL.

44. Montgomery to Cathcart, September 22, 1795, in Cathcart Family Papers, box 1, NYPL.

45. Captain Timothy Newman to Cathcart, unknown date, in Cathcart Family Papers, box 1, NYPL.

46. Cathcart, "Negotiations in Barbary," James L. Cathcart Papers, container III: 132, 138, LOC, quoted verbatim in Cathcart, *Captives*, 172–174.

47. Cathcart, "Negotiations in Barbary."

48. Cathcart, "Negotiations in Barbary."

49. James Cathcart, "Compensation for His Services in Effecting a Negotiation with the Regency of Algiers from Oct 1794 to Feb 7, 1797," Cathcart Family Papers, box 1, folder 2, NYPL.

50. December 16, 1793, "Report from the Secretary of State, in Relation to Morocco and Algiers," and December 16, 1793, "Report of the Secretary of State on the Privileges and Restrictions on the Commerce of the United States in Foreign Countries," in Lowrie and Clarke, *American State Papers*, I: 288, 300–304; James R. Sofka, "The Jeffersonian Idea of National Security: Commerce, the Atlantic Balance of Power, and the Barbary War, 1786–1805," *Diplomatic History* 21, no. 4 (Fall 1997): 520; Humphreys, *Life and Times of David Humphreys*, vols. 1–2; Randolph, *Memoir, Correspondence, and Miscellanies, From the Papers of Thomas Jefferson*, IV: 477–478.

51. Humphreys, *Life and Times of David Humphreys*, vols. 1–2; David Humphreys, *The Miscellaneous Works of David Humphreys* (New York: T. and J. Swords, 1804).

52. *South-Carolina State Gazette and Timothy's Daily Adviser* (Charleston, SC), July 7, 1794, p. 3; David J. Dzurec, "'An Entertaining Narrative of . . . Cruel and Barbarous Treatment': Captivity, Narrative, and Debate in the Early American Republic, 1775–1816" (PhD diss., Ohio State University, 2008), 72–74.

53. Humphreys, *Miscellaneous Works*, 41.

54. Humphreys, *Miscellaneous Works*, 41, 53–54, first published in winter 1788 in the *Albany Journal*; Peskin, *Captives and Countrymen*, 55–67; David Dzurec, "'A Speedy

Release to Our Suffering Captive Brethren in Algiers': Captives, Debate, and Public Opinion in the Early American Republic," *Historian* 71, no. 4 (Winter 2009).

55. For an astute analysis of the intersection of Humphreys, republican sensibility, and the captives, see Peskin, *Captives and Countrymen*, 55–67. For more on the evolution of public debate regarding the captives, see Dzurec, " 'Speedy Release.' "

56. Humphreys, *Miscellaneous Works*, 53–54.

57. Luther G. Riggs, ed., *The Anarchiad: A New England Poem, written in concert by David Humphreys, Joel Barlow, John Turnbull, and Dr. Lemuel Hopkins, now first published in book form* (New Haven, CT: Thomas H. Pease, 1861), 14–15; Linebaugh and Rediker, *The Many-Headed Hydra*, 239–240.

58. Humphreys to Washington, November 23, 1793, in Humphreys, *Life and Times of David Humphreys*, II: 188–189.

59. Mention of the address is conspicuously absent from Frank Landon Humphreys's laudatory biography, *Life and Times of David Humphreys*, which has been a source of controversy. For publications of the address in period newspapers, see *Albany Gazette* (Albany, NY), November 3, 1794, p. 2; *Catskill Packet & Western Mail* (Catskill, NY), November 8, 1794, vol. 3, no. 118, p. 1–2; *Federal Orrery* (Boston, MA), November 17, 1794, vol. 1, no. 9, p. 33; *American Minerva* (New York, NY), October 28, 1794, vol. 1, no. 276, p. 2; *The Medley or Newbedford Marine Journal* (New Bedford, MA), November 21, 1794, vol. 3, no. 3, p. 1; *Worcester Intelligencer, or Brookfield Advertiser* (Brookfield, MA), November 11, 1794, vol. 1 no. 6, p. 1–2; *Western Star* (Stockbridge, MA), November 11, 1794, vol. 5, no. 51, p. 1. For an edited collection of twentieth century British valedictory dispatches, see Matthew Parris and Andrew Bryson, *Parting Shots: Undiplomatic Diplomats: The Ambassadors' Letters You Were Never Meant to See* (London: Viking, 2010). For more on the address and national lotteries, see Humphreys, *Life and Times of David Humphreys*, II: 222–223; Robert J. Allison, *The Crescent Obscured: The United States and the Muslim World 1776–1815* (New York: Oxford University Press, 1995), 130–151; Gary E. Wilson, "American Hostages in Moslem Nations, 1784–1796: The Public Response," *Journal of the Early Republic* 2, no. 2 (Summer 1982): 123–141; Dzurec, " 'Speedy Release,' " 735–756.

Chapter 4 · From Captives to Consuls and Coup-Makers

Epigraphs. James Cathcart to William Eaton, March 15, 1801, William Eaton Papers, box 4, letters March 15, 1801 to July 30, 1801, Huntington Library, San Marino, California; Ambrose Bierce, *The Unabridged Devil's Dictionary*, ed. David E. Shultz and S. T. Joshi (Athens: University of Georgia Press, 2000), 41.

1. Harry Kopp and Charles A. Gillespie, *Career Diplomacy: Life and Work in the US Foreign Service* (Washington, DC: Georgetown University Press, 2011), 13. For further data and visual representations of the proportions of various foreign agents during the early republic, see "The Early American Foreign Service Database," accessed December 21, 2017, www.eafsd.org.

2. Charles Stuart Kennedy, *The American Consul: A History of the United States Consular Service, 1776–1914* (New York: Greenwood Press, 1990), 20.

3. Burt E. Powell, "Jefferson and the Consular Service," *Political Science Quarterly* 21, no. 4 (December 1906): 626.

4. Mathew Taylor Raffety, *The Republic Afloat: Law, Honor, and Citizenship in Maritime America* (Chicago: University of Chicago Press, 2013), 148.

5. Morrell Heald and Lawrence S. Kaplan, *Culture and Diplomacy: The American Experience* (Westport, CT: Greenwood Press, 1977), 92–93; Josiah Quincy, ed., *The Journals of Major Samuel Shaw: The First American Consul at Canton* (Boston: W. M. Crosby and H. P. Nichols, 1847). On the unsuccessful role of consuls in facilitating commerce, see Chester Lloyd Jones, *The Consular Service of the United States* (Philadelphia: John C. Winston Co., 1909), 60, 65, 83.

6. O'Brien to Secretary of State Pickering, April 6, 1799 in Dudley W. Knox, ed., *Naval Documents Related to the United States Wars with the Barbary Powers* (Washington, DC: US Government Printing Office, 1939), I: 320. O'Brien later assured Eaton that "Your light house of truth will do away the misty lies of" local commercial agents. O'Brien to Eaton, May 11, 1800, William Eaton Papers, box 2, Huntington Library, San Marino, California, hereinafter cited as HL. Though O'Brien was unusually devoted to maritime metaphors, he was certainly not alone. Merchant sailors often described adultery in the same terms as the theft of cargo from their ships. And ships being violently assaulted in a storm were vividly described in the language of a woman being raped, while ships lost at sea were referred to as miscarriages. Conversely, when teaching midwifery to men in the eighteenth century, maritime metaphors were used to highlight the importance of vaginal examination and proper use of instruments. Toby L. Ditz, "Shipwrecked; or, Masculinity Imperiled: Mercantile Representations of Failure and the Gendered Self in Eighteenth-Century Philadelphia," *Journal of American History* 81, no. 1 (June 1994): 65, 76–78.

7. For an excellent survey of Madeira's economic, administrative, and demographic history, as well as the role of consuls in trade, see David Hancock, *Oceans of Wine: Madeira and the Emergence of American Trade and Taste* (New Haven, CT: Yale University Press, 2009), especially ch. 1.

8. See Eaton's, O'Brien's, and Cathcart's letters of instruction upon being appointed consuls in Knox, *Naval Documents*, I: 231–234, 268–273.

9. Kopp and Gillespie, *Career Diplomacy*, 13.

10. In addition to matters of national interest, these discretionary powers in *practice*, if not in *theory*, also covered a consul's treatment of ships' crews within the consul's jurisdiction. See Charles Edwards Lester, *My Consulship*, 2 vols. (New York: Cornish, Lamport & Co., 1853), II: 297–302; Raffety, *Republic Afloat*, 166.

11. Hancock, *Oceans of Wine*, xxii, 157–161.

12. O'Brien to Humphreys, January 6, 1794, Despatches from US Ministers to Portugal, M43, roll 3, National Archives at College Park, Maryland, hereinafter cited as NACP. Cathcart's and O'Brien's inclusions of "hell" and "city of bondage" in the address lines of their correspondence from captivity can be found in Richard O'Brien, November 3, 1790, *Remarks and Observations in Algiers*, Historical Society of Pennsylvania, and Cathcart to Joseph Donaldson, April 23, 1796, in "The Diplomatic Journal and Letter Book of James Leander Cathcart, 1788–1796," *Proceedings of the American Antiquarian Society* 64, pt. 2 (Worcester, MA, 1955): 393–394, hereinafter cited as "Diplomatic Journal."

13. O'Brien to Humphreys, January 9, 1794, Despatches from US Ministers to Portugal, M43, NACP.

14. Pierre Eric Skjoldebrand to Humphreys, September 10, 1795, in Walter Lowrie and Matthew St. Clair Clarke, eds., *American State Papers: Documents, Legislative and Executive, of the Congress of the United States* (Washington, DC: Gales and Seaton, 1833), I: 530.

15. Joel Barlow to Secretary of State, May 4, 1796, in Knox, *Naval Documents*, I: 155

16. Knox, *Naval Documents*, I: 231–234, 273; Cathcart to Eaton, August 27, 1800, in James Cathcart, *Tripoli: Letter Book*, ed. J. B. Newkirk (LaPorte, IN: Herald Print, 1901), 168.

17. *City Gazette and Daily Advertiser* (Charleston, SC), February 18, 1797, vol. 15, no. 2981. News of O'Brien's return almost a year prior had also been circulated by newspapers in Connecticut, Massachusetts, New York, and Pennsylvania. See *Gazette of the United States* (Philadelphia, PA), June 8, 1796, vol. 9, no. 1170; *Register of the Times, a Gazette for the Country* (New York, NY), June 10, 1796, no. 2; *Independent Gazetteer* (Philadelphia, PA), June 11, 1796, no. 1781; *Weekly Museum* (New York, NY), June 11, 1796, vol. 8, no. 415; *Political Gazette* (Newburyport, MA), June 16, 1796, vol. 2, no. 8; *Middlesex Gazette* (Middletown, CT), June 17, 1796, vol. 11, no. 552.

18. Daniel Webster to Habijah Fuller, August 29, 1802, in Fletcher Webster, ed., *The Writings and Speeches of Daniel Webster*, 18 vols. (Boston: Little, Brown & Company, 1903), XVII: 121.

19. John Adams, "Communication to Congress," June 23, 1797, in Lowrie and Clark, *American State Papers*, II: 65; O'Brien to the Dey of Algiers, December 4, 1797, in Knox, *Naval Documents*, I: 223.

20. Cathcart to unknown, December 13, 1796, Cathcart Family Papers, item 100, box 1, folder 2, New York Public Library, hereinafter cited as NYPL.

21. Untitled and undated poetry, Cathcart Family Papers, box 3, NYPL.

22. James Cathcart to Jane Woodside, July 27, 1797, and James Cathcart to Jane Woodside, January 21, 1798, Cathcart Family Papers, box 3, NYPL.

23. James Cathcart, "A Most Sacred Truth," November 13, 1797, and James Cathcart to Jane Woodside, July 27, 1797, Cathcart Family Papers, box 3, NYPL.

24. Eaton to John Harris, April 12, 1799, "Letterbook April 8, 1799–February 13, 1802," p. 20, William Eaton Papers, HL [underline in original], also quoted in Louis B. Wright and Julia H. Macleod, *The First Americans in North Africa: William Eaton's Struggle for a Vigorous Policy against the Barbary Pirates, 1799–1805* (Princeton, NJ: Princeton University Press, 1945), 30.

25. John Gilbert McCurdy, *Citizen Bachelors: Manhood and the Creation of the United States* (Ithaca: Cornell University Press, 2009), ch. 5.

26. Paul Gilje, *Liberty on the Waterfront: American Maritime Culture in the Age of Revolution* (Philadelphia: University of Pennsylvania Press, 2004), 37–57.

27. Cathcart to Timothy Pickering, July 9, 1799, in Cathcart, *Tripoli*, 51; Eaton to John Harris, April 12, 1799, "Letterbook April 8, 1799–February 13, 1802," pp. 15–20, William Eaton Papers, HL; Wright and Macleod, *First Americans in North Africa*, 30.

28. Eaton to O'Brien, May 1, 1799, "Letterbook December 18, 1798–December, 9, 1799," p. 146, William Eaton Papers, HL [underline in original].

29. Cathcart to Timothy Pickering, July 9, 1799, in Cathcart, *Tripoli*, 51–52.

30. Cathcart to Eaton, November 5, 1799, in Cathcart, *Tripoli*, 95.

31. Consular Act of 1792 (April 14), in *Annals of Congress, 2nd Congress, 1st Session*, 1360–1363, accessed December 19, 2012, http://memory.loc.gov/ammem/amlaw/lwaclink .html.

32. Wilbur J. Carr, "The American Consular Service," *American Journal of International Law* 1, no. 4 (October 1907): 896; Raffety, *Republic Afloat*, ch. 7.

33. Kennedy, *American Consul*, 3–4.

34. Gillian Weiss, *Captives and Corsairs: France and Slavery in the Early Modern Mediterranean* (Stanford, CA: Stanford University Press, 2011), 13, 47.

35. Kennedy, *American Consul*, 3–4.

36. Carr, "The American Consular Service," 896–897; Bernadette Whelan, *American Government in Ireland, 1790–1913: A History of the US Consular Service* (Manchester, UK: Manchester University Press, 2010), 11–17; Henry E. Mattox, *The Twilight of Amateur Diplomacy: The American Foreign Service and Its Senior Officers in the 1890s* (Kent, OH: Kent State University Press, 1989), 9–10.

37. Similarly, Swedish merchant sailors could avoid paying certain fees and duties imposed by their government by using the local Swedish consul as their commercial broker rather than nominating a local merchant. Leos Müller, *Consuls, Corsairs, and Commerce: The Swedish Consular Service and Long-distance Shipping, 1720–1815* (Uppsala, Sweden: Acta Universitatis Upsaliensis, 2004), 90–93.

38. Cathcart to Eaton, August 12, 1799, William Eaton Papers, box 2, HL, also reprinted verbatim in Cathcart, *Tripoli*, 64–65.

39. Cathcart to Eaton, October 27, 1799, William Eaton Papers, box 2, HL; Cathcart translation of Nicholai Christian Nisen, November 13, 1801, in *State Papers and Publick Documents of the United States*, 3rd ed. (Boston: Thomas B. Wait, 1819), IV: 371–374.

40. C. R. Pennell, "The Social History of British Diplomats in North Africa and How It Affected Diplomatic Policy," in *The Diplomats' World: A Cultural History of Diplomacy, 1815–1914*, ed. Markus Mosslang and Torsten Riotte (Oxford: Oxford University Press, 2008), 348–349.

41. John Adams, "Message, recommending a compliance with the request of the Dey of Algiers to be supplied with two American built vessels," June 23, 1797, in Lowrie and Clark, *American State Papers*, II: 65.

42. President Thomas Jefferson to the Senate and House of Representatives, January 13, 1806, in Lowrie and Clark, *American State Papers*, II: 696.

43. O'Brien to Cathcart, December 29, 1800, Cathcart Family Papers, item 215, box 1, folder 3, NYPL.

44. O'Brien, Dispatch, January-March 1799, Knox, *Naval Documents*, I: 290–295; Eaton to Secretary of State, February 10 and February 14, 1799, "Letterbook December 18, 1798–December 9, 1799," p. 69, William Eaton Papers, HL.

45. Thomas Jefferson to William Carmichael, November 4, 1785, in Thomas Jefferson Randolph, ed., *Memoir, Correspondence, and Miscellanies, From the Papers of Thomas Jefferson* (Charlottesville, VA: F. Carr, and Co., 1829), I: 350.

46. Cathcart, "Journal of our negotiations with the Regency of Tripoli in Barbary, as transmitted to the Hon. Timothy Pickering, Secretary of State, by James Leander Cathcart," in Cathcart, *Tripoli*, 2–5.

47. Cathcart to O'Brien, July 7, 1799, in Cathcart, *Tripoli*, 49; Wright and Macleod, *First Americans in North Africa*, 63; Robert J. Allison, *The Crescent Obscured: The United States and the Muslim World, 1776–1815* (New York: Oxford University Press, 1995), 163, 170–171; O'Brien to Cathcart, September 30, 1800, and Eaton to Cathcart, October 1, 1800, "Letterbook, December 14, 1799–June 28, 1801," pp. 168–175, 177, William Eaton Papers, HL; Wright and Macleod, *First Americans in North Africa*, 63; Cathcart to Pickering, April 18, 1800, in Cathcart, *Tripoli*, 134–136.

48. Cathcart, April 10, 1799, in Cathcart, *Tripoli*, 19.

49. Entry of February 19, 1799, "Letterbook Dec. 18, 1798–Dec. 9, 1799," p. 36, William Eaton Papers, HL; Allison, *Crescent Obscured*, 163–164.

50. Entry of February 16, 1799, "Letterbook Dec. 18, 1798–Dec. 9, 1799," p. 31, William Eaton Papers, HL.

51. Eaton quoted in Allison, *Crescent Obscured*, 168; entry of April 3, 1799, "Letterbook Dec. 18, 1798–Dec. 9, 1799," p. 113, William Eaton Papers, HL; Wright and Macleod, *First Americans in North Africa*, 37.

52. James Cathcart, *Note Book Giving Weights and Measurements of Algiers and Time, Also*, January 14, 1798, La Porte County Historical Society, Indiana.

53. Pennell, "Social History of British Diplomats," 378.

54. Barlow to Secretary of State, August 24, 1797, in Knox, *Naval Documents*, I: 209.

55. O'Brien, "Statement of Particulars Relative to the Regency of Algiers in July 1802," in Knox, *Naval Documents*, II: 200. This sum is unverifiable and included $2.5 million in debts owed by the governments of France, Spain, Portugal, Holland, Sweden, and the United States.

56. United States Department of Commerce and Bureau of the Census, *Historical Statistics of the United States, Colonial Times to 1970* (Washington, DC: Government Printing Office, 1975), II: 1104.

57. O'Brien to William Smith, US Minister to Lisbon, January 10, 1801, in Knox, *Naval Documents*, I: 411; Morton Rosenstock, "The House of Bacri and Busnach: A Chapter from Algeria's Commercial History," *Jewish Social Studies* 14, no. 4 (October 1952): 345–346; Wright and MacLeod, *First Americans in North Africa*, 42; Cathcart to Eaton, August 12, 1799, in Cathcart, *Tripoli*, 63–64; Eaton to Secretary of State Pickering, July 15, 1799, "Letterbook December 18, 1799–December 9, 1799," p. 180, William Eaton Papers, HL, reprinted verbatim in Charles Prentiss, *The Life of the Late Gen. William Eaton* (Brookfield, MA: E. Merriam & Co., 1813), 113; entry of February 26, 1799, "Letterbook December 18, 1798–December 9, 1799," p. 39, William Eaton Papers, HL.

58. Cathcart, "Diplomatic Journal," 433.

59. Eaton to Cathcart, October 10, 1799, William Eaton Papers, box 2, HL; Allison, *Crescent Obscured*, 170.

60. Cathcart to Eaton, July 22, 1799, William Eaton Papers, box 1, HL.

61. Cathcart to Eaton, February 17, 1800, in Cathcart, *Tripoli*, 130.

62. Cathcart to Eaton, undated, likely between late November and early December 1800, in Cathcart, *Tripoli*, 215–220. For another lengthy letter that chronicles Cathcart's objections to O'Brien, see Cathcart to Eaton, November 9, 1799, in Cathcart, *Tripoli*, 91–98.

63. Cathcart to Eaton, August 7, 1801, William Eaton Papers, box 4, HL.

64. O'Brien to Eaton, October 15, 1799, William Eaton Papers, box 2, HL.

65. Eaton to O'Brien, May 21, 1801, "Letterbook, December 14, 1799–June 28, 1801," p. 308, William Eaton Papers, HL; Wright and Macleod, *First Americans in North Africa*, 77.

66. Cathcart to Eaton, October 27, 1799, in Cathcart, *Tripoli*, 82.

67. For several examples, see Cathcart to Eaton, July 22, 1799, William Eaton Papers, box 1, HL; Cathcart to Eaton, June 13 and June 15, 1801, William Eaton Papers, box 4, HL; Cathcart to Eaton, October 23, 1801, William Eaton Papers, box 5, HL.

68. Jacob Wagner to Eaton, September 16, 1801, William Eaton Papers, box 5, HL; Eaton to Cathcart, October 2, 1801, "Letterbook, July 4, 1800–October 2, 1801," p.75, William Eaton Papers, HL.

69. O'Brien to William Smith (US minister plenipotentiary to Lisbon), December 23, 1800, Cathcart Family Papers, item 213, box 1, folder 3, NYPL.

70. O'Brien to Jefferson, June 8, 1786, in Knox, *Naval Documents*, I: 3.

71. Cathcart to "all whom it doth or may concern," October 29, 1800, in Lowrie and Clark, *American State Papers*, II: 355.

72. Cathcart to Eaton, February 3, 1800, in Cathcart, *Tripoli*, 120; Cathcart to Eaton, November 5, 1799, William Eaton Papers, box 2, HL.

73. Cathcart to "all whom it doth or may concern," October 29, 1800, in Lowrie and Clark, *American State Papers*, II: 355–357.

74. O'Brien to Captain Bainbridge, October 9, 1800, in Lowrie and Clark, *American State Papers*, II: 353. O'Brien's update to the secretary of state upon the return of the *George Washington* to Algiers became his most-circulated correspondence in American newspapers until the outbreak of the First Barbary War. O'Brien to Secretary of State, January 27, 1801, in *Philadelphia Gazette* (Philadelphia, PA), December 28, 1801, vol. 18, no. 4090; *Poulson's American Daily Advertiser* (Philadelphia, PA), December 28, 1801, vol. 30, no. 7815; *American Citizen* (New York, NY), January 2, 1802, vol. 2, no. 560; *Mercantile Advertiser* (New York, NY), January 2, 1802, no. 2936; *Commercial Advertiser* (New York, NY), January 7, 1802, vol. 5, no. 13110; *Albany Centinel* (Albany, NY), January 8, 1802, vol. 5, no. 56; *Vermont Gazette* (Bennington, VT), January 25, 1802, vol. 1, no. 44; *Otsego Herald: or, Western Advertiser* (Cooperstown, NY), February 4, 1802, vol. 7, no. 358; *Newburyport Herald* (Newburyport, MA), February 16, 1802, vol. 5, no. 35.

75. O'Brien to Secretary of State, October 22, 1800, in Lowrie and Clark, *American State Papers*, II: 354.

76. *The Courier* (Norwich, CT), December 31, 1800, vol. 5, no. 6.

77. Bainbridge to Secretary of the Navy Ben J. Stoddert, October 10, 1800; O'Brien to Bainbridge, October 9, 1800; Bainbridge to O'Brien, October 9, 1800; O'Brien to Bainbridge, October 10, 1800, all in *The Bee* (New London, CT), May 6, 1801, vol. 4, no. 174. Also see *American Citizen and General Advertiser* (New York, NY), January 1, 1802, vol. 2 no. 559; *The Courier* (Norwich, CT), December 31, 1800, vol. 5, no. 6. Bainbridge also referred to the dey's "arbitrary demand" in a letter from Constantinople to Rufus King, the US minister to the Court of St. James. Bainbridge to Rufus King, November 20, 1800, in Charles R. King, ed., *Life and Correspondence of Rufus King: Comprising His Letters, Private and Official, His Public Documents and His Speeches* (New York: G. P. Putnam's Sons, 1896), III: 381.

78. Eaton to Secretary of State Pickering, November 11, 1800, in Knox, *Naval Documents*, I: 398 [italics in original].

79. Secretary of State Madison to O'Brien, May 20, 1801, in *National Intelligencer and Washington Advertiser* (Washington, DC), January 4, 1802.

80. *The Courier* (Norwich, CT), December 31, 1800, vol. 5, no. 6.

81. Eaton and the *George Washington*'s logbook differ on the precise number of these additional animals. O'Brien to Eaton, October 19, 1800, William Eaton Papers, box 3, HL; entry of November 12, 1800, in *Occurrences and Remarks on Board United States Frigate Geo. Washington Commanded by Wilson Jacobs Esq. 1800, June 14–1801, Apr. 19*, HL.

82. Wright and Macleod, *First Americans in North Africa*, 71; E. D. Clarke, *Travels in Various Countries of Europe, Asia and Africa*, 4th ed. (London: R. Watts, 1817), III: 77–79.

83. *Gazette of the United States* (Philadelphia, PA), September 4, 1801, no. 8; *Maryland Gazette* (Annapolis, MD), September 10, 1801, no. 2852.

84. *Philadelphia Gazette* (Philadelphia, PA), December 28, 1801, vol. 18, no. 4090.

85. *Philadelphia Gazette* (Philadelphia, PA), December 28, 1801, vol. 18, no. 4090; Cathcart to Secretary of State, January 4, 1801, in Lowrie and Clark, *American State Papers*, II: 354.

86. Thomas Jefferson, "First Annual Message, December 8, 1801," in Merrill D. Peterson, ed., *Addresses, Messages, and Replies* (New York: Literary Classics of America, 1984), 501–502; Cathcart to Captain Edward Preble, November 18, 1803, in Knox, *Naval Documents*, III: 229.

87. Cathcart's and Eaton's trade relationship at this time is detailed in Eaton to William Turner, December 13, 1801, and Eaton to Secretary of State Madison, February 3, 1802, "Letterbook, June 28, 1801–August 23, 1802," pp. 90–92, 100–103, William Eaton Papers, HL; Eaton to Cathcart, April 27, 1801, "Letterbook, December 14, 1799–June 28, 1801," p. 301, William Eaton Papers, HL; Wright and Macleod, *First Americans in North Africa*, 102.

88. Eaton to William Smith, January 17, 1801, "Letterbook, December 14, 1799–June 28, 1801," p. 257, William Eaton Papers, HL; Wright and Macleod, *First Americans in North Africa*, 79–80.

89. Eaton to Secretary of State Pickering, March 28, 1799, and October 12, 1799, "Letterbook, April 8, 1799–February 13, 1802," pp. 10–11, 45–47, William Eaton Papers, HL; Wright and Macleod, *First Americans in North Africa*, 56–57. The wheat and barley seeds were also procured for Secretary of State Pickering.

90. Eaton to Cathcart, April 27, 1801, "Letterbook, December 14, 1799–June 28, 1801," p. 301, William Eaton Papers, HL.

91. Eaton to Mrs. Eaton, March 10, 1801, April 14, 1801, and February 15, 1802, "Letterbook, April 8, 1799–February 13, 1802," pp. 125, 137, William Eaton Papers, HL; Wright and Macleod, *First Americans in North Africa*, 103.

92. Cathcart to Eaton, June 19, 1801, William Eaton Papers, box 4, HL; Cathcart to Eaton, March 12, 1802, William Eaton Papers, box 5, HL.

93. The same day that Eaton penned a report for the secretary of state on the promises of a regime change in Tripoli with Hamet at the helm, Eaton also claimed that his health necessitated a trip to Leghorn, where the *George Washington* could conveniently take him to his co-conspirator and business partner, Cathcart, that very night. Eaton to William Turner, December 13, 1801, and Eaton to Secretary of State Madison, February 3, 1802, "Letterbook, June 28, 1801–August 23, 1802," pp. 90–92, 100–103, William Eaton Papers, HL. According to Wright and MacLeod, "during his stay in Leghorn, Eaton divided his time between public affairs and private business, and found both to his liking." Wright and Macleod, *First Americans in North Africa*, 102.

94. Eaton to Secretary of State, June 8, 1802, in Knox, *Naval Documents*, II: 168.

95. Cathcart to Secretary of State, August 25, 1802, Cathcart Family Papers, item 435, box 2, folder 1, NYPL, quoted verbatim in Knox, *Naval Documents*, II: 250–251.

96. Secretary of State James Madison to Cathcart, August 22, 1802, Cathcart Family

Papers, item, 432, box 2, folder 1, NYPL, reprinted verbatim in Knox, *Naval Documents*, II: 244.

97. Cathcart to Secretary of State, August 25, 1802, Cathcart Family Papers, item 435, box 2, folder 1, NYPL, quoted verbatim in Knox, *Naval Documents*, II: 250–251.

98. Cathcart to Eaton, April 10, 1802, in Knox, *Naval Documents*, II: 111–112.

99. Eaton to Samuel Barron, April 29, 1805, "Letterbook January 2, 1804–June 17, 1805," William Eaton Papers, HL.

100. Eaton to Madison, March 18, 1802, William Eaton Papers, box 5, HL, reprinted verbatim in Knox, *Naval Documents*, II: 90–91.

101. Jefferson to the Senate and House of Representative of the United States, January 13, 1806, in Lowrie and Clark, *American State Papers*, II: 696.

102. Wright and Macleod, *First Americans in North Africa*, 176–198; *Scrapbooks of Clippings Compiled by Thomas Jefferson's Family, 1800–1808*, Jefferson Library, Charlottesville, Virginia, microfilm.

103. See data compiled from the Early American Newspapers database by David J. Dzurec III, "'An Entertaining Narrative of . . . Cruel and Barbarous Treatment': Captivity, Narrative, and Debate in the Early American Republic, 1775–1816" (PhD diss. Ohio State University, 2008), 131, 227.

104. Eaton later returned to a brief period of prominence as a witness in the trial of Aaron Burr.

105. Lear to Bainbridge, December 16, 1803, in Knox, *Naval Documents*, III: 274–275.

106. Dey of Algiers to President Jefferson, October 17, 1802, in *The Papers of Thomas Jefferson* (Princeton, NJ: Princeton University Press, 2011), XXXVIII: 509–510 [italics in original, underline added]. I thank the *Papers'* editor, Barbara Oberg, for bringing this to my attention.

107. Cathcart to Jefferson, August 12, 1805, Despatches from US Consuls in Funchal, Madeira, T205, roll 1, NACP.

108. Louis B. Wright and Julia H. Macleod, "Mellimelli: A Problem for President Jefferson in North African Diplomacy," *Virginia Quarterly Review* 20, no. 4 (Fall 1944): 557.

109. Mellimelli to President Jefferson, December 31, 1805, and Mellimelli to Secretary of State Madison, March 11, 1806, Notes From the Legation of Tunis (July 17, 1805–Sept 30, 1806), M67, NACP.

110. Everett Somerville Brown, ed., *William Plumer's Memorandum of Proceedings in the United States Senate, 1803–1807* (New York: Macmillan, 1923), 333.

111. For an extensive physical and character assessment of Mellimelli by Senator William Plumer, see Brown, *William Plumer's Memorandum*, 358.

112. Jason Zeledon, "'As Proud as Lucifer': A Tunisian Diplomat in Thomas Jefferson's America," *Diplomatic History* 41, no. 1 (October 2015): 156n7.

113. Dr. Samuel L. Mitchill quoted in Wright and Macleod, "Mellimelli," 560.

114. Cathcart to Jacob Wagner, July 20, 1806, Notes From the Legation of Tunis (July 17, 1805–September 30, 1806), M67, NACP.

115. Zeledon, "'As Proud as Lucifer,'" 12–14; James R. Sofka, "'The Jeffersonian Idea of National Security' Revisited," in *Rough Waters: American Involvement with the Mediterranean in the Eighteenth and Nineteenth Centuries,* Research in Maritime History 44, ed. Silvia Marzagalli, James R. Sofka, and John McCusker (Liverpool, UK: Liverpool

University Press, 2010), 183; Irving Brant, ed., *James Madison, Secretary of State, 1800–1809* (Indianapolis: Bobbs-Merrill, 1941–1961), IV: 306; Wright and Macleod, "Mellimelli," 559; Timothy Marr, *The Cultural Roots of American Islamicism* (Cambridge: Cambridge University Press, 2006), 66.

116. Brown, *William Plumer's Memorandum*, 359. In a State Department list of the eleven members of Mellimelli's entourage, the final member, presumably the prostitute in question, is listed as "Georgia—a Greek taken into service at Washington." This is the only mention of her in government records. January 14, 1806, Notes From the Legation of Tunis (July 17, 1805–September 30, 1806), M67, NACP.

117. Brown, *William Plumer's Memorandum*, 336–337, 345.

118. Cathcart to Secretary of State Madison, April 26 and May 5, 1806, Notes From the Legation of Tunis (July 17, 1805–September 30, 1806), M67, NACP.

119. Cathcart to Secretary of State Madison, June 15, 1806, Notes From the Legation of Tunis (July 17, 1805–September 30, 1806), M67, NACP.

120. Mellimelli to Secretary of State Madison, July 26, 1806, Notes From the Legation of Tunis (July 17, 1805–September 30, 1806), M67, NACP.

121. Cathcart and Nathaniel Ruggles, September 10, 1806, Notes From the Legation of Tunis (July 17, 1805–September 30, 1806), M67, NACP.

122. Cathcart to Secretary of the Navy and Secretary of State, August 20, 1806, Notes From the Legation of Tunis (July 17, 1805–September 30, 1806), M67, NACP.

123. Zeledon, "'As Proud as Lucifer,'" 22.

124. Wright and Macleod, "Mellimelli," 565.

125. Cathcart to President Jefferson, December 19, 1806, and Cathcart to Secretary of State Madison, December 19, 1806, Despatches from US Consuls in Funchal, Madeira, T205, roll 1.

126. Unknown government official, July 2, 1811, and unknown member of Woodside family to Secretary of State Madison, November 16, 1812, in Letters of Application and Recommendation during the Administration of James Madison, 1809–1817, M438, roll 2, NACP.

127. Cathcart to Eaton, July 5, 1807, William Eaton Papers, box 9, HL.

128. Cathcart to Madison, February 5, 1808, Despatches from US Consuls in Funchal, Madeira, T205, roll 1, NACP.

129. *Daily National Intelligencer* (Washington, DC), December 17, 1813; *Daily National Intelligencer* (Washington, DC), June 16, 1815, no. 762; *Providence Patriot, Columbian Phoenix* (Providence, RI), June 17, 1815, no. 23; *Niles' Weekly Register* (Baltimore, MD), March–September, 1815, vol. 8, p. 280; *National Advocate* (New York, NY), August 2, 1816; *National Advocate* (New York, NY), August 3, 1816.

130. *Daily National Intelligencer* (Washington, DC), December 17, 1813.

131. *National Advocate* (New York, NY), August 2, 1816; *National Advocate* (New York, NY), August 3, 1816.

132. Cathcart, *Seamen's Disbursements at Madeira from June to 31 December 1807*, Despatches from US Consuls in Funchal, Madeira, T205, roll 1, NACP.

133. Cathcart to unknown, June 3, 1816, Despatches from US Consuls in Cardiz, T186, roll 3, NACP.

134. Bloomfield to Cathcart, January 29, 1816, Despatches from US Consuls in Cardiz, T186, roll 3, NACP.

135. Charles Francis Adams, ed., *Memoirs of John Quincy Adams: Comprising Portions of His Diary From 1795 to 1848*, 12 vols. (Philadelphia: J. B. Lippincott & Co., 1875), IV: 426, V: 163.

136. Adams, *Memoirs of John Quincy Adams*, V: 163; John Quincy Adams to Cathcart, December 14, 1819, Papers of Charles William Cathcart, box 1, folder 1, Michigan State University Archives, hereinafter cited as MSUA. Also see Adams quoted in Eugene Schuyler, *American Diplomacy and the Furtherance of Commerce* (New York: Charles Scribner's Sons, 1886), 209.

137. Wright and Macleod, *First Americans in North Africa*, 199–200; Lowrie and Clark, *American State Papers*, II: 20; Richard Peters, ed., *The Public Statutes at Large of the United States, 1789 to March 3, 1845* (Boston: Charles C. Little and James Brown, 1848), VI: 250, 267; United States Congress, Senate, Committee on Foreign Relations, *Compilation of Reports of Committee on Foreign Relations, 1789–1901* (Washington, DC: Government Printing Office, 1901), III: 625–626.

138. Committee on Foreign Relations, *Committee on Foreign Relations, 1789–1901*, III: 625–626.

139. Committee on Foreign Relations, *Committee on Foreign Relations, 1789–1901*, III: 625–626.

140. John Tipton, Commissioner of Claims, United States Senate, to Cathcart, April 7, 1836; Cathcart to John Tipton, April 8, 1836; Cathcart to Senator Isaac Hill, April 9, 1836, all in Papers of Charles William Cathcart, box 1, folder 3, MSUA; Wright and Macleod, *First Americans in North Africa*, 199–200; Peters, *Public Statutes at Large*, VI: 250, 278, 668; Lowrie and Clark, *American State Papers*, II: 20.

141. Walter Prichard, Fred B. Kniffen, and Clair A. Brown, eds., "Southern Louisiana and Southern Alabama in 1819: The Journal of James Leander Cathcart," *Louisiana Historical Quarterly* 28, no. 3 (July 1945): 737.

Chapter 5 · *Accidentally Useful and Interesting to the World*

Epigraphs. James Riley, *An Authentic Narrative of the Loss of the American Brig Commerce: Wrecked on the Western Coast of Africa, in the Month of August, 1815* (New York: T. & W. Mercein, 1817), iii; Alexander von Humboldt, *Cosmos: Sketch of a Physical Description of the Universe*, vol. 1 (London: Longman, Brown, Green and Longmans, 1846), 304.

1. Riley, *Narrative*, 13–14.

2. In addition to Captain Riley, the *Commerce*'s crew included Archibald Robbins (able seaman), George Williams (first mate), Aaron Savage (second mate), Thomas Burns (able seaman), William Porter (able seaman), James Clark (able seaman), James Hogan (ordinary seaman), James Barrett (ordinary seaman), Richard Delisle (an African American cook), Horace Savage (cabin boy), and Antonio Michel (a French passenger who joined the voyage at Gibraltar, and whom Robbins described as "elderly"). Archibald Robbins, *A Journal Comprising an Account of the Loss of the Brig* Commerce (Hartford, CT: F. D. Bolles & Co., 1817), 7.

3. Donald Ratcliffe, "Selling Captain Riley, 1816–1859: How Did His 'Narrative' Become So Well Known?," *Proceedings of the American Antiquarian Society* 117, pt. 1 (Worcester, MA: American Antiquarian Society, 2007), 183–184.

4. For an excellent breakdown of the *Narrative*'s distribution and sales figures across its various editions, see Ratcliffe, "Selling Captain Riley."

5. Frank Lambert, *The Barbary Wars: American Independence in the Atlantic World* (New York: Hill and Wang, 2005), 50–59.

6. Riley, *Narrative*, 62–63, 82–84, 221, 531.

7. Christine E. Sears, *American Slaves and African Masters: Algiers and the West Sahara, 1776–1820* (New York: Palgrave Macmillan, 2012), ch. 6.

8. Riley, *Narrative*, 16.

9. Riley, *Narrative*, 20–21.

10. Riley, *Narrative*, 23. For more on the role of alcohol in the life of sailors, see Mathew Taylor Raffety, *The Republic Afloat: Law, Honor, and Citizenship in Maritime America* (Chicago: University of Chicago Press, 2013), 111–112; Paul A. Gilje, *Liberty on the Waterfront: American Maritime Culture in the Age of Revolution* (Philadelphia: University of Pennsylvania Press, 2004), 7, 92–94, 258; W. J. Rorabaugh, *The Alcoholic Republic: An American Tradition* (New York: Oxford University Press, 1979), 194.

11. Riley, *Narrative*, 35–38.

12. Riley, *Narrative*, 38; Robbins, *Journal* (1817), 17.

13. Riley, *Narrative*, 44–49.

14. Dean King, *Skeletons on the Zahara: A True Story of Survival* (New York: Back Bay Books, 2005), 72.

15. Myra C. Glenn, "Forging Manhood and Nationhood Together: American Sailors' Accounts of Their Exploits, Sufferings, and Resistance in the Antebellum United States," *American Nineteenth Century History* 8, no. 1 (March 2007): 31; Linda Colley, "Going Native, Telling Tales: Captivity, Collaborations and Empire," *Past and Present* 168 (August 2000): 187–188.

16. Ratcliffe, "Selling Captain Riley," 186–187.

17. *Columbian Centinel* (Boston, MA), May 7, 1817, no. 3469; *New-York Columbian* (New York, NY), September 18, 1817, vol. 8, no. 2345.

18. Jared Sparks, review, *North-American Review and Miscellaneous Journal* 5, no. 15 (September 1817): 390–391.

19. Judah Paddock, *A Narrative of the Shipwreck of the Ship* Oswego (New York: Captain James Riley, 1818).

20. Robbins, *Journal* (1817).

21. Mary Louise Pratt, "Fieldwork in Common Places," in *Writing Culture: The Poetics and Politics of Ethnography*, ed. James Clifford and George E. Marcus (Berkeley: University of California Press, 1986), 38.

22. Pauline Turner Strong, *Captive Selves, Captivating Others: The Politics and Poetics of Colonial American Captivity Narratives* (Boulder, CO: Westview Press, 1999), 1.

23. Strong, *Captive Selves, Captivating Others*, 10, 159–160.

24. Riley, *Narrative*, iii.

25. Riley, *Narrative*, 10.

26. Archibald Robbins, *A Journal Comprising An Account of the Loss of the Brig* Commerce, 18th ed. (New York: Silas Andrus, 1825), 151.

27. Riley, *Narrative*, 43, 53, 96, 118, 120.

28. Riley, *Narrative*, 63.

29. Riley, *Narrative*, 67, 136–138, 187, 207, 224.

30. Riley, *Narrative*, 400–402.

31. Riley, *Narrative*, 171.

32. Riley, *Narrative*, 376–377.

33. Riley, *Narrative*, 158, 171–172.

34. Riley, *Narrative*, 170, 270–271, 472–482; *New-York Herald* (New York, NY), May 24, 1817, no. 1607, p. 2; *Camden Gazette* (Camden, South Carolina), November 8, 1817, vol. 2, no. 70, p. 4.

35. *New-York Columbian* (New York, NY), September 18, 1817, vol. 8, no. 2345, p. 2.

36. *St. Louis Globe-Democrat* (St. Louis, MO), August 8, 1875, no. 81, p. 9; *Galveston Daily News* (Houston, TX), August 8, 1875, no. 180.

37. Riley, *Narrative*, 101, 103, 105–106, 175, 184, 197–200.

38. Donald J. Ratcliffe, "The Strange Career of James Riley," *Timeline* 3, no. 4 (August–September 1986): 49.

39. Mordecai Manuel Noah, *Travels in England, France, Spain, and the Barbary States, in the Years 1813–14 and 15* (New York: Kirk and Mercein, 1819), 40–41, 376–377; Riley, *Narrative*, 415–416, 467–468.

40. Lawrence A. Peskin, "American Exception? William Eaton and Early National Antisemitism," *American Jewish History* 100, no. 3 (July 2016): 299–317.

41. Noah, *Travels*, 378–379.

42. Riley, *Narrative*, 399–416, 445–452, 464–469.

43. Riley, *Narrative*, 414.

44. *Spirit of the Times and Carlisle Gazette* (Carlisle, PA), August 31, 1818, vol. 1, no. 43, p. 2.

45. For a list of American-Barbary narratives and their publication histories, see Paul Baepler, *White Slaves, African Masters: An Anthology of American Barbary Captivity Narratives* (Chicago: University of Chicago Press, 1999), appendix.

46. W. Willshire Riley, ed., *Sequel to Riley's Narrative: Being a Sketch of Interesting Incidents in the Life, Voyages and Travels of Capt. James Riley* (Springfield, OH: George Brewster, 1851), iv.

47. Riley, *Narrative*, 301.

48. Riley, *Narrative*, 301.

49. Riley, *Narrative*, 310.

50. Robbins, *Journal* (1817), 17. William Willshire later forwarded a report of an elderly man found dead on Riley's wreck, suggesting that Michel might have broken free and swam to the wreck, only to succumb to his wounds or die of starvation. Willshire to James Green, British Consul General to Tangier, in David Maislish, *White Slave* (London: Pen Press, 2005), 408.

51. John W. Francis, *Old New York, or, Reminiscences of the Past Sixty Years: Anniversary Discourse Delivered Before the New York Historical Society, November 17, 1857* (New York: Charles Roe, 1858), 69.

52. Granting some credibility to Riley's broad authorship, Thurlow Weed, later a prominent journalist and feared political operator, remembered the day that Riley "brought the manuscript of his book to the office, and reading the first chapter, I ventured to suggest that it was carelessly written and needed revising, and although at first annoyed, he finally took it away and availed himself of the services of a school-teacher, who improved the whole narrative in its style and grammar. The work was a great success, keeping its author before the people for fifteen or twenty years." That school teacher, presumably Josiah Shippey, whom Riley describes as a friend, may have been the manuscript's

anonymous scribe. Harriet A. Weed, ed., *Autobiography of Thurlow Weed* (Boston: Riverside Press, 1884), I: 58.

53. Ratcliffe, "Selling Captain Riley," 188–189. It is Ratcliffe's reasonable speculation that almost all of the manuscript was penned by a professional scribe, and he ultimately concludes that Riley, not Bleecker, was the principle author and held final editorial control.

54. James Riley, *Riley's Narrative: Manuscript, 1817*, New-York Historical Society, pp. 291, 509–511, 565.

55. Riley, *Riley's Narrative: Manuscript*, 307–309, 312–315, 390, 475–476, and especially 493.

56. Ann Eliza Bleecker, *The History of Maria Kittle*, in *The Posthumous Works of Ann Eliza Bleecker*, ed. Margareta V. Faugeres (New York: T. & J. Swords, 1793).

57. Bleecker, *History of Maria Kittle*.

58. Sharon M. Harris, ed., *American Women Writers to 1800* (New York: Oxford University Press, 1996), 338–402.

59. Ratcliffe, "Selling Captain Riley," 200.

60. Ratcliffe, "Selling Captain Riley," 202–209; King's amalgamation was quickly turned into a History Channel documentary, and since 2010, it has been flagged as a potential motion picture. King, *Skeletons on the Zahara*; "Skeletons on the Zahara Movie Adaptation," accessed November 12, 2017, http://www.filmofilia.com/skeletons-on-the -zahara-movie-adaptation-24256/.

61. Baepler, *White Slaves, African Masters*, 307.

62. Ratcliffe, "Selling Captain Riley," 202.

63. David Jaffee, "The Village Enlightenment in New England, 1760–1820," *William and Mary Quarterly* 47, no. 3 (July 1990): 339.

64. Jaffee, "Village Enlightenment," 345.

65. Allan R. Pred, *Urban Growth and the Circulation of Information: The United States System of Cities, 1790–1840* (Cambridge, MA: Harvard University Press, 1973), 43.

66. *Connecticut Mirror* (Hartford, CT), January 22, 1816, vol. 7, no. 30, p. 3; *American Mercury* (Hartford, CT), January 23, 1816, vol. 32, no. 1647, p. 3; *American Beacon and Commercial Diary* (Norfolk, VA), January 26, 1816, vol. 1, no. 150, p. 3; *Washington City Weekly Gazette* (Washington, DC), January 27, 1816, no. 10, p. 76; *The Repertory* (Boston, MA), January 30, 1816, vol. 13, no. 13, p. 2.

67. Pred, *Urban Growth*, 43–47, 58–59.

68. Ratcliffe, "Selling Captain Riley," 202.

69. *Commercial Advertiser* (New York, NY), March 20, 1816, vol. 19, no. 7294, p. 2; *Evening Post* (New York, NY), March 20, 1816, no. 4303, p. 2; *Baltimore Patriot* (Baltimore, MD), March 22, 1816, vol. 7, no. 71, p. 2; *Boston Daily Advertiser* (Boston, MA), March 23, 1816, vol. 12, no. 72, p. 2; *New-York Herald* (New York, NY), March 23, 1816, no. 1490, p. 1; *The Repertory* (Boston, MA), March 23, 1816, vol. 13, no. 37, p. 2; *American Mercury* (Hartford, CT), March 26, 1816, vol. 32, no. 1656, p. 3; *Hampden Federalist* (Springfield, MA), March 28, 1816, vol. 11, no. 13, p. 2; *Boston Weekly Messenger* (Boston, MA), March 28, 1816, vol. 5, no. 24, p. 390; *Newburyport Herald* (Newburyport, MA), March 29, 1816, vol. 19, no. 104, p. 4; *Salem Gazette* (Salem, MA) March 29, 1816, vol. 30, no. 26, p. 1; *Enquirer* (Richmond, VA), March 30, 1816, p. 4; *Washington City Weekly Gazette* (Washington, DC), March 30, 1816, no. 19, p. 150; *New-Bedford Mercury* (New Bedford, MA), April 5, 1816, vol. 9, no. 37, p. 1; *American Advocate* (Hallowell, ME),

April 6, 1816, vol. 7, no. 12, p. 2; *Albany Argus* (Albany, NY), April 12, 1816, vol. 4, no. 336, p. 2; *New-Hampshire Gazette* (Portsmouth, NH), April 23, 1816, vol. 61, no. 21, p. 4

70. *Albany Advertiser* (Albany, NY), May 14, 1816, no. 198, p. 2; *Connecticut Journal* (New Haven, CT), May 21, 1816, vol. 50, no. 2534, p. 3; *Connecticut Mirror* (Hartford, CT), May 27, 1816, vol. 7, no. 48, p. 3; *Middlesex Gazette* (Middletown, CT), May 30, 1816, vol. 31, no. 1592, p. 3; *Newburyport Herald* (Newburyport, MA), May 31, 1816, vol. 20, no. 18, p. 2; *American Mercury* (Hartford, CT), June 4, 1816, vol. 32, no. 1666, p. 2; *New-York Daily Advertiser* (New York, NY), July 7, 1817, vol. 1, no. 86, p. 3; *The Times* (Hartford, CT), July 22, 1817, vol. 1, no. 30, p. 4. By 1817, newspapers began printing serialized extracts of Riley's narrative over several days, with each extract expanding on a single event or theme, such as Riley's discovery of towns, their residents, and the savagery of their masters. See *Boston Patriot* (Boston, MA), January 11, 1817, vol. 16, no. 37, p. 2; *Norwich Courier* (Norwich, CT), January 15, 1817, vol. 21, no. 10, p. 1; *Connecticut Mirror* (Hartford, CT), January 20, 1817, vol. 8, no. 30, p. 3; *Middlesex Gazette* (Middletown, CT), January 23, 1817, vol. 31, no. 1626, p. 3; *Independent Chronicle* (Boston, MA), February 6, 1817, vol. 49, no. 3736, p. 4; *The Times* (Hartford, CT), April 22, 1817, vol. 1, no. 17, p. 1; *Providence Gazette* (Providence, RI), June 7, 1817, vol. 53, no. 2789, p. 1; *Newburyport Herald* (Newburyport, MA), June 13, 1817, vol. 21, no. 22, p. 3; *Pittsfield Sun* (Pittsfield, MA), June 25, 1817, vol. 17, no. 875, p. 2.

71. *Alexandria Herald* (Alexandria, VA), June 30, 1817, vol. 7, no. 875, p. 2.

72. Dorothy Bowen, "Thomas Jefferson: 1743–1943: A Bicentennial Exhibition," *Huntington Library Quarterly* 6, no. 4 (August 1943): 503–504.

73. Ratcliffe, "Selling Captain Riley," 207.

74. *Maryland Gazette and Political Intelligencer* (Annapolis, MD), July 17, 1817, no. 29.

75. *Village Register and Norfolk County Advertiser* (Dedham, MA), February 6, 1824, vol. 5, no. 16, p. 2.

76. Samuel Goodrich, *The Story of Captain Riley, and His Adventures in Africa* (1832; repr., Philadelphia: Desilver, Thomas & Co., 1837), 237; Samuel Goodrich, *The Tales of Peter Parley* (1830; repr., Philadelphia: Charles Desilver, 1856).

77. *The Emancipator* (New York, NY), November 23, 1837, no. 30, p. 2; Paddock, *Narrative*.

78. *The Emancipator* (New York, NY), November 23, 1837, no. 30, p. 2.

79. *The Emancipator* (New York, NY), October 25, 1838, vol. 26, no. 26, p. 1.

80. John Locke Scripps, *The First Published Life of Abraham Lincoln* (1860; repr., Detroit: Cranbrook Press, 1900), 20.

81. Louis A. Warren, *Lincoln's Youth, Indiana Years: Seven to Twenty-one, 1816–1830* (New York: Appleton, 1959), 111; R. Gerald McMurtry, "Some Books That Lincoln Read," *Journal of Developmental Reading* 1, no. 2 (Winter 1958): 22; R. Gerald McMurtry, "The Influence of Riley's Narrative upon Abraham Lincoln," *Indiana Magazine of History* 1, no. 3 (June 1934): 133–138; Robert Bray, *Reading with Lincoln* (Carbondale: Southern Illinois University Press, 2010), 32–34; Robert J. Allison, "Review of Baepler, *White Slaves, African Masters,*" *William and Mary Quarterly* 57, no. 2 (April 2000): 460.

82. Robert J. Allison, *The Crescent Obscured: The United States and the Muslim World, 1776–1815* (New York: Oxford University Press, 1995), 221–222.

83. Allison, *Crescent Obscured*, 221–222.

84. King, *Skeletons on the Zahara*, xi.

85. Allison, *Crescent Obscured*, 222; Jennifer Costello Brezina, "A Nation in Chains: Barbary Captives and American Identity," in *Captivating Subjects: Writing Confinement, Citizenship, and Nationhood in the Nineteenth Century*, ed. Jason Haslam and Julia M. Wright (Toronto: University of Toronto Press, 2005), 201–219.

86. Timothy Marr, *The Cultural Roots of American Islamicism* (Cambridge: Cambridge University Press, 2006), ch. 6; Susan Nance, *How the "Arabian Nights" Inspired the American Dream, 1790–1935* (Chapel Hill: University of North Carolina Press, 2009), 20–21, 38–46.

87. King, *Skeletons on the Zahara*, 312; *Pittsfield Sun* (Pittsfield, MA), December, 2, 1818, vol. 19, no. 950, p. 2.

88. King, *Skeletons on the Zahara*, 306–308.

89. Those former captives who lived for decades after returning to the United States include Aaron Savage (1795–1836), William Porter (1784–1847), Archibald Robbins (1793–1860), Horace Savage (1800–1882), and James Riley (1777–1840). Horace Savage was the last surviving member of the *Commerce*'s crew, dying in 1882 at the age of 82. After returning from captivity, Savage divided his time between Connecticut and Mexico as a trader and merchant sailor.

90. King, *Skeletons on the Zahara*, 312–313.

Chapter 6 · Sailing the Inland Sea

Epigraph. George Washington to François Jean, marquis de Chastellux, October 12, 1783, "Envisaging the West," accessed December 22, 2017, http://jeffersonswest.unl.edu /archive/view_doc.php?id=jef.00153.

1. The first usage of this phrase is disputed, and attributions range from a private conversation in the 1830s to Greeley's editorial in the *New York Tribune* in 1865. Thomas Fuller, " 'Go West, Young Man!' An Elusive Slogan," *Indiana Magazine of History* 100, no. 3 (September 2004); Josiah Busnell Grinnell, *Men and Events of Forty Years: Autobiographical Reminiscences of an Active Career From 1850 to 1890* (Boston: D. Lothrop Company, 1891), 87.

2. Alexis de Tocqueville, *Democracy in America* (Cambridge: Sever and Francis, 1863), 164.

3. Anne Farrer Hyde, *Empires, Nations, and Families: A History of the North American West, 1800–1860* (Lincoln: University of Nebraska Press, 2011), 257.

4. John Lauritz Larson, *Internal Improvements: National Public Works and the Promise of Popular Government in the Early United States* (Chapel Hill: University of North Carolina Press, 2001), 5.

5. Alan Taylor, *Liberty Men and Great Proprietors: The Revolutionary Settlement on the Maine Frontier, 1760–1820* (Chapel Hill: University of North Carolina Press, 1990), 83.

6. For two exceptions to this scholarly indifference, see Donald J. Ratcliffe, "Riley and Antislavery Sentiment," *Ohio History* 81, no. 2 (Spring 1972); Jacob Rama Berman, *American Arabesque: Arabs and Islam in the Nineteenth Century Imaginary* (New York: New York University Press, 2012).

7. Anthony M. Joseph, *From Liberty to Liberality: The Transformation of the Pennsylvania Legislature, 1776–1820* (Lanham, MD: Lexington Books, 2012), 49–50.

8. *Salem Gazette* (Salem, MA), February 10, 1809, vol. 23, no. 1824.

9. *Journal of the Nineteenth House of Representatives of the Commonwealth of Pennsyl-*

vania. Tuesday, the 6ᵗʰ of December, 1808 to April 4ᵗʰ, 1809 (Lancaster: Benjamin Grimler, 1809), 588.

10. *Journal of the Nineteenth House of Representatives of the Commonwealth of Pennsylvania*, 34, 54, 212–213, 238, 306, 333, 524, 526–529.

11. *Journal of the Nineteenth House of Representatives of the Commonwealth of Pennsylvania*, 26, 50–51, 150–153, 217, 333.

12. *Salem Gazette* (Salem, MA), February 10, 1809, vol. 23, no. 1824, p. 4.

13. *Salem Gazette* (Salem, MA), February 10, 1809, vol. 23, no. 1824, p. 4.

14. Joseph, *From Liberty to Liberality*, 14, 19.

15. Joseph, *From Liberty to Liberality*, 34.

16. Joseph, *From Liberty to Liberality*, 34–35.

17. *Journal of the Nineteenth House of Representatives of the Commonwealth of Pennsylvania*, 26.

18. *Journal of the Nineteenth House of Representatives of the Commonwealth of Pennsylvania*, 51–53, 152–153.

19. *Journal of the Nineteenth House of Representatives of the Commonwealth of Pennsylvania*, 168, 210–211.

20. *The Tickler* (Philadelphia, PA), September 28, 1808, vol. 1, no. 33; *Journal of the Nineteenth House of Representatives of the Commonwealth of Pennsylvania*, 37–38, 55.

21. Quoting a classic O'Brien-ism, a Philadelphia newspaper referred to O'Brien's *"queer way"* of critiquing Jefferson's insidious influence and Madison's passivity if the latter were elected president: "Jefferson, you *o*nderstand me, will remain at Monticello, and Madison, you *o*nderstand me, will be at Washington. Jefferson will stick a pretty long tiller into Madison, and steer him, you *o*nderstand me, from Monticello, just as well as if he was at Washington, you *o*nderstand me." *The Tickler* (Philadelphia, PA), October 19, 1808, vol. 1, no. 36 [italics in original].

22. *The Tickler* (Philadelphia, PA), September 28, 1808, vol. 1, no. 33, p. 2. There is no evidence that O'Brien was a shipowner at any time in his life. For a detailed analysis of the various political factions in Pennsylvania at this time and speculation on why party support for the embargo was near-universal, see Andrew Shankman, *Crucible of American Democracy: The Struggle to Fuse Egalitarianism and Capitalism in Jeffersonian Pennsylvania* (Lawrence: University Press of Kansas, 2004), 181.

23. *Journal of the Nineteenth House of Representatives of the Commonwealth of Pennsylvania*, 168, 210–211.

24. *Journal of the Nineteenth House of Representatives of the Commonwealth of Pennsylvania*, 55.

25. *Carlisle Herald* (Carlisle, PA), September 11, 1812, p. 3.

26. *Carlisle Gazette* (Carlisle, PA), February 17, 1824, p. 3. O'Brien also failed to rank among over one hundred notable members of the Carlisle community during this period. Alfred Nevin, *Men of Mark of Cumberland Valley, Pa. 1776–1876* (Philadelphia: Fulton Publishing Company, 1876).

27. Samuel P. Bates, *History of Cumberland and Adams Counties, Pennsylvania* (Chicago: Warner, Beers, & Co., 1886), 329.

28. Judith Ridner, *A Town In-Between: Carlisle, Pennsylvania, and the Early Mid-Atlantic Interior* (Philadelphia: University of Pennsylvania Press, 2010), 4.

29. H. C. O., "The Romantic Tourist: Holly Gap to the Hogshead Spring," in *Two*

Hundred Years in Cumberland County: A Collection of Documents and Pictures Illustrating Two Centuries of Life in Pennsylvania, ed. D. W. Thompson (Carlisle, PA: Hamilton Library and Historical Association, 1951), 111.

30. Charles Wilkes, "A Traveller in Cumberland County, 1844," *Cumberland County History* 12, no. 1 (Summer 1995): 59–62.

31. D. W. Thompson, *Two Hundred Years in Cumberland County*, 131–135.

32. Ridner, *A Town In-Between*, 191–197; Theodore B. Klein, *Early History and Growth of Carlisle: Early Footprints of Developments and Improvements in Northwestern Pennsylvania* (Harrisburg: WM. Stanley Ray, State Printer of Pennsylvania, 1905), 6.

33. Ridner, *A Town In-Between*, 180.

34. "Microfilm Index to Wills, 1750–1905" and "Indexes to estate inventories and vendues," Cumberland County Historical Society, Ohio. In spite of the significant wealth gap *within* Carlisle, the wealthiest and poorest of the town were relatively alike when compared to the nation as a whole. Whereas taxable assets in Carlisle in 1798 ranged from $30 to $100, across the nation they ranged from just $1 to over $30,000. Ridner, *A Town In-Between*, 197. For further demographic analysis of Cumberland County during this period, see Paul Marr, "Reconstructing the Demographics of Cumberland County, 1750–1800," *Cumberland County History* 21, no. 2 (Winter 2004): 50–61.

35. James Cathcart, "Southern Louisiana and Southern Alabama in 1819: The Journal of James Leander Cathcart," ed. Walter Prichard, Fred B. Kniffen, and Clair A. Brown, *Louisiana Historical Quarterly* 28, no. 3 (July 1945): 737–738.

36. Cathcart, "Southern Louisiana and Southern Alabama," 739.

37. Cathcart quoted in Berman, *American Arabesque*, 51.

38. Cathcart, "Southern Louisiana and Southern Alabama," 751, 768, 801, 826–827.

39. Cathcart, "Southern Louisiana and Southern Alabama," 740–741.

40. John C. Frémont, *A Report on an Exploration of the Country Lying between the Missouri River and the Rocky Mountains on the Line of the Kansas and Great Platte Rivers* (Washington, DC: Printed by order of the United States' Senate, 1843); John C. Frémont, *Narrative of the Exploring Expedition to the Rocky Mountains, in the Year 1842, and to Oregon and North California, in the Years 1843–44* (Syracuse, NY: Hall & Dickson, 1848).

41. Cathcart's colleague John Landreth also penned a surveyor's journal that is invaluable in complementing and verifying Cathcart's account. Milton B. Newton Jr., ed., *The Journal of John Landreth, Surveyor: An Expedition to the Gulf Coast, November 15, 1818–May 19, 1819* (Baton Rouge, LA: Geoscience Publications, 1985).

42. Cathcart, "Southern Louisiana and Southern Alabama," 753, 763–764, 860.

43. Cathcart, "Southern Louisiana and Southern Alabama," 749, 751.

44. Christopher Morris, *The Big Muddy: An Environmental History of the Mississippi and Its Peoples from Hernando de Soto to Hurricane Katrina* (New York: Oxford University Press, 2012), 92.

45. Morris, *Big Muddy*, 86–89.

46. Morris, *Big Muddy*, 106.

47. John Hebron Moore, "The Cypress Industry of the Old Southwest and Public Land Law, 1803–1850," *Journal of Southern History* 49, no. 2 (May 1983): 206.

48. Though Cathcart surveyed the region over a decade after the Louisiana Purchase, much of it was being surveyed for the first time, and until surveyed, the government was not permitted to sell public lands to private interests. It was not until the latter half of the

nineteenth century that there were legal means for the government to lease public lands to loggers or to simply sell the trees themselves. Surveyors and residents in the early 1820s bemoaned how the delay in releasing public lands to private loggers had fostered conflict between illegal loggers and ranchers and produced massive waste in high quality timber that was left to rot. Moore, "Cypress Industry," 207, 216.

49. Moore, "Cypress Industry," 212–213; Morris, *Big Muddy*, 105.

50. Cathcart quoted in Berman, *American Arabesque*, 54.

51. Cathcart quoted in Berman, *American Arabesque*, 51.

52. Cathcart quoted in Berman, *American Arabesque*, 51.

53. Cathcart quoted in Berman, *American Arabesque*, 51.

54. Cathcart, "Southern Louisiana and Southern Alabama," 826–827.

55. Cathcart, "Southern Louisiana and Southern Alabama," 826–827.

56. Cathcart, "Southern Louisiana and Southern Alabama," 756, 780–783; Caleb Forshey quoted in Morris, *Big Muddy*, 113; Berman, *American Arabesque*, 51.

57. Cathcart, "Southern Louisiana and Southern Alabama," 756–757.

58. Cathcart, "Southern Louisiana and Southern Alabama," 756.

59. Berman, *American Arabesque*, 33.

60. Cathcart claimed the US acquisition of the Floridas, with their allegedly ideal soil and climate, would soon make the region "the vineyard of the United States." Cathcart's speculation sparked an ongoing debate among supportive and skeptical readers, which played out in the pages of newspapers from Washington, DC, to Philadelphia, and Raleigh, North Carolina. *Daily National Intelligencer* (Washington, DC), May 16, 1821, no. 2603; *Raleigh Register and North-Carolina Gazette* (Raleigh, NC), June 22, 1821, no. 1135; *Daily National Intelligencer* (Washington, DC), May 29, 1821, no. 2614; *Daily National Intelligencer* (Washington, DC), May 31, 1821, no. 2616; *Daily National Intelligencer* (Washington, DC), June 6, 1821, no. 2621, p. 2; *Daily National Intelligencer* (Washington, DC), June 19, 1821, no. 2632, p. 2.

61. These petitions were sent to James Monroe, Thomas Jefferson, James Madison, and John Quincy Adams. Thomas Jefferson to Cathcart, September 10, 1821; Madison to Cathcart, September 23, 1821; John Adams to Cathcart, March 25, 1822, all in Papers of Charles William Cathcart, box 1, Michigan State University Archives, hereinafter cited as MSUA; Marvin R. Cain, "The Cathcart Family: A Family Account of 100 Years of American History," *Cultural Studies* 1, no. 2 (1962): 138.

62. Cathcart even went as far as to meticulously sketch a design of the unbuilt homestead, under which he again vented his frustrations at not receiving his government reimbursements, noting, "No claims, no house!" Cathcart Family Papers, box 3, folder F.62, New York Public Library, hereinafter cited as NYPL.

63. James Cathcart to Charles Cathcart, April 1, 1836, Papers of Charles William Cathcart, box 1, folder 3, MSUA.

64. James Cathcart to Charles Cathcart and James Cathcart, April 15, 1833, Papers of Charles William Cathcart, MSUA.

65. Cain, "Cathcart Family," 139.

66. The possibly hundreds of letters from James Cathcart to his son Charles came as a decades-long torrent, and they were not responded to with the same diligence, eliciting the elder Cathcart to frequently express his anxiety at delays. He wrote to Charles: "We are very anxious to hear from you, it is now 77 days since the date of your last letter, I

have frequently requested you to write once a month, it is passing strange that in return for all my anxiety for my four sons I cannot be gratified in this small request!!!!!!!!" Cathcart rarely used more than one exclamation mark, and this number was not used during his captivity or decades-long frustrations over federal reimbursement claims. This greater frustration over correspondence from his son also speaks to Cathcart's dependence upon Charles to carry the future of the family. James Cathcart to Charles Cathcart, August 22, 1834, Cathcart Family Papers, box 3, NYPL.

67. James Cathcart to Charles Cathcart, August 9, 1836, Papers of Charles William Cathcart, box 1, folder 4, MSUA [underline in original].

68. James Cathcart to Charles Cathcart and James Cathcart, April 15, 1833, Papers of Charles William Cathcart, MSUA.

69. Cain, "Cathcart Family," 141.

70. Cain, "Cathcart Family," 144.

71. Cain, "Cathcart Family," 144–5.

72. Eric Hinderaker, *Elusive Empires: Constructing Colonialism in the Ohio Valley, 1673–1800* (Cambridge: Cambridge University Press, 1997), 185.

73. Hinderaker, *Elusive Empires*, 244.

74. George Washington quoted in Hinderaker, *Elusive Empires*, 239.

75. Michael A. Blaakman, "Land Mania, Fledgling Governments, and the Problem of the Public Coffers in the Revolutionary American Republic," McNeil Center for Early American Studies Seminar Series, Philadelphia, October 16, 2015, pp. 23–25.

76. Malcolm J. Rohrbough, *The Land Office Business: The Settlement and Administration of American Public Lands, 1789–1837* (New York: Oxford University Press, 1968).

77. Cain, "Cathcart Family," 141–142.

78. Cain, "Cathcart Family," 142.

79. Cain, "Cathcart Family," 148–155.

80. James Cathcart to Charles Cathcart, August 19, 1843, Cathcart Family Papers, box 3, NYPL.

81. Michael Kimmel, *Manhood in America: A Cultural History* (New York: Free Press, 1996), 61–62.

82. Correspondence of this lobbying is compiled in W. Willshire Riley, ed., *Sequel to Riley's Narrative: Being a Sketch of Interesting Incidents in the Life, Voyages and Travels of Capt. James Riley* (Columbus, OH: George Brewster, 1851), 333–341; Gaillard Hunt, ed., *The First Forty Years of Washington Society* (New York: Charles Scribner's Sons, 1908), 148; *Annals of Congress, House of Representatives, 16th Congress, 1st Session*, 933–934, accessed December 23, 2017, http://memory.loc.gov/cgi-bin/ampage?collId=llac&file Name=035/llac035.db&recNum=464.

83. Riley, *Sequel to Riley's Narrative*, 18–19.

84. Riley, *Sequel to Riley's Narrative*, 18–19. New York governor DeWitt Clinton similarly referred to the Great Lakes as "our Mediterranean seas" in his speech at the Erie Canal's official opening ceremony in 1825. David Hosack, ed., *Memoir of DeWitt Clinton* (New York: J. Seymour, 1829), 408.

85. James Riley to Rebecah Riley, June 17, 1832, and surveying and land purchase journals, Captain James Riley Archival Collections, Mercer County Historical Society, hereinafter cited as MCHS; Riley, *Sequel to Riley's Narrative*, 20.

86. James Riley to Rebecah Riley, June 17, 1832, Captain James Riley Archival

Collections, MCHS; Riley, *Sequel to Riley's Narrative*, 21–22. For a centuries-long history of the region, including its demographics and political organization from Native American tribes to the Reconstruction era, see *History of Van Wert and Mercer Counties, Ohio* (Wapakoneta, OH: R. Sutton & co., 1882), 17–23, 124–127, microfilm 84531, reel 54, item no. 168, Library of Congress, hereinafter LOC.

87. Riley to unknown, July 3, 1824, in "Founding of Willshire," *Northwest Ohio Quarterly* 16 (1944): 42.

88. Riley to unknown, July 3, 1824, in "Founding of Willshire," *Northwest Ohio Quarterly* 16 (1944): 42.

89. Peter L. Bernstein, *Wedding of the Waters: The Erie Canal and the Making of a Great Nation* (New York: W. W. Norton, 2005), 325, 344–345, 347, 352; Brian Phillips Murphy, *Building the Empire State: Political Economy in the Early Republic* (Philadelphia: University of Pennsylvania Press, 2015), ch. 5.

90. *New-York Columbian* (New York, NY), August 23, 1819, vol. 12, no. 2888, p. 2; *Otsego Herald* (Cooperstown, NY), August 30, 1819, vol. 25, no. 1275, p. 2; *Daily National Intelligencer* (Washington, DC), August 26, 1819, no. 2066; *National Standard* (Middlebury, VT), September 1, 1819, vol. 7, no. 2, p. 3; *Maryland Gazette and State Register* (Annapolis, MD), August 12, 1824, no. 33; *Connecticut Courant* (Hartford, CT), August 3, 1824, vol. 60, no. 3106, p. 2; *Newburyport Herald* (Newburyport, MA), December 21, 1824, vol. 28, no. 76, p. 1; *Salem Gazette* (Salem, MA), December 24, 1824, vol. 2, no. 102, p. 2.

91. Riley to unknown, July 3, 1824, in "Founding of Willshire," 42 [italics in original].

92. Riley, *Sequel to Riley's Narrative*, 21.

93. Riley, *Sequel to Riley's Narrative*, 21–22.

94. Riley, *Sequel to Riley's Narrative*, 22.

95. Donald J. Ratcliffe, "The Strange Career of James Riley," *Timeline* 3, no. 4 (August–September 1986): 44.

96. Ratcliffe, "Strange Career of James Riley," 46.

97. James Riley, *An Authentic Narrative of the Loss of the American Brig Commerce: Wrecked on the Western Coast of Africa, in the Month of August, 1815* (New York: T. & W. Mercein, 1817), 531–533.

98. Ratcliffe, "Riley and Antislavery Sentiment," 80; *Scioto Gazette* (Chillicothe, OH), June 11, 1819, vol. 19, no. 38, p. 3.

99. Riley to Governor Ethan Allen Brown, December 24, 1819, Ethan Allen Brown Papers, MIC 96 ser. 1, roll 2, Ohio Historical Society, hereinafter OHS.

100. Riley to Governor Ethan Allen Brown, December 24, 1819, Ethan Allen Brown Papers, MIC 96 ser. 1, roll 2, OHS.

101. Caitlin A. Fitz, "The Hemispheric Dimensions of Early US Nationalism: The War of 1812, Its Aftermath, and Spanish American Independence," *Journal of American History* 102, no. 2 (September 2015); Caitlin A. Fitz, "Our Sister Republics: The United States in an Age of American Revolutions" (PhD diss., Yale University, 2010).

102. *Ohio General Assembly, House of Representatives Journal*, vol. 22, 1824, FLM 250 roll 5, pp. 225–226, OHS.

103. "Oration of Capt. Riley, Delivered at Willshire, July 4, 1825," *History of Van Wert and Mercer Counties, Ohio* (Wapakoneta, OH: R. Sutton & co., 1882), 251, Microfilm 84531, reel 54, item no. 168, LOC.

104. Riley, *Narrative*, 532–533.

105. Calvin Stowe, "Professor Stowe on Colonization," June 9, 1834, accessed December 23, 2017, http://utc.iath.virginia.edu/abolitn/abescsat.html; Matthew Carey, ed., *Letters of the Colonization Society*, vols. 1–2 (Philadelphia: L. Johnson, 1832); Amos Jones Beyan, *The American Colonization Society and the Creation of the Liberian State: A Historical Perspective, 1822–1900* (Lanham, MD: University Press of America, 1991); Claude A. Clegg III, *The Price of Liberty: African Americans and the Making of Liberia* (Chapel Hill: University of North Carolina Press, 2004); Lamin O. Sanneh, *Abolitionists Abroad: American Blacks and the Making of Modern West Africa* (Cambridge, MA: Harvard University Press, 1999); Howard Temperley, "African-American Aspirations and the Settlement of Liberia," *Slavery and Abolition* 21, no. 2 (2000).

106. William Lloyd Garrison, "Exposure of the American Colonization Society" (1832), accessed November 7, 2015, http://utc.iath.virginia.edu/abolitn/abeswlgbt.html; Frederick Douglas, "Colonization," January 26, 1849, accessed December 23, 2017, http://utc.iath.virginia.edu/abolitn/abaro3at.html.

107. Riley to Rev. R. Gurley, March 11, 1833, in Riley, *Sequel to Riley's Narrative*, 56, also see 183, 186.

108. Any actual improvements in Riley's health must have been by placebo, as he was complaining of jaundice and "phrenitis," which is now diagnosed as either encephalitis or meningitis, both brain inflammations caused by viral or bacterial infection. Riley and his physicians failed to identify the jaundice and brain inflammation as independent from one another, and of course, neither can be treated by sea air or strenuous duties on a merchant ship. Riley, *Sequel to Riley's Narrative*, 25–28, 30.

109. The final age range studied by Daniel Vickers and Vince Walsh was sailors aged 45 to 49, who represented just 1.7 percent of the profession. Vickers and Walsh, "Young Men and the Sea: The Sociology of Seafaring in Eighteenth-Century Salem, Massachusetts," *Social History* 24, no. 1 (January 1999): 26–27.

110. James Riley to unknown, March 14, 1832, and invoices of brigs *James Monroe* and *William Tell*, 1830–1833, Captain James Riley Archival Collections, MCHS.

111. Riley, *Sequel to Riley's Narrative*, 194–197.

112. James Riley to Thomas Carr, US consul to Tangier, November 19, 1839, Simon Gratz Autograph Collection 1343–1928, case 8, box 16, folder 52, Historical Society of Pennsylvania; David H. Finnie, *Pioneers East: The Early American Experience in the Middle East* (Cambridge, MA: Harvard University Press, 1967), 10–11; Susan Nance, *How the "Arabian Nights" Inspired the American Dream, 1790–1935* (Chapel Hill: University of North Carolina Press, 2009), 38–39; Riley, *Sequel to Riley's Narrative*, 148, 222.

113. Riley, *Sequel to Riley's Narrative*, 31–33.

114. Riley to Secretary of the Navy Levi Woodbury, February 1833, in Riley, *Sequel to Riley's Narrative*, 52–53.

115. Riley to Secretary of State John Forsythe, March 28, 1832, Captain James Riley Archival Collections, MCHS, and in Riley, *Sequel to Riley's Narrative*, 39–45, 126, 201.

116. For details of Riley's trades in North Africa, see the logs of his brigs *James Monroe* and *William Tell*, 1830–1834, Captain James Riley Archival Collections, MCHS; Riley, *Sequel to Riley's Narrative*, 46, 49, 51.

117. Riley, *Sequel to Riley's Narrative*, 101–112.

118. Riley, *Sequel to Riley's Narrative*, 327.

119. *Daily National Intelligencer* (Washington, DC), April 20, 1840, no. 8480; *New England Weekly Review* (Hartford, CT), April 18, 1840, no. 16; *Boston Courier* (Boston, MA), April 13, 1840, no. 1667, p. 1; *Indiana Journal* (Indianapolis, IN), May 2, 1840, no. 933; *New-Hampshire Statesman and State Journal* (Concord, NH), April 18, 1840, no. 50.

120. *New England Weekly Review* (Hartford, CT), April 18, 1840, no. 16; *Boston Courier* (Boston, MA), April 13, 1840, no. 1667, p. 1; *Indiana Journal* (Indianapolis, IN), May 2, 1840, no. 933; *New-Hampshire Statesman and State Journal* (Concord, NH), April 18, 1840, no. 50.

121. Riley, *Sequel to Riley's Narrative*, 326.

122. "Cathcart Family Clippings," Milstein Division, NYPL.

Conclusion · Opportunities of Empire

Epigraph. James Cathcart to Charles Cathcart, June 17, 1833, Cathcart Family Papers, box 3, New York Public Library.

1. D. Ebsworth, "National Prosperity," *Aurora General Advertiser* (Philadelphia, PA), May 15, 1804.

2. Michael A. McDonnell, "War and Nationhood: Founding Myths and Historical Realities," in *Remembering the Revolution: Memory, History, and Nation Making from Independence to the Civil War*, ed. Michael A. McDonnell, Clare Corbould, et al. (Amherst: University of Massachusetts Press, 2013); Donald F. Johnson, "Ambiguous Allegiances: Questioning Loyalties in Revolutionary Cities under British Military Rule," McNeil Center for Early American Studies Seminar Series, January 23, 2015.

3. Alexis de Tocqueville, *Democracy in America* (New York: Colonial Press, 1900), II: 144–145.

4. Matthew Raffety, "Recent Currents in the Nineteenth-Century American Maritime History," *History Compass* 6, issue. 2 (2008): 609.

5. Myra C. Glenn, "Troubled Manhood in the Early Republic: The Life and Autobiography of Sailor Horace Lane," *Journal of the Early Republic* 26, no. 1 (Spring 2006): 74.

Epilogue

1. Maria Antonia Garces, *Cervantes in Algiers: A Captive's Tale* (Nashville: Vanderbilt University Press, 2002); Christopher Lloyd, *English Corsairs on the Barbary Coast* (London: Collins, 1981), 15.

2. Scholars dispute the authenticity of circumstances and events recounted after Smith's initial captivity, with one describing Smith's 1630 account as "pure fantasy, but does serve to suggest what readers had come to expect of the captivity narrative genre by this time." Brian L. Davies, "The Prisoner's Tale: Russian Captivity Narratives and Changing Muscovite Perceptions of the Ottoman-Tartar *Dar-al-Islam*," in *Eurasian Slavery, Ransom and Abolition in World History, 1200–1860*, ed. Christoph Witzenrath (Surrey, UK: Ashgate, 2015), 286; John Ashton, *The Adventures and Discoveries of Captain John Smith, Sometime President of Virginia, and Admiral of New England* (London: Cassell & Company, 1833).

3. Timothy Marr, *The Cultural Roots of American Islamicism* (Cambridge: Cambridge University Press, 2006), 2–3.

4. Daniel Defoe, *Robinson Crusoe* (1719; repr., London: Macmillan and Co., 1868),

17–18; Linda Colley, *Captives: Britain, Empire, and the World, 1600–1850* (New York: Pantheon, 2002), 140–141.

5. Paul Baepler, ed., *White Slaves, African Masters: An Anthology of American Barbary Captivity Narratives* (Chicago: University of Chicago Press, 1999), 303–307.

6. James Turner quoted in Marr, *Cultural Roots of American Islamicism*, 58; Benilde Montgomery, "White Captives, African Slaves: A Drama of Abolition," *Eighteenth-Century Studies* 27, no. 4 (Summer 1994): 615–630; Elizabeth Maddock Dillon, "*Slaves in Algiers*: Race, Republic Genealogies, and the Global Stage," *American Literary History* 16, no. 3 (Fall 2004): 407–436; Royall Tyler, *The Algerine Captive: or, the Life and Adventures of Doctor Updike Underhill* (Hartford: Peter B. Gleason and Co., 1816); Susanna Rowson, *Slaves in Algiers, or A Struggle for Freedom* (Philadelphia: Wrigley and Berriman, 1793), 23.

7. Lotfi Ben Rejeb, "America's Captive Freemen in North Africa: The Comparative Method in Abolitionist Persuasion," *Slavery and Abolition* 9, no. 1 (1988): 57–71.

8. Historicus (Benjamin Franklin), "On the Slave-Trade," *Federal Gazette* (Philadelphia, PA), March 23, 1790, also in *The Works of Benjamin Franklin; Containing Several Political and Historical Tracts Not Included in Any Former Edition, and Many Letters Official and Private Not Hitherto Published; with Notes and a Life of the Author*, ed. Jared Sparks (Boston: Whittemore, Niles, and Hall, 1856) II; James Parton, *Life and Times of Benjamin Franklin* (New York: Mason Brothers, 1864), II: 606–614.

9. Baepler, *White Slaves, African Masters*, 25–30; Paul Baepler, "The Barbary Captivity Narrative in American Culture," *Early American Literature* 39, no. 2 (2004): 237–239; Paul Baepler, "White Slaves, African Masters," *ANNALS of the American Academy of Political and Social Science* 588 (July 2003).

10. David Dzurec, "'A Speedy Release to Our Suffering Captive Brethren in Algiers': Captives, Debate, and Public Opinion in the Early American Republic," *Historian* 71, no. 4 (Winter 2009); Gary E. Wilson, "American Hostages in Moslem Nations, 1784–1796: The Public Response," *Journal of the Early Republic* 2, no. 2 (Summer 1982).

11. Charles Sumner, *White Slavery in the Barbary States: A Lecture Before the Boston Mercantile Library Association* (Boston: William D. Ticknor, 1847), 38.

12. Charles Sumner, *The Works of Charles Sumner* (Boston: Lee and Shepard, 1870), II: 57–58.

History books chart an author's journey through the archives as much as they chart an intellectual journey through a particular era. It is therefore just as important to acknowledge the sources that I could not find, and how that has shaped the direction of this book, as it is to acknowledge the sources I could find, but chose not to include, and why. To that end, I must confess that this project started with two failures that led me to write a radically different book than I had planned. The original plan was to spend years in North Africa, and perhaps also Turkey, digging through manuscripts that documented Americans' captivity, and then to explore the role of those captives in America's early antislavery movement.

Instead, North Africa specialists quickly informed me that there are not enough surviving primary sources authored by Barbary officials about their American captives to anchor a whole project. Then I quickly learned that, with the exception of James Riley, the captives themselves were not a significant presence in the American antislavery movement. The literary genre of fictional captivity narratives of Americans in Barbary certainly warrants greater attention by scholars of literature (which I sadly am not) who are interested in representations of race, religion, and gender in the early American republic. But it is telling that there has been relatively little sustained work on the relationship between Barbary captivity and American abolitionism since Lotfi Ben Rejeb's excellent article "America's Captive Freemen in North Africa: The Comparative Method in Abolitionist Persuasion" was published in 1988 (*Slavery and Abolition*).

Primary Sources

The research that underpins this book draws on more than twenty archives and perhaps the same number of digital databases that aggregate historic newspapers (such as America's Historical Newspapers and America's Historical Imprints, maintained by Readex) and government documents (such as the American State Papers, digitized and maintained by the Library of Congress). From the notes, it will be clear that the most significant primary sources for this book are the correspondence and narratives written by O'Brien, Cathcart, and Riley and the correspondence and official government documents written about them. Cathcart's narrative and subsequent letter book (both edited and published by his granddaughter) are freely available online, as are many editions of Riley's *Narrative* and the sole edition of the *Sequel to Riley's Narrative*, which was compiled and published by his son. Additional primary source collections that underpinned this book include the Cathcart

Family Papers, held by the New York Public Library, and the James L. Cathcart Papers, 1785–1817, held by the Library of Congress, while the Michigan State University Archives hold the Papers of Charles William Cathcart, which contain correspondence between Cathcart and his sons. The New-York Historical Society holds the original 1817 handwritten manuscript of Riley's *Narrative*, and the Historical Society of Pennsylvania holds O'Brien's fourteen-month captivity diary. For the period of O'Brien's and Cathcart's captivity and their later years as diplomats, the most comprehensive collection of correspondence and government reports can be found in Dudley W. Knox's six-volume official history of *Naval Documents Related to the United States Wars with the Barbary Powers* (1939–1944).

Secondary Sources

As mentioned in this book's introduction, the last twenty years have seen nothing less than a torrent of publications (both popular and scholarly) on the US conflict with Barbary. While the bulk of these publications have been post-9/11, several books and essays published in the preceding years include fresh perspectives on the US-Barbary conflict and American Orientalism. This suggests that the revived interest in Americans in Barbary might still have occurred even without 9/11 giving the topic (a highly distorted) relevance in the public imagination. These earlier texts include Robert J. Allison's *The Crescent Obscured: The United States and the Muslim World, 1776–1815* (1995); James Sofka's essay, "The Jeffersonian Idea of National Security: Commerce, the Atlantic Balance of Power, and the Barbary War, 1786–1805" (*Diplomatic History*, 1997); and Paul Baepler's anthology, *White Slaves, African Masters: An Anthology of American Barbary Captivity Narratives* (1999). These were followed by, to just name a few, Martha Elena Rojas, "'Insults Unpunished': Barbary Captives, American Slaves, and the Negotiation of Liberty" (*Early American Studies*, 2003); Richard B. Parker, *Uncle Sam in Barbary: A Diplomatic History* (2004); Frank Lambert, *The Barbary Wars: American Independence in the Atlantic World* (2005); William Ray, *Horrors of Slavery; or, The American Tars in Tripoli*, ed. Hester Blum (2008); Lawrence A. Peskin, *Captives and Countrymen: Barbary Slaves and the American Public* (2009); Christine E. Sears, *American Slaves and African Masters: Algiers and the West Sahara, 1776–1820* (2012); Hannah Farber, "Millions for Credit: Peace with Algiers and the Establishment of America's Commercial Reputations Overseas" (*Journal of the Early Republic* 2014).

The works of Marcus Rediker and Peter Linebaugh (*The Many-Headed Hydra: Sailors, Slaves, Commoners, and the Hidden History of the Revolutionary Atlantic*, 2000) and Daniel Vickers (*Farmers and Fishermen: Two Centuries of Work in Essex County, Massachusetts, 1630–1850*, 1994) together with Vince Walsh ("Young Men and the Sea: The Sociology of Seafaring in Eighteenth-Century Salem, Massachusetts," 2005) were instrumental in informing the seafaring components of this book. I also found my interest in and use of maritime history aligning with that of Matthew Raffety and Myra Glenn. Raffety justly accuses maritime historians of being too insular, speaking only to other scholars of the sea, becoming entrenched in narrow channels that prevent researchers from engaging with the broader historiography of the United States ("Recent Currents in the Nineteenth-Century American Maritime History," *History Compass*, 2008). The biographical approach of *From Captives to Consuls* and each of its component chapters were precisely designed to overcome this failing. Glenn does not write biographical microhistories, but she nonetheless concurs that "Sailor narratives, therefore, offer historians a wide angle lens from which to view multiple but connected discourses about different groups of nonprivileged men in the early republic" (*Jack Tar's Story: The Autobiographies and Memoirs of Sailors in Antebellum America*, 2010, p. 23).

The biographical approach taken in this book drew upon the growing body of scholarly biographical (and collective biographical) microhistories, including Gary Nash and Graham Russell Gao Hodges, *Friends of Liberty: A Tale of Three Patriots, Two Revolutions, and the Betrayal That Divided a Nation; Thomas Jefferson, Thaddeus Kosciuszko, and Agrippa Hull* (2008); Alfred F. Young, *The Shoemaker and the Tea Party: Memory and the American Revolution* (1999); Linda Colley, *The Ordeal of Elizabeth Marsh: A Woman in World History* (2007); Emma Rothschild, *The Inner Lives of Empires: An Eighteenth-Century History* (2011). Colley and Rothschild provided particularly invaluable models by embracing "exceptional-typical" biographical subjects and rebutting the idea that the subjects of a microhistory must, should, or even *can*, be ordinary in every way.*

---

*Carlo Ginzburg and Carlo Poni define *exceptional-typical* as "a truly exceptional (and thus statistically infrequent) document" that "can be much more revealing than a thousand stereotypical documents." Carlo Ginzburg and Carlo Poni, "The Name Game," in *Microhistory and the lost peoples of Europe*, ed. Edward Muir and Guido Ruggiero, trans. Eren Branch (Baltimore: Johns Hopkins University Press, 1991), 7–9.

Page numbers in *italics* indicate illustrations

Bunker Hill (ship), 12
Burns, Thomas, 130, 184n2
Burr, Aaron, 182n104
business interests: Cathcart, 76–77, 83–84,
   88–89, 91–92, 95, 106, 110; Eaton, 91–92,
   96–97, 106; O'Brien, 76–77, 83–84, 89,
   90, 95, 108–11; Riley on African, 120
Busnach. *See* banking houses

Cadiz, Cathcart as consul to, 8, 76, 106,
   107–8
cannibalism, 112, 113, 114, 130
captivity: earnings in, 40, 41–42; and
   Morocco treaty, 113; North African
   system, 9, 39–40; Ottoman system, 4–5;
   papaluna status in, 39–40, 66; pressure to
   convert to Islam while in, 39, 46, 50–51.
   See also captivity, Cathcart in; captivity,
   O'Brien in; captivity correspondence;
   captivity narratives; imprisonment
captivity, Cathcart in: appeals to various
   nations, 63–67; capture, 35, 44; diplomacy during, 49, 53–59, 66–67, 72; duties,
   40–42, 48, 57–58, 65–66; earnings, 41–42,
   66, 67; help for O'Brien, 46–47; journals,
   34, 35–36, 39, 44–45, 51; overview of, 7–8,
   53–56; as victim of American independence, 61–63; writing style, 35–36, 39, 42,
   51, 54, 56–59
captivity, O'Brien in: capture, 35; diaries,
   34, 35–36, 39, 42, 44–45, 51; diplomacy
   during, 53–59, 65; duties of, 39–40,
   46–47; Irwin on, 19; overview of, 7–8,
   53–56; as spokesman, 35, 40; as victim of
   American independence, 61–63; writing
   style, 35–36, 39, 42, 51, 54, 56–59
captivity correspondence: influence of, 68;
   and newspapers, 54, 55, 58, 62–63, 69;
   patriotism in, 55, 60, 67, 72; Revolution
   in, 55, 62–63, 72; victim language in,
   61–63
captivity narratives: and antislavery, 127–29,
   157–58; and Bleecker family, 125; embellishment in, 52, 116; ethnography in, 39,
   117, 119, 129–30; format and style, 35–36,
   39, 51, 112, 115; as genre, 156–58; as
   informative, 39, 111, 117–23; liberty in,
   49–51; masculinity in, 7, 35–38, 45–49,

51–52, 64, 157; and national identity, 8, 9,
   11, 33, 36, 157; Native American, 35, 39,
   117, 156; O'Brien's diaries, 34, 35–36, 39,
   42, 44–45, 51; Orientalism in, 7, 43–45,
   51; Othering in, 39, 115, 117; and politics,
   117, 157; religion in, 52, 117, 157, 170n76.
   See also *Authentic Narrative of the Loss of
   the American Brig* Commerce
Carey, Mathew, 38
Carlisle, PA, 9, 102, 130–31, 136–37
Carmichael, William, 55
Carpenter, Jonathan, 27
Cathcart, Charles, 142–43, 144
Cathcart, Henry, 142
Cathcart, James, *16*; on buoyancy, 152;
   business interests, 76–77, 83–84, 88–89,
   91–92, 95, 106, 110; charity by, 169n56;
   conflict with O'Brien, 8, 78, 79, 82–83,
   89–91, 95, 102, 109–10; death of, 133;
   early career, 16; education and background, 15, 16, 32, 35, 58; and frontier, 1,
   5–6, 9–10, 130–31, 132–34, 137–43, 153;
   later career, 9, 73, 102–9, 137–43, 150–51;
   marriage and family, 80–81, 142–43; multiple identities of, 32–33, 44, 140–41, 153;
   and Revolution, 6–7, 13–14, 16, 20–22,
   26–27, 62–63, 72, 92; shifting loyalties of,
   14, 63–67, 72, 79, 140–41, 153; as subject,
   1, 2, 5–6, 11, 153, 154. See also captivity,
   Cathcart in; consul, Cathcart as
Cathcart, James (son), 142
Cathcart, Jane, 80, *81*
Cathcart, John (son), 142
Cathcart, John (uncle), 16, 20–22, 23–24
Cervantes, Miguel de, 156
Cervantes, Rodrigo de, 156
changing works, 133–34
Charlotte Temple (Rowson), 112
citizenship, 47–48, 63–64, 75
Clark, James, 130, 184n2
Clarydge, Francis, 25
Clinton, DeWitt, 193n84
Coffin, Zaccheus, 39
Colvill, Charles, 174n40
Commerce (ship): fate of crew, 115, 123–24,
   130; list of crew, 184n2; shipwreck of, 111,
   114. See also *Authentic Narrative of the Loss
   of the American Brig* Commerce

Confederacy (ship), 22, 24–25
Congress (ship), 19
Connecticut Wits, 68, 69
Connor, Timothy, 27
consul, Cathcart as: and business interests,
   76–77, 83–84, 88–89, 91–92, 95, 96–97,
   106; to Cadiz, 8, 76, 106, 107–8; to
   Madeira, 8, 76, 105–7; overview of, 1, 7–8,
   73, 75–77; reimbursements, 108–9, 141;
   to Tripoli, 8, 73, 76, 78, 84–101; war with
   Tripoli, 95–101
consul, Eaton as: and business interests,
   91–92, 96–97; coup attempt in Tripoli, 73,
   85, 97–100, 101; to Tunis, 8, 73, 75–77,
   84–85, 88, 96–100, 101
consul, O'Brien as: Algerian flag incident, 73,
   93–95, 96; and business interests, 76–77,
   83–84, 89, 90, 95, 108–11; difficulty of
   post, 84–85, 88; overview of, 1, 7–8, 73,
   75–77; reimbursements, 108–9; and re-
   working of treaty, 86, 87; shipbuilding
   supervision, 79, 86
consuls: autonomy of, 8, 76–77, 85–86, 95,
   97; British, 83, 85; Cathcart on, 74; citizenship of, 75; communication delays,
   75–76, 84–85, 87–88, 97–98, 101, 102; and
   Consular Acts on, 83, 91, 106; correspondence style, 60–61; and corruption, 84,
   90–92; duties of, 74–75, 83, 106; French,
   83; and gifts, 87; networking by, 75–76,
   84; numbers of, 75, 76; reforms proposed
   by Riley, 149; salaries, 83–84, 88–89, 96,
   149; Swedish, 178n37; Willshire as, 10,
   115, 130. *See also* consul, Cathcart as;
   consul, Eaton as; consul, O'Brien as;
   diplomacy
Continental Navy: Cathcart's claims of, 7,
   14, 22, 23, 153; and Penobscot Expedition,
   20; prizes, 18, 19; and Sherburne, 18
Corey, Ebenezer Hill, 29–30
corruption and consuls, 84, 90–92
corsairs: capture of *Dauphin* and *Maria,* 35,
   44; history of, 2–5; *vs.* pirates, 2; *vs.* privateers, 2; shipbuilding, 40, 46; as term, 42.
   See also captivity
coup attempt in Tripoli, 73, 85, 97–100, 101
Crescent (ship), 79
Cutting, Nathaniel, 60–61

Dauphin (ship): capture of, 35; Irwin on, 19;
   officers, 39; petition of crew, 64; ransom of
   Colvill, 174n40
Declaration of Independence, 37–38, 169n68
defection, 14, 25, 26
Defoe, Daniel, 156–57
de la Cruz, Giovanni, 40
Delisle, Richard, 184n2
DeWitt, Clinton, 116
D'Expilly, Miguel, 40, 44
diaries and journals. *See* captivity narratives
diplomacy: Cathcart and Tunis delegation,
   8, 76, 102–3, 104–5, 137; by Cathcart as
   captive, 49, 53–59, 66–67, 72; correspondence style, 60–61; and information
   gathering, 54–56, 59–60; by O'Brien as
   captive, 53–59, 66–67, 72; O'Brien on,
   44; use of captivity narratives, 39. *See also*
   consuls
Donaldson, Joseph, 49, 58, 66–67, 84
Downs, Barnabas, 6, 12–13, 14

Eaton, William, *100*; on Algerian flag
   incident, 94, 96; and Burr trial, 182n104;
   business interests, 91–92, 96–97, 106; on
   Cathcart, 80, 82; and Cathcart-O'Brien
   conflict, 89, 90–91, 95, 109–10; and culture shock, 88; earnings, 97; and First
   Barbary War, 73, 76, 77, 85, 97–100; later
   career, 106; on O'Brien, 82, 87–88. *See also*
   consul, Eaton as
Eliza (ship), 29–30
Embargo Act of 1807, 31, 135
employment correspondence, 77–78, 102, 141
Erie Canal, 126, 130, 145
escapes from prison, 14, 22, 25–27, 48
Essex (ship), 23–24
ethnography, 39, 117, 119, 129–30, 149

Farfara, Leon, 90, 91–92
First Barbary War (1801–1805), 73, 76, 77,
   85, 95–101
Florida: acquisition of, 147; Cathcart on,
   192n60; salvage in, 149
Forbes, Robert, 28
France: consuls from, 83; impressment by, 29;
   imprisonment of Riley, 31, 32; privateers,
   29, 31; Quasi-War, 29, 54, 86